CULTURE IN EIGHTEENTH-CENTURY ENGLAND

Culture in Eighteenth-Century England

A Subject for Taste

Jeremy Black

hambledon
continuum

Hambledon Continuum

The Tower Building
11 York Road
London, SE1 7NX

80 Maiden Lane
Suite 704
New York, NY 10038

First Published 2005 in hardback
This edition published 2007

ISBN 1 85285 463 4 (hardback)
ISBN 1 8528 5534 7 (paperback)

A description of this book is available from the
British Library and from the Library of Congress.

Typeset by Carnegie Publishing, Lancaster,
and printed in Great Britain by MPG Books, Cornwall.

Contents

Illustrations

For Tom

The most stylish of the Black family

Preface

Culture in eighteenth-century England is a matter not only of Handel and Hogarth, Pope and Reynolds, Capability Brown and Sheridan, books and paintings, landscape gardens and plays, but also of the society that sustained such works, that bought the books, saw the paintings, gardens and plays, the operas and the concerts, and that played a major role in the cultural and artistic heritage that has been left to us. In the space available, I cannot seek to be comprehensive, but I have sought to tackle the major themes and both to provide a guide to developments and to show how they can be understood. This book will work if it encourages you to turn and look anew at the cultural heritage of this most fascinating of periods.

England's culture is one that commands attention, but what should be the method of approach and where should be the emphasis? On the one hand, the culture of the eighteenth century appears close enough to grasp: its dynamism attracts with the writings of Defoe and Fielding or the pictures of Hogarth; and its grace is seductive, with elegant portraits, couplets, minuets, colonnades and landscape. Television offers versions of John Gay's *Beggar's Opera* (1728) and Jane Austen's novels. Begun in 1796–97, Austen's *Pride and Prejudice* came second in the best book (in fact novel) of all time competition staged by the BBC in 2003, beating all Victorian works, particularly the novels of Charles Dickens, and suggesting that it 'connects' very well with modern readers. The world it depicts seems reassuredly modern, certainly in contrast to the civil strife, religious zeal and witch trials of the seventeenth century, and if different to that of today, only quaintly, safely and, indeed, attractively so. Yet other aspects of the culture of the period, for example Handel's operas, seem remote, and, indeed, with every year, the eighteenth century gets closer to the Middle Ages than to today.

The title of this book comes from an influential work of the period, Thomas Whately's *Observations on Modern Gardening* (1770). The introduction was not only an assertion of the importance and artistry of landscape gardening, but also a more general statement about cultural goals:

> Gardening, in the perfection to which it has been lately brought in England, is entitled to a place of considerable rank among the liberal arts. It is as superior to landskip painting, as a reality to a representation: it is an exertion of fancy, a subject for taste; and being released now from the restraints of regularity, and enlarged beyond the purposes of domestic convenience, the most beautiful, the most simple, the most noble scenes of nature are all within its province: for it is no longer confined to the spots from which it borrows its name, but regulates also the disposition and embellishments of a park, a farm, or a riding; and the business of a gardener is to select and to apply whatever is great, elegant, or characteristic in any of them, to discover and to show all the advantages of the place upon which he is employed; to supply its defects, to correct its faults, and to improve its beauties.

Whately's work, which was rapidly translated into French and which reached a fifth English edition by 1793, was also symptomatic of a wider process of the discussion and classification of culture and knowledge in a public format and to a general audience, as his attempt to discuss aims and methods sought to validate English achievements and to fix their public understanding. Whately (c. 1728–72) himself was no aesthete removed from the world, but a Cambridge-educated lawyer who became an MP and an important second-rank politician, serving as Secretary to the Treasury and also as an Under-Secretary of State.

This book proceeds after two introductory chapters by considering the varied spheres of patronage, before looking specifically at books and newspapers and then, more generally, at changes in artistic styles. The book then considers two key contrasts: London and the provinces, followed by the interplay of cosmopolitanism and xenophobia. The range is from royal patronage to low-life entertainment, the splendours of the imperial metropolis to the ruins of medieval abbeys, the sailing ships of transoceanic trade to the hard toil of peasants, high literature to pornography and doggerel, Handel to home duets; while the span of the energy of the age includes clothes, landscape design, gardening and books.

My interest in eighteenth-century English culture owes much to the inspiring teaching of the late Michael Fitch who decided to squeeze the A level English course into one year and to devote the other year of sixth-form English to a tour through the canon. Alas, modern 'reforms' would make such a horizon-expanding activity impossible. In my case, it led not to the study of English literature at university but to a lifelong interest in the literature and culture of the period. While researching this book, I have benefited from the opportunity to speak at the second Münster symposium on Jonathan Swift held in 1989; the colloquium on 'Culture and Politics: Ideology and Practice in Britain 1660–1800' held at Newcastle Polytechnic in 1989; the Handel Institute Conference, 'Handel in the 1730s' in 1993; the conference on 'L'Europe des politesses et le caractère des nations' held in Paris at the Sénat in 1995; to the University of Virginia's School of Continuing and Professional Studies summer schools on the English Country House, held in 1995 and 1999, and on Jefferson in England held in 1997 and 1998; the conference 'Chunnel Vision: France and England and the Reciprocity of Taste, 1763–1851' in New York in 1998, sponsored by the Bard Graduate Center for Studies in the Decorative Arts; the Horace Walpole bicentennial lecture series at Strawberry Hill; the conference of the Société d'Etudes Anglo-Américaines des XVIIᵉ et XVIIᵉ siècles in the Sorbonne; and the 2004 British Museum conference on 'The Enlightenment: Discovering the World in the Eighteenth Century', as well as to meetings of the Newport Preservation Society. Attendance at the Eighteenth-Century Seminar at the University of Exeter has provided an opportunity to listen to several fruitful papers. I would like to thank the late Earl Waldegrave for permission to cite material from the Waldegrave papers and Lady Lucas for permission to do likewise for the Lucas papers. I am most grateful to Nigel Aston, Donald Burrows, Stephen Clarke, Pamela Clemit, Grayson Ditchfield, Bill Gibson, Bob Harris, Holger Hoock, Steven Parissien and Murray Pittock for commenting on an earlier draft, to Howard Erskine-Hill and Harry Johnstone for comments on particular chapters, and to Martin Sheppard for his editorial advice and encouragement.

Introduction

> Whatever distinctions the extent may occasion between a park and a garden, a state of highly cultivated nature is consistent with each ... the same species of preservation, of ornament, and of scenery, may be introduced; and though a large portion of a park may be rude; and the most romantic scenes are not incompatible with its character; yet it should seem rather to be reclaimed from a forest, than a neglected corner of it; the wildness must not be universal; it is but a circumstance; and it is a happy circumstance only when it is kept within due bounds; some appearance of improvement is essential; and a high degree of polish is at times expected, and generally agreeable. All scenes wherein it prevails, naturally coalesce.
>
> Thomas Whately, *Observations on Modern Gardening* (1770).[1]

Contrasts of light and dark, the elegance of Palladian architecture and the chaos of Gin Lane, characterise eighteenth-century English culture, and two very different scenes and settings serve to introduce this book. The first is the capital of empire, the centre of the English-speaking world, London. In 1738, the French ambassador was not amused by a dramatic display of metropolitan xenophobia and cultural nationalism, but, in truth, the auspices had not been encouraging. The arrival in London of a company of French comedians in the autumn of 1738 led first to a sustained barrage of press criticism, and then to the Haymarket riot. Condemnation of the arrival in the press was widespread, and a contrast with the supposed poor fate of British theatre following the Licensing Act of the previous year was often made. The *Daily Advertiser* noted:

> The French Company of Comedians newly arrived from Paris, it's said, consists of seventy persons. It seems to be a little unnatural that French strollers should have a superior Privilege to those of our own Country; and it were to be wish'd, that these should meet with no more encouragement

here than ours would in France, whose intrinsick merits are generally allow'd to be not a lot inferior to those of the French.

The monthly *Political State of Great Britain* printed a letter from 'Anglicus' on the subject that linked the issue to a more general critique of French influences in British life:

French comedians ... there must naturally such reflections arise in the breast of every Englishman, who is attached to the love and interest of his country ... foreign Vagrants and French Papists ... To how abject a state of Degeneracy are then the English sunk, if they can once harbour a thought of being entertained with foreign Grimace ... the mimickry of a harlequin ... An unnatural affection for French follies has, I own, been a just censure on our gentry and nobility: Yet, by any ridiculous extravagance in French dress, or French cookery, they only distinguished themselves for the particularity of their taste.

The provincial press repeated these attacks. The leading Chester newspaper, *Adam's Weekly Courant*, carried in its issues of 15 November and 27 December items attacking the French players which derived from London sources. The *Weekly Courant*, a Nottingham weekly with marked opposition leanings, printed attacks in its issues of 29 October and 23 November, alleging that the Court was supplying money for the players. In the issue of 16 November it printed a poem 'On the French Players Coming to England':

> Their dowdy Actresses come over from France,
> To shew their Ar – s in immodest Dance;
> Think Harlequin's Grimace would please the Town,
> ...
> Let Gallia know that Britons are born free, and will maintain
> Their right and Liberty.'

In London, the attempt by the players to stage a performance led to a riot:

On the ninth, at the New Theatre in the Haymarket, was attempted to be played, by the French Company lately arrived, the comedy of 'L'Embaras des Richesses'; but, notwithstanding the rhetorick of a noted Middlesex Justice, the Audience were so polite and so much English, that they would not permit them to go on with the play which shews the true spirit of the English Nation, in discouraging a French set of Vagabonds, who attempt to play contrary to an Act of Parliament ... met with such rude Treatment, and were so interrupted with hissing, catcalling, ringing small Bells,

knocking out of candles, pelting etc. notwithstanding the Guard of three
Files of Musqueteers, that they were forced at last to quit the stage with
precipitation.[2]

The French envoy, the Comte de Cambis, was present, along with his
wife, the entire diplomatic corps and most of their wives, the head of
the Hanoverian Chancery in London, Baron Ernst von Steinberg, and
many distinguished British subjects. Indeed Cambis claimed that
George II had wished to attend the performance. Cambis was at pains
to point out that the company, under its leader Le Sage, had been given
permission to perform by the Lord Chamberlain, Charles, Duke of
Grafton. Cambis's vivid account made it clear that the performance had
to be called off because of the noise.[3] In his next dispatch, Cambis noted
that there had been no further performances, and that the king was
livid that the permission he had given to the company had been ignored,
but would do nothing.[4] This was not a culture dominated by the royal
court, but one in which the volatile world of London opinions played a
crucial role.

The second scene occurred fifty-one years later, in 1789, and the setting was very different. At the furthest reach of both empire and the
English-speaking world, in Sydney Cove, the convicts staged a play. This
was in order to celebrate the birthday of the king, George III. The
London-born first Governor of New South Wales, Arthur Phillip, gave
permission and the occasion was recorded by Captain Watkin Tench,
one of the captains of marines in charge of the convicts. As an aspect of
the vigorous and entrepreneurial literary culture that both excited and
satisfied reader interest, both men in 1789 also published accounts of the
expedition to New South Wales. The play that was staged in Syndey
Cove was a classic comedy of the eighteenth-century repertoire, George
Farquhar's *The Recruiting Officer*, first performed in London in 1706.
Tench recorded:

> The exhilarating effect of a splendid theatre is well known; and I am not
> ashamed to confess that the proper distribution of three or four yards of
> stained paper, and a dozen farthing candles stuck around the mud walls
> of a convict hut, failed not to diffuse general complacency on the counte-
> nances of sixty persons ... who were assembled to applaud the
> representation. Some of the actors acquitted themselves with great spirit,
> and received the praises of the audience: a prologue and an epilogue, writ-
> ten by one of the performers, were also spoken on the occasion; which,
> although not worth inserting here, contained some tolerable allusions to

the situation of the parties, and the novelty of a stage representation in New South Wales.[5]

Two very different scenes that testified to the variety and energy of cultural commitment and response. The contours of English culture are the subject of this book, but, at every stage, it is necessary not to take a disembodied stance, but to remember that it was individuals – artists and patrons, performers and public – that provided the variety.

By the time the convicts acted Farquhar on the shores of Sydney Cove, England boasted a dynamic economy, the focus of what was subsequently termed the Industrial Revolution, while London, the centre of a global trading system, was the world city. Although the Thirteen Colonies that became the core of the modern USA successfully fought for independence in 1775–83, Britain at the end of the century was developing its colonial presence in Australia and Canada and was the leading colonial power in India. With the most powerful navy in the world, the British, at war again from 1793, were able to defend their colonies in the West Indies and West Africa, and to seize some of those of France, Spain and the Dutch.

At home, change was coming from a series of transformations that are collectively known as the Industrial Revolution. The development of industry and trade, agricultural improvement, and the construction of canals and better roads, led to a growth in national wealth and a gradually emerging new economy. The economy acquired powerful advantages in trade and manufacturing compared to foreign states, and greatly impressed informed foreign visitors. The cumulative impact of often slow and uneven progress was impressive by the end of the century, by when the rate of industrial growth had risen markedly. Although by 1800 fewer than 2000 steam engines had been produced, they each represented a decision for change.

A sense of the possibilities of progress was widely experienced in the later eighteenth century, and can be glimpsed in depictions of industrial scenes, such as the ironworks at Coalbrookdale. Joseph Wright produced heroic paintings in praise of scientific discovery and technological advance. In the Frog Service that Josiah Wedgwood designed for Catherine the Great of Russia, each piece of china was painted with a different British scene. These included not only aristocratic landscapes such as Stowe, but also the Prescot glassworks on Merseyside.

These changes were very apparent by 1800, but a century earlier the situation was very different. In 1700, England was already a major trading country, but the sense of industrial and agricultural development was far less than it was to be a century later, and population growth was still modest. The population of England and Wales, about 5.18 million in 1695, only rose to about 6.20 million in 1751. Thereafter, as death rates fell and birth rates in particular rose, the population rose rapidly, to reach 8.66 million in 1801. At the outset of the eighteenth century, economy and society were still largely traditional. Much of the economy was agrarian, economic productivity was low, there was little substitute for manual labour, and the value gained through most work was limited. In what was a very inegalitarian society, most of the population neither controlled nor produced much wealth. The dominant ethos was religious, patriarchal, hierarchical, conservative, and male-dominated. The law and the teachings of the churches decreed monogamy, prohibited marriage between close kin, stipulated procreation as a purpose of matrimony while condemning it outside, denounced abortion, infanticide, homosexuality and bestiality, made divorce very difficult, venerated age, and ordered respect for authority, both religious and secular. The rate of social change was relatively low, although there was significant movement by individuals.

Social mobility was helped by primogeniture (inheritance by the eldest son) which forced different roles on younger sons, a major dynamic in the plots of novels and plays, and also by the relative openness of marital conventions that, in particular, allowed the sons of land to marry the daughters of commerce, another important theme in plots. The poor, however, found it difficult to improve their condition. Despite the development of charity schools, they had only limited access to education, especially if they were female. This though was a society that took inegalitarianism for granted, and it was not until the crisis in the 1790s created by the response to the French Revolution that a notion of class-based politics developed.

To understand England at the start of our period it is necessary to appreciate that, despite the size and importance of London, it was still a largely rural country, with the towns heavily dependent on their rural hinterlands. Most people spent most of the time in their own neighbourhoods, where travel, particularly by land, was difficult, and where the dark, the damp and the cold pressed hard. It is appropriate to think of a country where injuries and illnesses that we now regard as posing few problems instead were killers. It is necessary to be wary of finding signs of modernity in the social and domestic life of the period, and this should make readers of eighteenth-century novels and viewers of plays and paintings cautious before they too readily read experience and feeling across the centuries. There are few signs for the superficial viewer of more profound contrasts with modern society, contrasts, however, that assure us that the very experience of life was totally different to today.

The demographics were certainly chilling. Individual and collective experiences were affected by the age of the observer, and the average experience of life for the people of the period came at a younger age than for their descendants today, and was shaped within a context of the ever-present threat of death, disease, injury, and pain. Alongside long-lasting individuals, there were lives quickly cut short, in the case of women especially in childbirth. This was also true of those who lived in the splendid houses that survive from the period. Sir Hugh Acland (1637–1713), the gentleman-owner of Killerton, survived his son John and was succeeded by his grandson, another Hugh, who lived from only 1696 until 1728. Of the Parkers of Saltram, four of the five who headed the family between 1649 and 1840 had two wives. Several of these wives died young; after Frances, first wife of Joshua Reynolds's friend, John Parker, 1st Lord Boringdon (1734–88), died in 1764, he married Theresa (1744–75), but she died soon after the birth of her second child, another Theresa. There were some improvements in health care during the century, not least the use of inoculation against smallpox, but defences against disease remained flimsy.

The situation for the 'lower orders' was bleaker on average. As far as the poor were concerned, there was scant understanding of the problems posed by unemployment and under-employment, and such hardships were treated as self-inflicted and thus deserving of neglect or punishment. The standard precept of care was that it should discriminate between the deserving and the undeserving. Educational access and provision reflected social power and assumptions. Because so many children worked, their access to formal education was limited. Attendance at school was lowest in summer, the high point of agricultural work, and the aspect of agrarian life most frequently presented by writers and artists. Far from being supported by taxation, education had to be paid for by the pupil's family, or by a benefactor, dead or alive.

The economy of the poor was such that employment was also the essential condition for most women. The arduous nature of most of the work, and the implications of family and social life together defined the existence of the majority of women. The use of the household as the basis for social organisation led to an emphasis on the role of men, because they were regarded as heads when they were present. The legal rights of women were limited, not least their rights to own and dispose of property. Yet, it would be mistaken to minimise the role of women. Aside from their great importance as consumers, the extent to which the individual family lived together in close proximity led to a need for cooperation and mutual tolerance that necessarily affected the authority of husbands and fathers. In addition, the emphasis on deference, discipline and piety by authoritarian parents was not incompatible with affection. The idea of equality between men and women was increasingly approved of, although the general notion of equality was one of respect for separate functions and development. The cultural position of women is considered in Chapter five.[6]

This was a society whose structures, needs, problems and opportunities moulded its cultural life, but they did not dictate artistic endeavour, nor the choices of patrons. Instead, the varied interaction of these factors made for the exciting dynamism and fertile diversity of eighteenth-century English culture.

1

Arts and Amusements

There is no set way to assess and discuss cultural activity and artistic achievement. It is possible to emphasise artistic styles, but, alternatively, a stress on the social context and the ways in which works were produced leads to an emphasis on patronage or the market, with a focus on the influence they had on culture and the arts; or, rather, on the different forms of patronage, the varied artistic markets and distinct marketplaces, and the multiple influences they had. The nature of the so-called consumer society, indeed, has become a much-studied theme of late.[1] Much recent scholarship has associated the cultural patterns of the century with the various forces of social and economic change. Above all, this branch of scholarship has tended to link cultural development with the new forms of leisure and recreation in the period. It has been suggested that cultural diffusion can be seen as one way of accounting for the so-called stability of eighteenth-century England, the growth of leisure and refinement helping to defuse the political tensions of the previous century.

The role of the market was certainly demonstrated and given ironic force at the close of John Gay's *The Beggar's Opera* (1728), with Macheath the highwayman being saved from hanging when one of the actors demanded a happy ending to 'comply with the taste of the town'. Nineteen years later, Samuel (Dr) Johnson, in his *Prologue at the Opening of Drury Lane Theatre*, declared:

> The stage but echoes back the public voice.
> The drama's laws the drama's patrons give,
> For we that live to please, must please to live.

Yet caution is needed in seeing society as consumer-led, with culture as largely a response to market forces. In practice, a more complex relationship existed between producers, suppliers and the market. Furthermore, because there were different artistic market-places and several important sources of patronage, there was no clear causal relationship, but, rather, a more fluid and contested situation. The situation varied not only by artistic form, but also by place: towns provided a different cultural world from remote rural areas, and, even among them, towns varied greatly. Churches featured as patrons of music, but not of novels (although clerics, such as Parson Adams in Henry Fielding's novel *Joseph Andrews* of 1742, could play a major role in the plots of the latter)

At the same time, individuals moved between patrons, and sought to profit from the varied demands of a diverse and expanding society. The painter Francis Hayman (1708–1776) produced in about 1741 a series of scenes from contemporary life, such as children kite-flying, to ornament the supper boxes at Vauxhall Gardens. He also designed illustrations for books, was a portraitist, produced a set of historical works focusing on British history, including *Caractacus* and *The Conversion of the Britons to Christianity*, and was one of the founders of the Royal Academy.[2] Similarly, theatre scene-painters, such as Nicholas Dall, John Inigo Richards, and Philip James de Loutherbourg, were also important painters of other works, including landscapes. Scene-painting itself reflected shifts in the depiction of landscape as well as in the settings believed appropriate for particular types of drama.[3]

Writers also produced works in different genres. Alexander Pope (1688–1744), the son of a London linen-draper, who had been debarred by his Catholicism from attending university, was a leading literary figure. His works included a translation of Homer into heroic couplets, and an edition of Shakespeare, as well as the satirical celebration of the inconsequential in a mock-epic, *The Rape of the Lock* (1714), the *Dunciad* (1728), a satire on dullness in contemporary English culture, and the *Essay on Man* (1733–34), which was more philosophical in its subject and tone.[4] Pope's interest in the Classics – he wrote many of his works in conscious imitation of Classical genres – reflected a more general dominance of Classical themes in national culture. Aside from their prestige, these themes had resonance and the genres were regarded as workable.

Less successfully, in terms of literary fame or response, Moses Browne (1704–87) also illustrated the range of individual activity. Not only a wide-ranging poet, he was also the author of sermons and other theological works. A keen angler, he sought to present his hobby in an uplifting literary form. The third edition of Browne's *Piscatory Eclogues* (1729) was entitled *Angling Sports: In Nine Piscatory Eclogues. A new attempt to introduce a more pleasing variety and mixture of subjects and characters into pastoral. On the plan of its primitive rules and manners. Suited to the entertainment of retirement, and the lovers of nature in rural scenes. With an essay in the defence of this undertaking* (1773).

Aside from individual artists and writers working in different genres, particular forms could also be used for very different purposes. John, 2nd Earl of Buckinghamshire noted the pleasure of the South Coast of England:

> There is a peculiar geniality in Weymouth which softens even the Eastern and Northern Blasts. It is to this warmth we own the semblance of living in a state of primeval innocence, wherever you turn your eyes nakedness greets them without fig leaves or blushes, it seems indeed (to apply two lines of poor Granby's elegant poetry)
>
> > That, e'een as you list you may stick in your T
> > To a Jolly Brown C or a Lilly White A.[5]

This brings together two facets that receive insufficient attention in works on culture: private versifying and pornographic interest. The two were also combined in an unpublished ode Sir Charles Hanbury Williams wrote in 1743 to Henry, 9th Earl of Lincoln (1720–1794). Exuding a sense of male sexual confidence, if not self-satisfaction, this began:

> Oh! Lincoln Joy of Womankind
> To thee this humble Ode's design'd
> Let Cunt inspire the Song
> Gods! with what Power's art thou indue'd

and included such lines as

> 'Tis Fucking now my Pen employs
>
> . . .
>
> Prick and the man I'll sing
>
> . . .
>
> Four times each Night some amorous Fair
> He swives, throughout the circling year.
>
> . . .
>
> His Prick that always stands.
> That never baulks him with Delays
> Its willing Lord alone obeys
> And all the Fair commands
>
> . . .
>
> With Whores be Lewd, with Whigs be hearty

And both in Fucking and in Party
Confess this Noble's Race.[6]

This phallocentric approach was not untypical of elite male comments:
the approach of many men to sexuality, at least as evinced in private
correspondence, was clearly priapic. While politeness was part of society's self-image, a coarseness of utterance, and indeed of thought, was
equally part of its reality: indeed politeness in part consciously existed
in deliberate separation from a private coarseness. Impolite conduct and
culture are too readily overlooked. Aside from an extensive publication
of pornographic material,[7] the humour published in the press was, by
modern standards, frequently cruel. Excremental jokes and verses
directed against cuckolds were commonplace. The elopements and sexual scandals of the great were also covered in considerable detail,
providing items not too different from the more dramatic episodes of
some novels: indeed gossip, newspaper stories and novels were often
closely related in plot and tone. As an instance of the extent to which
the culture of sexuality crossed social divides, the cast of William Hogarth's painting of 'The Rake at the Rose Tavern' from his 'Rake's
Progress' (1733–34) includes a poor female street singer singing indecent
songs to the heedless company.

The Reformation of Manners movements of the 1700s, 1710s and
1780s, for example the Proclamation Society against Vice and Immorality established in 1787, were, at least in part, a response to the anxieties
which coarse behaviour induced in religious and evangelical circles. The
listing of numbers of prosecutions by Societies for the Reformation of
Manners[8] suggested a misplaced authoritarian faith in the state regulation of behaviour. Frequent campaigns against swearing, lewdness and
profanity, and an insistence on Sabbath observance, were the counterpart to sexually explicit and forthright language. There was an
important gender dimension, as women used propriety and the cult of
politeness to help manage the behaviour and symbolic authority of
fathers, husbands, and men in general.[9] The contrast between male
coarseness and, at least apparent, female refinement was frequently displayed on stage, as in William Congreve's comedy *The Way of the World*
(1700), when the drunken, singing Sir Wilfull Witwoud annoys Lady
Wishfort, although in fact she is seeking a lover. Farces and burlesques,
such as those of Henry Carey, frequently mocked politeness, and would
probably have done so even more clearly in production as actors
resorted to gesture to make their points.

Male correspondence suggests that many men did not internalise the politeness that they apparently valued in public, and this presaged the contrast between public morality and private vice seen with the Victorians. The use of a vulgar discourse was, in part, a conscious rejection of public morality, as in the 1713 tract *Terrae Filius*, an attack on the Oxford authorities that included a poem attributed to the Vice-Chancellor's 'nag' in which the latter asks if he has not 'F-d handsome, ugly, rich and poor'. The intended tract was burned on the Vice-Chancellor's orders, but its author, John Willes, later both Lord Chief Justice of Common Pleas and a notorious womaniser, had it printed in London where it had a wide circulation. London was also the site of the 'Mohock Club', members of which, young gentlemen, in 1711–12 brawled and were held to slit the noses of victims and other such activities. In an instructive comment on the impact of a wider world, this was traced to the influence of their perception of the conduct of Native Americans.

The social positioning of politeness was complex. If politeness and gentility, or at least discussion of their value, are seen for the eighteenth century as 'middle-class' virtues, and the discussion as characteristic of 'middle-class' writers, then public restraint can also be seen as evidence of the emergence of values defining a broad social spectrum, and of their greater importance within society. There are also ideas of moral and social superiority implicit in the attitudes to those deemed vulgar. It is as dangerous to assume that politeness was simply a show as to assume that it was genuine; while, if politeness was a public act, the fact that such a show was thought necessary tells us much about social attitudes and change. Politeness was also at odds with self-indulgence not simply over matters of sexual decorum, but also in response to the opportunities and pressures created by economic growth. This consumerism was typecast as luxury with its associations of excess, and this language could at times be employed as an aspect of cultural criticism and artistic comment. Criticism of luxury came from a 'polite' not a Puritan context: indeed the opposition of taste to luxury legitimated consumption at the same time as it criticized its excesses.

Far from being primarily an offshoot of middle-class leisure activity, cultural life had a wider context. In reading or looking today at the works of the period, it is important to bear in mind that they were often closely bound up with the worlds of local politics and religion. For example, assembly rooms might serve not (or not only) as a place of relaxation and show driven by entrepreneurial energy, but as an opportunity for a particular political group to meet and socialise. Indeed, the spread and diffusion of culture could have more to do with political and religious issues, indeed crises, than with consumption. Those who agreed on the ethics of politeness and the morality of moderation, which are seen today as the criteria of eighteenth-century middle-class culture, might disagree on much else. The printed version of Dr Henry Sacheverell's controversial 1709 sermon on the threat to the Church of England from Whiggish tendencies sold 40,000 copies.

As an aspect of the cultural plurality of the century, culture indeed could become an expression of conflict, rather than a panacea for strife. The political background was stormy. Monarchy, Parliament, the Church of England and the position of the social elite were all seen as mutually reinforcing, but the Catholicism of James II (1685–88) had made this an elusive harmony. James had inherited his father Charles I's worst characteristics – inflexibility and dogmatism – and pressed forward unpopular authoritarian changes designed to further his goals of greater royal authority and paving the way for re-Catholicisation. The political culture of the age assumed deference in return for good kingship: expectations of political behaviour involved a measure of contractualism. James had spurned these boundaries. James's base of support was narrow, and it collapsed in 1688 as a result of challenge from without by his nephew William III (1689–1702), stadholder of many of the provinces of the Dutch Republic and the husband of James's daughter Mary (1689–94). William's invasion of England was successful, in large part because he ably exploited James's failure of nerve. James was encouraged to flee and Parliament declared that James had abdicated, rather than adopting the more radical notion that he had been deposed. Parliament, however, debarred Catholics from the succession and placed restrictions on royal power. The financial settlement left William with an ordinary revenue that was too small for his peacetime needs, obliging him to turn to Parliament for support, and a standing army was prohibited unless permitted by Parliament. In other words, Parliament was by this time stronger than the monarchy.

As at the time of the Tudor triumph in 1485, England had been successfully invaded in 1688. But in 1688 the political situation was very different for a number of reasons, not least the validating role of Parliament, and the need to ensure that Scotland and Ireland were brought in line. Nevertheless, there was also a fundamental continuity. Political issues were settled by conflict. Furthermore, the dynastic position was crucial: political legitimacy could not be divorced from the sovereign and the succession. Both these factors ensure that the elements of modernity suggested by the constitutional products of the 1688 invasion have to be qualified by reminders of more traditional features of the political structure.

What was to be termed by its supporters the Glorious Revolution of 1688–89 was to play a central role in the Whiggish, heroic, self-congratulatory account of English development. It was clearly important in the growth of an effective parliamentary monarchy in which the constitutional role of Parliament served as the anchor of co-operation between the crown and the socio-political elite. Yet a less benign account is also possible, and not only from the perspective of the exiled James and his Jacobite supporters. The instability of the ministries of the period 1689–1721 suggests that the political environment necessary for an effective parliamentary monarchy had in some ways been hindered by the events of 1688–89. A parliamentary monarchy could not simply be legislated into existence. It required the development of conventions and patterns of political behaviour that would permit a constructive resolution of contrary opinions. This took time and was not helped by the burdens of the lengthy and difficult wars with France from 1689 to 1697 and 1702 to 1713 that followed the Glorious Revolution. William III's seizure of power did not assist this process of resolution for other reasons: alongside praise for him as a Protestant and a providential blessing, there was criticism of him as a usurper. This criticism was marginalised because the circumstances of William's reign permitted him a political and polemical victory over his opponents. As a result, the Protestant and Whiggish vision associated with the victors eventually came to seem natural to the English. However, there were opponents who offered a very different account of the Revolution Settlement and the subsequent political establishment. The Glorious Revolution also had a wider cultural resonance, not only in encouraging links with the Protestant world, especially the United Provinces, but also because a tenuous link can be drawn between the willingness to conceive of new political structures and governmental arrangements, seen, for example with the parliamentary Union of England and Scotland in 1707 and the foundation of the Bank of England in 1694, and the increased interest in taking an active role in first understanding the world and then seeking to profit from this understanding that flowered with the scientific revolution.

The cultural world was not separate to that of political strife. This was true of individual careers, the response to individual works, and the willingness with which political issues were presented in terms of cultural commitment. The partisan character of culture can be readily seen with the content and staging of plays. Nicholas Rowe's *Tamerlane* (1701), in which Christopher Marlowe's protagonist was reworked to appear as William III, with his eventually defeated rival Bajazet as Louis XIV of France, was not performed during the Tory ascendancy in Anne's last years, a period in which peace was made with France. Once George I had come to the throne in 1714, Whig control was restored, and the work was staged anew, while Rowe's *Lady Jane Grey* (1715) offered in the person of Lady Jane a model of Protestant constancy and pathos in opposition to the wiles of the Catholic Queen Mary I. Reference to the persecution of Protestants during Mary's reign (1553–58) served as a way to discredit the Catholic Pretender, 'James III'. Rowe himself was appointed Poet Laureate in 1715. Similarly, John Philips's play *The Inquisition* (1717), the action of which opened in Child's Coffeehouse in London, showed the popular sense of the tension between High and Low Churchmen.

The response to plays provided an opportunity to display political allegiance. A clear instance occurred in 1713 with the tragedy *Cato*. Its author, Joseph Addison (1672–1719), the co-editor of the influential periodical the *Spectator* (1711–12), a master of restrained prose and an essayist of widely acclaimed quality, was also an active Whig MP. *Cato* was correctly seen as a markedly political play, and acclaimed or criticised accordingly. Both play and protagonist became a touchstone of conspicuous virtue and literary value. *The Flying Post: or The Postmaster*, a leading London Whig newspaper, in the issue of 20 February 1714 published verses (unidentified in the fashion of the period, but allegedly by a lady) in support of the Whig polemicist and writer Sir Richard Steele (co-editor of the *Spectator*) that included comparisons with Cato:

> Steele, who amidst Britannia's enemies,
> Dares for her laws, like Rome's great Cato, rise
> . . .
> Cato and Steele pursue the self same end.

The play's message continued to resonate strongly, and, in the fashion of the period, inspired self-conscious reflections, such as the poem 'On Reading *Cato*' printed in *Brice's Weekly Journal,* an Exeter newspaper, in its issue of 2 July 1725.

The staging of plays was seen as particularly politically charged in the first half of the century, and the sense of an overlap between culture and politics, of the staging of politics as well as the politics of the stage, was captured in the title of a Whig pamphlet of 1715, *The Tragicomedy Acted by the Late Ministry: or An Answer to a Scandalous Pamphlet Entitled A Defence of the King.* The *Post-Man and the Historical Account,* a Whig London newspaper, in its issue of 6 November 1722, noted the response of London's theatre world to the Atterbury Plot, a Jacobite attempt to seize power:

> The players of both houses being willing to show their loyalty, the Tragedy of Tamerlane was last night acted both at Drury Lane and Lincolns Inn Fields: the character which gives that play its name was drawn from nature for the character of King William.

This was a reference to the Whig hero William III as depicted in the 1701 play by the Whig Nicholas Rowe. The theatre therefore acted out current events, while the ministry deployed troops in Hyde Park to overawe London.

Poetry was also partisan to an extent that is sometimes underrated: thus the Bangorian controversy of 1716–20, a key Church-State party political issue of the 1710s, led to a huge number of verses. Newspapers contained many partisan verses, and these drew on a widespread habit of versifying on many topics. There are some particularly striking examples from the 1710s, and fewer in the second half of the century. G.C. from Enfield applauded the return of John, Duke of Marlborough to military command after George I replaced Anne's Tory ministry in 1714. The *Flying-Post: or The Postmaster* of 2 November 1714, a leading London Whig newspaper, carried his contribution:

> These following lines are wrote by a lover of loyalty, courage, conduct, and the present ministry, and a soldier's friend.

> > I need not sing what is already known,
> > Of what bright jewels sparkle in the crown;
> > How lately sullied, now it will appear
> > Which were the true, and which the false ones were,
> > Marlborough's return unto the soldiers sight,

Welcome to all their eyes as wished for light;
Renowned for council, and for courage great,
And merit only made him fortunate.
Louis [XIV] in earnest never would have mourned
Great Anne's death, had Marlborough not returned:
He loyal, true, and trusty ever was,
And, now for rightful George his sword he draws,
The same his courage, and the same his cause.
Louis 'tis thought, laughed in his sleeve to see,
Mardyke imposed on our late ministry.
The times are changed, no more his laughing day,
Great George now reigns, and Marlborough doth obey.

Nine days later, the same newspaper illustrated the national sway of partisan poetry when it published an article from Frome criticising the strength of Tory sentiment in nearby Bristol. It ended with a description of an hypocrite:

Among the beasts that range the hills and woods,
Or scaly fish that shame the liquid floods;
The treacherous crocodile the worst appears,
That aims at mischief with deluding tears:
So if mankind in various forms we view,
The hypocrites appear a dreadful crew;
Who, juggler-like, surprise us with delight,
Yet cast a cheat upon our easy sight,
If in the state these double gamesters play,
Their thoughts are different to whate'er they say;
In boasting words their loyalty reveal,
Yet the false traitor in their hearts conceal;
A thousand different tongues their conscience keeps,
And every tongue a different language speaks;
So artificial glasses fall, or rise,
As fair, or cloudy weather rules the skys.

'A New Ballad to an Old Tune' followed in the issue of 26 February 1715, offering an account of politics and the struggle between George I and 'James III', the Stuart Pretender, which ended with the Pope making the latter a cardinal (something which did not occur although James's younger son, Henry, 'Henry IX', later became one). The advertisements also recorded not only the role of songs, but also the extent to which political partisanship overlapped with the world of print.

Readers of this Whig newspaper would have known what to expect from the following, advertised in the issues of 24 March, 14 April and 23 April 1715:

Political Merriment: or Truths Told to Some Tune; being a collection of above 150 of the choicest songs and poems that were composed and writ during the four last years of the late reign, many of which never before appeared in print.

Perkin's Cabal ... A satirical poem on [the Earl of] O[xfor]d ...

A key to the Lock; or a treatise proving beyond all contradiction, the dangerous tendency of a late poem, entitled, *The Rape of the Lock*, to government and religion. By Esdras Barnivelt.

Facetious notices also played a role, as with the paper's suggestion on 30 January 1714 that Jonathan Swift, the Tory author of *The Tale of a Tub*, was both an opportunist and a Jacobite:

The newest edition of the *T—le of a T—b*, so long reprinted and modestly laid by in sheets, will be published very swiftly by that famous hand who has boasted in one of the former editions, that he was wrote fourscore and eleven pamphlets under three reigns, and for the service of six and thirty factions, subscriptions are carried on in Italy, France, Lorraine [seat of the Jacobite court] and Lancashire [an area with many Catholics], and as soon as the books are ready to be delivered out to subscribers, notice will be given in the *Examiner* of London [Swift's newspaper], and at Pasquin's statue in Rome.

In the late 1720s and early 1730s, ministerial concern about opposition use of the stage led to criticism of the theatre in the pro-government press and also to action.[10] The latter included the refusal of a performing licence for John Gay's play *Polly* in 1729. Eventually, the ministry resorted to legislation, the Licensing Act of 1737, of which Andrew Stone, an MP and an Under Secretary of State, wrote 'the late insolence and immorality of the stage ... called aloud for such a remedy'.[11] Few followed the advice in Alexander Pope's *An Essay on Man* (1733–34):

> For forms of government let fools contest;
> Whate'er is best administered is best.

Samuel Johnson commented in 1739 'The present poets I reckon amongst the most inexorable enemies of our most excellent ministry'.[12] Johnson is a controversial figure, but his Toryism and his Nonjuring position on Church politics[13] seem clearer than the modern characteristics sometimes emphasised.[14] The Walpole ministry (1720–42) was particularly vilified by men of letters. Most of the leading literary figures of the period, including Gay, Pope and Swift, joined in the 1730s by others such as Glover, Mallet, Thomson and Johnson, attacked Sir Robert Walpole, alleging that he governed through corruption and that his attitudes were debasing public life and society.[15] The strength of the literary opposition to Walpole has consistently impressed posterity, and if it reflected both wider pressure for cultural revival, some of it xenophobic in character, and Walpole's neglect of the literati of the age, rather than any particular faults of his administration, the former showed the political resonance of cultural issues (and vice-versa). The neglect of the literati was important in several prominent cases. John Gay abandoned his support of the government when he was denied the promotion he felt he merited,[16] and, as John Andrews later wrote:

> Sir Robert Walpole, by neglecting men of letters, drew the whole load of their odium upon him. Hence it is, that no mercy hath been shown to his character; and that he is, according to the representations of the majority of writers, accounted the chief author and modeller of that regular system of corruption which has nearby subverted the constitution.[17]

More than this, however, was at stake. There was also a fundamental disdain for the disruptive character of change, one made more specific in an opposition to the apparent capacity of money and the monied to rework values. In his pamphlet *The Conduct of the Allies* (1711), Swift condemned the monied interest:

> A set of upstarts who had little or no part in the [Glorious] Revolution, but valued themselves by their noise and pretended zeal when the work was over, were got into credit at court, by the merit of becoming undertakers and projectors of loans and funds. These, finding that the gentlemen of estates were not willing to come into their measures, fell upon those new schemes of raising money, in order to create a monied interest, that might in time vie with the landed, and of which they hoped to be at the head.

Similarly, Johnson, in his pamphlet *Thoughts on the Late Transactions Respecting Falkland's Islands* (1771), asked:

> how are we recompensed for the death of multitudes and the expense of millions, but by contemplating the sudden glories of paymasters and

agents, contractors and commissaries, whose equipages shine like meteors and whose palaces rise like exhalations.

Johnson's dictionary definition of stockjobber was also very critical. Aside from the moral revulsion towards those who profited from the sufferings of others, Swift and Johnson also offered the classic Tory critique of financial activity and speculation. This looked back on a rich tradition and one with a strong Classical genealogy, not least in opposition to the alleged urban values of ancient Rome and modern London, but the critique was in many respects outdated in a society where such activity and wealth were of growing importance. If opposition to the corruption of values apparently represented by change represented an important literary strand throughout the century, one that encouraged references back to supposed golden ages, or at least to admirable models, the political resonance, indeed bite, of such a strand varied greatly. Party politics, for example, played a role in the depiction of relationships in early female amatory fiction, and Delarivier Manley, a prominent female novelist and playwright, was a keen Tory.[18] In contrast, the novels of the 1760s and 1770s were not party political.

After the Walpole ministry, which fell in 1742, and the intense disappointment created that year by the willingness of much of the opposition to enter office alongside the government Whigs, this political bite diminished in intensity and became more episodic in character. Political references continued important in literary culture, while poetry remained an important medium of political communication;[19] but these references became less insistent, and the role of political reference and relationship across the range of artistic activity diminished. Politics played a role in the cultural life of the latter half of the century, although it is sometimes exaggerated.[20] There was, however, to be a marked revival in political commitment in response to the French Revolution.

While party politics was not at the forefront of cultural concerns in the 1760s, 1770s and 1780s, politics in the wider sense of views on the arrangement and purpose of society remained important, and was related to aesthetic assumptions and categorisation.[21] Furthermore, the presentation of the artist, especially, but not only, the novelist, the playwright and the essayist, throughout the century as a commentator on the manners and mores of contemporary society ensured that politics in this more extensive sense was widely covered. This role indeed was presented as a continuation of Classical models. Thus, on the completion of its first year of publication, the achievements of the *Tatler* (1709–11), an influential tri-weekly London periodical, were summed up by Joseph Addison, who was, after Richard Steele, its major contributor:

> I took upon me the Title and Dignity of *Censor* of *Great Britain*, reserving to myself all such Perquisites, Profits, and Emoluments, as should arise out of the Discharge of the said Office. These in Truth have not been inconsiderable ... I have made a narrow Search into the Nature of the old *Roman Censors*, whom I must always regard, not only as my Predecessors, but as my Patterns in this great Employment ... the Duty of the *Roman Censor* was Twofold. The first Part of it consisted in making frequent Reviews of the People ... In Compliance with this Part of the Office, I have taken many curious Surveys of this great City ... The Second Part of the *Roman Censor*'s Office was to look into the manners of the People, and to check any growing Luxury, whether in Diet, Dress, or Building. This Duty likewise I have endeavoured to discharge, by those wholesom Precepts which I have given my Countrymen in Regard to Beef and Mutton ... upon looking into my Catalogue of Subscribers, which I intend to print Alphabetically in the Front of my Lucubrations, I find the Names of the greatest Beauties and Wits in the whole Island of *Great Britain*.

If political rivalries were sometimes closely related to the often bitter ones between writers, artists and theatres, there were also differences between the latter and political tensions that in large part reflected the role of personal and entrepreneurial disputes.[22] It is more generally important to be cautious about asserting political relationships. This can be seen with architecture: English (neo-)Palladianism is usually seen as a clear sign of the Whig appropriation of a Venetian self-image, with the Whigs associating themselves with the oligarchic liberty of Venetian republicanism; while the Baroque is sometimes simplistically linked to Tories. This Palladianism in fact probably owed more to a concern with pure Classical models, and Tory patrons as well as Whigs patronised Palladian architects from the 1720s. Metropolitan fashion was the key element. Furthermore, Venetian painters worked all over Europe and on both sides of the so-called English party divide.[23] In the case of landscape design, a contrast has been drawn between elite amateurs keen to innovate, and professionals more reluctant to take risks.[24]

The cultural resonances of political strife varied greatly, and this could become a theme of writers. In 'Cicely, Joan and Deborah: An Eclogue upon Hearing of the Defeat of the Rebels at Culloden' (the dramatic culmination in 1746 of the struggle with the Jacobites), Mary

Leapor, a young servant-poet, depicted Cicely, upset that her beloved has been enlisted into the army to fight the Jacobites, and Deborah bringing news of the victory, while Joan adds an element of common-sense. The parody of Classical conventions and poetising of everyday life is striking in Joan's lines. Meeting the weeping Cicely, she asks:

> is old Brindle dead?
> (Since yester morn I have not heard her low)
> If so – who would not weep for such a cow?

and, after news of Culloden, adds

> My husband lost his purse at Cheatham Fair.
> Last night a beam broke down and killed the mare.
> These things are hard to such as thee and I:
> But yet we'll drink, because the rebels fly.

Deborah replying, adds to the parody

> This beer is good – say, how d'ye like it? ho!
> And shall I fetch the other pot, or no?
> Hark, the men shout, and bonfires light the plain:
> Then shall we sit, and lick our lips in vain?

Among the factors that need to be borne in mind when considering politics in its widest sense is that of potential conflict between popular and elite culture. The late Edward Thompson focused attention on the world of 'plebeian', as opposed to 'patrician', culture. His work has been crucial in alerting historians to a wider cultural sphere, specifically the social and political messages of ritual within society, showing the unwritten cultural and political assumptions behind what he valuably termed the 'moral economy' of the crowd.[25] Indeed, there was an, at least apparent, dichotomy in the world of amusements. The elite and the middling orders generally supported highly structured amusements, whether in assemblies, card games, or the entertainments offered at Ranelagh, Vauxhall, Marylebone, and many other pleasure gardens. In contrast, among the bulk of the population, amusement often went hand-in-hand with an, at least apparent, absence of structure. Cock-fighting, public drunkenness, attending hangings and such activities were amusements that in some senses reflected this absence of structure and control. Possibly the chaos of mass community activities was itself an important element in plebeian amusement. This extended into riot-ing, for example the Sacheverell riots of 1710, the Gordon riots in 1780, and the periodic disturbances of the London apprentices, which can be seen as in part entertainment, not least excitement for its own sake.

It is, however, also possible to modify this analysis of a bifocal cultural world by seeing, instead, cultural gradations and/or a world that encompassed populace and elite.[26] Furthermore, it is probable that the oft-cited dichotomy between written and oral culture, the former progressive and the latter conservative, should be replaced by an emphasis on gradations within a cultural world that encompassed both written and oral forms.

This is very abstract. To be reminded of what is now covered by cultural history, it is useful to turn to clothes, a surviving example of the material culture of the age, and to consider the argument that the display and utility they at once incorporate provide a way to consider strategies of class differentiation and stabilisation. Instead, therefore, of seeing clothes largely in terms of independent stylistic issues, it is valuable to present them as an aspect of a consumerist society in which style and ideology interacted. Crucially, this was not a matter defined by legislation: the consumerist society set sartorial standards that acted as a substitute for the sumptuary legislation seen in certain continental states which regulated what different social groups could wear. The aesthetics of taste, however, were debated – with fashion and concepts of virtue interacting, and, at times competing, as values and taste were defined and redefined. The style chosen can be presented as heavily politicised:

> at the heart of English political culture, guarding the boundaries of the aristocratic polity meant donning the image of noble simplicity, presenting the landed gentleman as true-born Englishmen and the moral backbone of the nation.

The political and social location of stylistic and cultural developments, however, are far from easy. For example, rather than seeing the tendency for men to adopt increasingly modest and uniform dress (the great masculine renunciation, as it is commonly presented) as middle-class and occurring in the later eighteenth century, its origins have been presented in the most recent study as in 'an aristocratic response to new ideas of manliness legitimated by the culture that emerged after the Glorious Revolution'.[27]

This serves in fact as a reminder of the difficulties of providing a context and causative framework for cultural developments, because, by their very nature, the links are not clear; the same being true of relating the abandonment of wigs for men, either in favour of lightly powdered and tied back hair or of it falling naturally, to the cultural movement of Romanticism towards the close of the eighteenth century, with its emphasis on individual expression. That is not, however, a reason to avoid the challenge of providing a context, not least because there are multiple connections between the worlds of culture, society and politics.

To return, indeed, to male clothes, there was a secularisation of clothing with, for example, gowns and hoods in the universities and the church becoming specialist clothes that were not worn for everyday wear.[28] More generally, alongside growing simplicity can be seen continued exuberance, and this in a field of design that allowed considerable range for the play of artistic ability. Thus, Anna Maria Gurthwaite (1690–1763), the well-educated daughter of a Lincolnshire parson who came to London in about 1730, was one of the leading mid-century silk designers. She produced and sold an average of eighty designs a year, relying on a contrast between bright, coloured floral motifs and a textured pattern in the ground, and from 1742 based her designs on flowers of correct botanical size and shape. Costume was linked to stance, both aspects of a body language held to denote politeness, breeding, judgement and intention.[29] Costume was also linked to display and status, and could signal eroticism and wealth. Whether in clothes or cameos, canons of taste changed, so that notions of and attitudes to colour, shape and sound all varied. For example, the exuberant use of colour by Robert Adam and others in interior decoration in the late eighteenth century contrasted with the more sombre interior colours of the start of the century.[30]

In displaying the world around, and life within, the arts also provided both guidance to the rich and varied fascination of the life and imagination of the period, and also indications about the tensions of the age. Joseph Wright's intimate and gentle portrayal of *Two Girls with their Black Servant* focuses not only modern concerns about race relations but also would have struck an increasingly ambivalent note in the latter decades of the century, as opposition to slavery and, even more, the slave trade grew. This painting, which may have been his *A Conversation of Girls*, exhibited in 1770, probably depicts the daughters of a merchant in Liverpool, where Wright worked in 1769–71. The Classical connotations of the portrayal were explicit, especially the motif of the girls decorating an ewer with flowers. Yet the ship in the background and the black servant serve today as a reminder of Liverpool's role as

Britain's foremost slaving port, and thus offer a reference to England's leading role in the slave economy that prefigures Jane Austen's novel *Mansfield Park* (1814).

Prior to that, at the same time that the profits of the slave trade funded cultural activity, for example the construction of William Beckford's massive stately home, Fonthill Abbey, abolitionist sentiment affected the arts. It led to the production of visual and literary images of the horrors of slavery, such as the medallion of the Society for the Abolition of the Slave Trade designed by William Hackwood and manufactured at Josiah Wedgwood's factory, as well as a mass of pamphlet literature and discussion of the issue in humanitarian novels, and also comments on the abolitionist fight. *Swinney's Birmingham and Stafford Chronicle* of 5 May 1791 included a poem by 'H.F.' praising William Pitt the Younger's recent parliamentary speech on the slave trade. As a reminder of cultural diversity, colour was also employed as a device in comic works, as in Henry Bate's opera *The Blackamoor Washed White*, which was produced at Drury Lane in 1776.

It is not always easy to understand how works were viewed by contemporaries. In mid century, George Stubbs (1724–1806), the popular painter of racehorses, visited Ceuta with a Moor with whom he was friendly. From the walls, he saw a lion seize a white Barbary horse, and this powerful scene provided the subject of numerous of his pictures, including *A Lion Seizing a Horse* (1764) and *A Lion Devouring a Horse* (1770). Once engraved, these proved popular prints. The paintings can be variously interpreted, and clearly Stubbs's skills, which stemmed in part from his anatomical expertise, explain part of their attraction, as does the dramatic exposition derived from his Classicism.[31] There is also a sense of observing the savagery of the non-European world that locates the focus of the contemporary impact of these pictures. This world was one in which the polite patina of European society played scarcely a role, while animals were still powerful, unlike in Europe where they were treated as objects and commodities. From that perspective, it was easy to imply that Europeans were best placed to define and spread civilisation.

An awareness of cultural and other tensions helps explain the emphasis on order that underlays the stylistic interplay of simplicity and exuberance. This emphasis can be seen not only in the content of literature, artistry of clothes and deportment, but also in the organization of works of art, ranging from the overtly geometric character of buildings and the tonal organization of music to the structuring of literary works, both in terms of story and of syntax, and the use of space within paintings. The notion of God as an orderly architect of the world,[32] rather than as a unpredictable wielder of the arms of Providence, was an important product of this culture, and one that also sustained its values. The emphasis on order reflected the central theme of aesthetics prior to the Romantic transformation at the end of the eighteenth century. Order was at once seen as psychological, social and political. If the feeling understood as sensibility was to be the guide to individual responses to culture (and to everything else), then this sensibility had to be guided so that it was appropriate and uplifting, rather than disruptive; although there were also counter-trends, such as the interest in the grotesque.

Aesthetics was linked to conduct, with the inspiration of spectator and reader not a matter of the order of arid reason, still less repression, but rather of fine delicacy that variously called forth and inculcated appropriate behaviour. Anthony, 3rd Earl of Shaftesbury (1671–1713) was a leading force here, offering an optimistic account of the capability of human nature, providing an aesthetic that linked this to a sense of universal harmony, and stressing how innate 'moral sense' should be encouraged. His key works included *Inquiry Concerning Virtue* (1699) and *Characteristics of Men, Manners, Opinions and Times* (1711).[33] Another influential writer, Francis Hutcheson (1694–1746), in his *Inquiry Concerning Beauty, Order, Harmony, Design* (1725), sought to reconcile the subjective individual response with the objective value of uniformity. Proper order and appropriate style were moral as well as aesthetic requirements and thus judgements. A failure to provide them was presented as the consequence of flawed values and improper goals, and this manifested itself in inappropriate form and sentiments.[34]

Societies that place an emphasis on order are generally, at least in part, concerned with disorder. This was a legacy of the seventeenth century, with its civil conflicts, religious strife and social uncertainty. All three were subjects of eighteenth-century opprobrium, especially in its early decades, when there was a strong emphasis on the virtue, as well as value, of restraint and balance. This overlapped with a partisan character to cultural activity that reflected the continuation of earlier tensions, especially dynastic challenge in the shape of the Jacobites who produced their own cultural legacy,[35] and party bitterness in the form of Whig-Tory rivalry. Any stress on England as a polite society,[36] a happy symbiosis of aristocratic ease and elegance with bourgeois energy, a balanced constitution sustaining those with property in liberty, has to address powerful elements of instability and division.

At the same time, partisanship was designed to be inclusive as well as exclusive. Thus, the anti-Catholic theme was unwelcome to a religious minority but sought to bind the Protestant majority together.[37] Due in large part to the Jacobite challenge, anti-Catholic literature was especially common in the first half of the century. The challenge lent an edge to work that might otherwise be simply comic. Thus Henry Fielding's *The Debauchees: or The Jesuit Caught*, a comedy set in Toulon and first performed at Drury Lane in 1732, presented the lascivious cleric Martin not only as a figure of fun but also as a disturbingly malevolent force, with lines such as 'Religion loves to warm itself at the fire of a heretic'. The play was reprinted in 1746, a time of acute sensitivity about Jacobitism. Originally, it was a response to the Cadière case: the trial of a Jesuit at Aix-en-Provence for seduction lent pornographic interest to national prejudice, and led to exuberant literature of broadsheets, prints, pamphlets and newspaper reports, the anonymous pamphlet *The Case of Mary Katherine Cadiere* (1731) running through at least nine editions. The newspapers reported the case, as well as advertising publications and noting theatrical performances: 'at the Theatre in Goodman's Field was acted an entertainment at the close of the play relating to Father Girard and Miss Cadiere'.[38] This was a frequent theme. In 1727, the *Case of Seduction: being the late Trial of the Reverend Abbé Des Rues, at Paris for committing rapes upon one hundred and thirty three virgins* had been published. References to religious persecution were also common, and became part of the idiom of theatre. In *The Fair Quaker of Deal*, Charles Shadwell's first play, which appeared at the Theatre Royal, Drury Lane in 1710 with some success, Rovewell says of his beloved: 'She uses me as tyrannically as if she was the French King, and I one of the Protestants'.

The continued role of religious tension occurred in surprising artistic contexts. In 1789, George Huntingford, then master of the school at Warminster, and later a bishop, added an instructive twist to the contemporary fascination with Gothick ruins and the picturesque when he wrote to his friend Henry Addington, then Speaker of the House of Commons and later prime minister, who had been travelling in Hampshire:

> The old ruins of Beaulieu I know well, and remember with an impression bordering on superstition: the Abbey was most extensive and its site

highly picturesque ... Netley Abbey ... the elevated situation of the latter gives it a very superior advantage not to mention 'the sullen murmur of the dashing waves' heard at the ebb and flow of the tide, and the sacred horror of the adjacent wood. I have often marked these circumstances on the very spot, and never think of the place but with the recollection of the poetical charms it must convey to a mind framed for the love of aweful and striking objects in art and nature combined. In that fatal year, when fanaticism led the way and villainy conspired to destroy the metropolis, some wretch set fire to the ivy that surrounded the abbey, by way of showing his detestation of popery.[39]

Thus, in 1780, the year of the large-scale anti-papal Gordon Riots in London and elsewhere,[40] the appearance of a resonant image of the Gothick picturesque had been altered.

Aside from religious and political issues, there were also signs of social tension. Visiting the Haymarket Theatre in London in 1786, Sophie La Roche noted a hostile interplay of fashionable spectators with the rest of the audience, and with the actors also responding rapidly:

four ladies ... entered a box during the third play, with such wonderfully fantastic caps and hats perched on their heads, that they were received by the entire audience with loud derision. Their neckerchiefs were puffed up so high that their noses were scarce visible, and their nosegays, were like huge shrubs, large enough to conceal a person. In less than a quarter of an hour, when the scene had changed to a market square in any case, four women walked on to the stage dressed equally foolishly, and hailed the four ladies in the box as their friends. All clapped loud applause.

She also noted the actors defending the value of the stage as social commentary, a goal that joined the moral mission of the theatre of sensibility, the exposure of hypocrisy seen in comedies such as Richard Brinsley Sheridan's *The School of Scandal* (1777), and interest that was to come in a more politically committed theatre:

After this delightful performance I saw the players hold a kind of trial and support the motion, 'That it is the duty of the stage to condemn social evils, and [to] seek improvement through the medium of its wit'.[41]

Theatrical performances were an index of social precedence in many respects. When a new theatre opened in Exeter in 1787, the newspaper advertisement proclaimed 'By Desire of the Rt Hon. Lord Viscount Courtenay ... will be opened the New Theatre', but, in a sign of the precedence of commercial considerations over hierarchy, the previous year the advertisement for a London showing of Loutherbourg's dramatic backdrops had noted 'Ladies and Gentlemen desirous of taking places, are requested to send their servants early to keep them, otherwise it will be impracticable to ascertain [sic] them'.[42]

The success of the shows of these backdrops serve as a reminder of the variety of entertainments on offer, a variety in which innovation was fuelled by commercialization. It would be questionable to isolate a number of these entertainments as culture, without being aware that the aesthetic criteria employed to make such distinctions were not always of weight with contemporaries. In Oliver Goldsmith's popular novel *The Vicar of Wakefield* (1766), the narrator is told by a travelling player he meets on the road that:

> Dryden and Rowe's manner are quite out of fashion; our taste has gone back a whole century, Fletcher, Ben Johnson [sic], and all the plays of Shakespeare, are the only things that go down ... the public think nothing about dialect, or character; for that is none of their business, they only go to be amused, and find themselves happy when they can enjoy a pantomime, under the sanction of Johnson's or Shakespeare's name ... it is not the composition of the piece but the number of starts and attitudes that may be introduced into it that elicits applause. I have known a piece, with not one jest in the whole, shrugged into popularity, and another saved by the poet's throwing in a fit of the gripes ... the works of Congreve and Farquhar have too much wit in them for the present taste.

In London in the 1770s, the young Samuel Johnson (not the famous writer) recorded the variety of shows on offer. In 1775, he went to see the regatta on the Thames:

> There has been so much said about this regatta, and people's expectations have been raised so high, that I had not the least hope of getting a tolerable sight of it without mobbing, which is dangerous at least. The name, the end, the plan etc I refer you to newspapers for a circumstantial account of.'Tis said that the end of it was to keep our gentry from trooping to the coronation [of Louis XVI of France] ... on the waterside I thought I should run the risk of being crushed to death or thrown into the water. One might almost have walked over the Thames and through every part of it on the boats, which could scarcely pass by each other; the streets were paved with heads, the houses were all ... covered with faces, on the shore all along on each side of the Thames was a moving quay which seemed to hem in the water, and Westminster Bridge was exactly like a rich fringe formed by the people who sat across the balustrades sideways

over the heads of those who were peeping through them ... When a number of people are brought together, there is always some end proposed by their assembling, I mean something to draw them together, something to be seen, but in this case they all appeared to me to be assembled for no other purpose than to see each other, which without doubt is a secondary consideration in most conventions, and in this a sight well worth going to see but it is a new way of entertaining the public, who indeed may console themselves with the thoughts of adding to the entertainment, and of looking on themselves to be as well the entertainers as the entertained.

The following year, Johnson went to see the trial of the Duchess of Kingston for bigamy. This was 'the grandest sight that I have ever yet seen, or expect ever to see'. He reported seeing about 120 peeresses, some with amazingly contrived hair.[43] The sense of Parliament as entertainment was captured with comparisons between speakers and actors, not only in oratory but also in action. William Pitt the Elder was compared to the leading actor David Garrick by Horace Walpole in 1755. The theatrical mood climaxed with Edmund Burke's dagger speech in December 1792 when he threw a dagger onto the floor of the House of Commons in order to warn of pro-French revolutionary subversion, only to be greeted with laughter.[44] For more dramatic spectacle, Londoners then could instead go to see Thomas Morton's successful new play *Columbus*, which included an earthquake and storm that satisfied both spectators and plot.

A sense of show was captured by Thomas Harris, a London lawyer, when he wrote to his brother James in 1746:

This has been one of the most entertaining weeks for the mob that has happened a great while: on Wednesday five soldiers were shot in Hyde Park, and on Thursday the whole town was full of bonfires and illuminations, and yesterday (which was the top of all) Matthew Henderson was hanged, at whose execution all the world (I speak of the low-life division) were got together; and he died to the great satisfaction of the beholders, that is he was dressed all in white with black ribbons, held a prayer book in his hand and, I believe, a nosegay.[45]

In fact hangings were occasions not only for the 'low-life division' but also for the social elite. Fireworks were another example of an event that attracted avid interest across the social spectrum. They were an elite pleasure that all could enjoy, as well as an instance of conspicuous consumption and luxury. Another grim form of show were the insane inmates at Bedlam, depicted by William Hogarth being visited by fashionable women in the last painting in *The Rake's Progress* (1733–34). The wide-ranging nature of entertainment in part reflected both demands for novelty and entrepreneurial energy. Once a market was identified, competitors often emerged. A troupe of dancing dogs had a very successful run at Sadler's Wells Theatre in 1784, and by 1785 there were two competing troupes of dogs, although only one in 1786. The dogs portrayed tradesmen and acted a series of scenes including the failed storming of a castle.[46] Popular interest in new acts could be harnessed to comic effect, as in 1749 when the New Theatre in the Haymarket was hired, probably by the Duke of Montagu, a noted prankster, for the performance of 'Harlequin's Escape into the Bottle':

> A person advertised that he would, on the stage, get into a tavern quart bottle without equivocation, and while there sing several songs, etc... Performances seen by the crowned heads of Asia, Africa and Europe.

The large crowed tricked by their gullibility into attending was not mollified by the offer of the return of their admission money and, in the resulting riot, the theatre was badly burned.[47]

2

The Crown

Eighteenth-century monarchs were important as subjects and patrons of culture. Their role as subjects was displayed on canvas and in statues, as well as in dedications and allusions, but, in the first half of the century, was contested by the frequent depiction of the Jacobite claimant (the descendant through the male line of James II), not only in nostalgic references and forms that were frequently so allusive as to be almost secret, but also at a more accessible vernacular level.[1] There was also a wideranging symbolic and metaphorical quality of both royalty and dynastic politics. For example, attitudes towards the contest over the succession between the Hanoverians and the Jacobites also affected discussion of sexual politics.[2]

Nevertheless, although the monarchs were important, they were less so than their continental counterparts. By European standards, the British monarchs were not great patrons, in part because of the limited nature of royal revenues and the dependence on parliamentary financial support. The royal court was a setting of elegance and sometimes splendour, but not to compare with its continental counterparts, although the situation varied by art form. The royal court was particularly important for music. Many performers and composers were trained and worked there. From 1708 the establishment of the Chapel Royal included two composers and two organists, although usually the same men held both organist and composer places.[3] Similarly, large numbers of royal portraits had to be painted, for palaces and as presents, and the monarchs appointed portrait painters. William Beechey, for example, painted a portrait of Queen Charlotte in 1793, which gained him the position of Portrait Painter to the Queen.

The literary role of the court was less significant. The limited literary reputations of successive Poet Laureates offers a good instance as in many other European countries the position would have been a key one in national cultural life, and would thus have demonstrated the importance, for good or ill, of royal patronage. Nahum Tate, Laureate from

1692 until 1715, wielded his pen across changes in monarch and ministry. His best work dates from the 1680s and 1690s, but, thereafter, much of his poetry lacked conviction or even inspiration. Royal birthdays and other official events were commemorated, but Tate did little in the 1700s and early 1710s to challenge the critical remarks later expressed by Alexander Pope and Robert Southey. His verses for George I's birthday in 1715 included reference to the succession in the shape of George, Prince of Wales (later George II) and his wife Caroline:

> Yet long before our royal sun,
> His destined course has run,
> We are blessed to see a glorious heir,
> That shall the mighty loss repair,
> When he that blazes now, shall this low sphere resign,
> In a sublimer orb eternally to shine.
> A Cynthia too, adorned with every grace
> Of person and of mind,
> And happy in a starry race,
> Of such auspicious kind,
> As joyfully presage,
> No want of royal heirs, in any future age.

The celebration of royal heirs was important as it countered the Jacobite theme, at once promise and strength, of rebirth through a second Stuart restoration.

Tate's successor, Nicholas Rowe, Laureate from 1715 until 1718, a keen Whig, was, on appointment, a more significant figure, his play *Lady Jane Grey* having recently appeared. The political functions of the post were conducive to Rowe, and he attacked Jacobitism in a prologue for Colley Cibber's partisan play *The Nonjuror* (1717), while his play *Tamerlane* (1701) was performed most years in or near early November, the period of the anniversaries of Guy Fawkes' Gunpowder Plot and the landing of William III. Nevertheless, as Laureate, Rowe produced little of importance, bar completing a verse translation of Lucan's *Pharsalia*, a project that testified to the prestige of work on Classical texts and the extent to which major (and minor) literary figures, such as Alexander Pope, were also active as translators. Rowe's translation was dedicated by his widow to George I, who had been honoured by Rowe in some commonplace New Year odes.

Rowe's successor, Laurence Eusden, Laureate from 1718 until 1730, gained the post through political patronage unencumbered by merit, a commonplace practice of the age but not one conducive to literary quality. He had signalled his loyalty with *The Royal Family: A Letter to Addison on the King's Accession* (1714) and won the support of the Lord Chamberlain, Thomas, Duke of Newcastle, a key patron, with a poem on his marriage. Thereafter, Eusden turned out the poems expected of him, but added a reputation for drunkenness to his existing one for mediocrity. Colley Cibber, Laureate from 1730 to 1757, was an important figure in the theatre, as actor, manager and playwright, but his poetry was weak and deserved the scorn of Pope.[4] His successor, William Whitehead, Laureate until 1785, gained the position because Thomas Gray had rejected it, and was similarly assailed, especially by Charles Churchill. The lacklustre quality of Whitehead's poetry was amply illustrated by his New Year ode for 1785 which predicted that the newly-independent American colonies would return to their loyalty, and that Britain:

> Shall stretch protecting branches round,
> Extend the shelter, and forget the wound,
> Two Britons thro' the admiring world,
> Shall wing their way with sails unfurl'd;

Whitehead's successor, Thomas Warton, was important for reviving interest in the sonnet, but his own poetry had less of an impact than his *History of English Poetry* (1774–81). Plumbing the depths, Henry Pye held the Laureateship from 1790 until 1813, but his undistinguished poetic writings made less of an impact than his *Summary of the Duties of a Justice of the Peace out of Sessions* (1808), and he probably owed his position to his loyal voting record as an MP. Pye certainly did his job as a Laureate, and dedicated to George III his *Naucratia: or Naval Dominion* (1798), but he also attracted the scorn of other poets. Pye's successors, Robert Southey (1813–43), William Wordsworth (1843–50) and Alfred Tennyson (1850–92), improved the credibility of the post, although, while Laureate, Wordsworth failed to write the poetry he should have produced.

The deaths as well as lives of royalty provided occasions for works by the Poet Laureates. Joseph Trapp, who in 1708 became the first Professor of Poetry at Oxford, wrote a poem on the death of the future Queen Anne's son, the young William, Duke of Gloucester (1700), and others after those of William III (1702), Prince George of Denmark (1708), and Queen Anne (1714). A Tory, his *The Royal Sin: or Adultery Rebuk'd in a*

Great King (1738), supposedly about the biblical King David, could not help but be seen as referring to George II, who, it was well known, had taken up with Madame Walmolden before the death of Queen Caroline in 1737. This was a period of much literature aimed against George. The Whig John Hughes, in contrast, wrote *An Ode for the Birthday of Her Royal Highness the Princess of Wales* (1716), as Caroline then was. He was the beneficiary of party patronage, being appointed Secretary to the Commissions of the Peace in the Court of Chancery by Lord Chancellor Cowper, a prominent Whig.

Aside for the work of the Poet Laureates, the monarchy provided occasions for massive outpourings of verse at moments of celebration and of transition, especially coronations and deaths. Thomas Newcomb contributed with 'A Congratulatory Ode to the Queen on her Voyage to England' (1761), a prelude to the marriage of Charlotte of Mecklenburg-Strelitz to George III. George's recovery in 1789 from apparent madness was also much celebrated in verse. Indeed, his mental health influenced the depiction of madness in the arts. George's later recovery in 1800–1 provided a background to the plot of Maria Edgeworth's novel *Belinda* (1801).[5]

The celebratory tone was very different between 1714 and 1727, when the accessions of George I and George II were applauded by the Whigs, but unwelcome to the Jacobites and left many Tories uncomfortable, and 1760, when George III's accession benefited from his youth, his ostentatious Britishness, and from the demise of Jacobitism. Nevertheless, on each occasion, celebratory poetry was extensively printed in the newspapers, while celebratory verses and songs also accompanied theatrical performances. Most of the poetry, in the fashion of the period, was anonymous. Much of it was weak, the sentiments pedestrian, and the rhymes unimpressive, but it clearly corresponded with the needs and wishes of the occasion. The leading London Whig tri-weekly newspaper, *The Flying-Post: or The Postmaster*, in its issue of 9 October 1714, offered verses on George I's recent Declaration in Council that made the King appear a rational thinker as well as an appropriate symbol. After a comparison with Classical Greece, came:

> So on King George, as through the streets he rode,
> Almost adored by us as a God;
> Our eager eyes with joyful hearts we place,
> Liking the features of his royal face;
> Yet curious still we waited till he spoke,

> To know the soul in that majestic look:
> This declaration shows complete the King,
> And tells the blessings which his reign will bring.

Nineteen days later, in yet another instance of depicting George as people wanted him to be rather than as he was, there was a poem to celebrate the coronation:

> Advance, great monarch, in majestic state,
> An able head supports the glorious weight:
> But underneath that stately towering prize,
> A greater weight, all Europe's safety, lies.
> We now the gold and jewels cease to view,
> And find the truest jewel lodged in you;
> The Crown no brightness to the monarch brings,
> The Crown takes lustre from the best of kings.

The issue of 11 June 1715 included a poem on how the accession had banished the eclipse of national honour, religion and liberties associated with the Toryism of Anne's later years, ending:

> To give Britannia once more light and day,
> And drive her former darkness quite away.

The remorseless character of this poetry is an indication of how verses were used to express political allegiance in a deliberate bridging of partisanship with established tunes and rhythms. The issue of 16 June 1715 included, as many other verses did, a helpful direction to the tune: *A lamentation for the Late Times. To the Tune of, To you fair Ladies now at hand.* The last verse offered a clear contrast between Hanoverian rule and that of the Catholic Stuarts, associated with the wooden shoes held to be characteristic of the oppressed French:

> Then God preserve our brave King George,
> And all his royal race;
> And may all those who dare to forge
> A papist for his place,
> O, may all men who have such views,
> O, may they die in wooden-shoes.

Architecture provided a more dramatic display of royal activity, and one in which the role of the monarch could be contested by only a few other patrons, rather than by a public market comparable to that which affected poetic reputations. Nevertheless, nothing was built to match either some of the ambitious projects of Continental rulers for new palaces, which would have been provoking in England, nor the particular character of Catholic royal Baroque seen with the sponsorship of massive royal-ecclesiastical buildings, such as the monastery-church of Mafra in Portugal, the huge church of Superga outside Turin (begun in 1717), the Karlskirche in Vienna and the palace-monastery of Klosterneuburg nearby, the last a complex dear to the heart of the Emperor Charles VI (1711–40).

In England there was impressive work, but not on this scale. At Hampton Court and Kensington, William III, King from 1689 to 1702, demolished earlier work and built essentially new palaces, both carefully integrated with their gardens. Sir Christopher Wren remodelled Hampton Court for William with scant concern for the Tudor fabric: he designed the Baroque Fountain Court which was surrounded by two sets of state rooms, because William was a joint monarch with his wife, Mary II (1689–94). As a consequence, there were two royal staircases and so on. The impression was dramatic as befitted both the grandeur of a ruler trying to establish his position as king, and the Baroque style. The King's staircase glorified William, the murals, by Antonio Verrio, presenting him as Alexander the Great. The enfilade of the King's state rooms was similarly designed to exalt William, not simply with the three throne rooms, but also with the large state bed. On the ground floor, William's living quarters were far more modest, as was in keeping both with his character and with the emphasis on display under the public gaze. A palace nearer London was also required, and, with Whitehall unacceptable because its damp exacerbated William's asthma, he bought the Earl of Nottingham's house in Kensington for £20,000 and had that greatly altered, not least with a series of reception rooms.

Queen Anne, who ruled from 1702 until 1714, in contrast was not a great builder. The extensive work of William III at Hampton Court and Kensington made it unnecessary that she should be, although she enhanced the latter with an Orangery by Nicholas Hawksmoor. The great palace that dates from her reign is that of John Churchill, 1st Duke of Marlborough at Blenheim: named after his great victory over the French and Bavarians on the Danube in 1704, the palace was built on land given by Anne and with money voted by Parliament. Anne's role was to have been celebrated in Godfrey Kneller's *Queen Anne Presenting the Plans of Blenheim to Military Merit*, but due to her rift with the Marlboroughs only the *modello*, not the painting, was ever executed. The cast of the painting, including Apollo, Minerva and Hercules, was very much a Baroque one. Anne did, however, retain a lifelong interest in music, and patronised both the Chapel Royal and secular musicians.

Britain was at war for most of Anne's reign, and it was therefore necessary to set her in a martial pose. This had also been a role that the last female sovereign ruler, Elizabeth I, had taken during the war with Spain that began in 1585. Anne was no Elizabeth, but the prologue to the play *Zelmane: or The Corinthian Queen* (1705), included:

> So that great day when Anna was the word
> And every conquering Britain drew his sword
> Her name with terror struck the nations
> And unknown fears their numerous troops confound.

The forceful Zelmane is presented as an able warleader, and the Classical comparison was deliberate.

The accession of the Hanoverian dynasty in 1714 did not have a dramatic cultural effect because of the relatively small scale of their royal patronage, the absence of a strong and distinctive indigenous Hanoverian culture, and the personality and interests of the kings. For example, George I (1714–27), George II (1727–60) and George III (1760–1820) did not compare in their building with George IV (Prince Regent 1811–20, King 1820–30), or with such continental monarchs as Elizabeth I and Catherine II of Russia, or even rulers of lesser states such as the prince-bishop of Würzburg, who began an enormous *Residenz* in 1719.

Yet it would be a mistake to ignore the role of the Hanoverian monarchs. George I, for example, was interested in both building and music. He was responsible for extensive work on Kensington Palace, including the completion and decoration of new state rooms by Colen Campbell and the rich painting of them by William Kent, and the remodelling of the grounds, where he liked to take long evening walks. George I was also a keen supporter of Italian opera and a patron of the German composer George Frideric (popularly spelt Frederick) Handel, whom he had appointed *Kapellmeister* at Hanover in 1710, and who had been awarded £200 annually for life by Queen Anne as a reward for his birthday ode of 1713 and for his thanksgiving for the Peace of Utrecht of that year. Handel was absent from Hanover from August 1710 until the end of 1711 and again from the autumn of 1712. There is a popular story that Handel had deserted Hanover for England, and that George I only became reconciled to him because of the quality of the *Water Music*, but this is inaccurate: in the early 1710s Handel remained in George's favour.[6]

Once George had come to the British throne, Handel taught George I's grand-daughters, while his *Water Music* was first performed in 1717 on the Thames, as part of an evening of entertainment for the King, and in 1723 he was appointed a composer to the Chapel Royal. George was an assiduous attender at the opera: during the 1714–15 season at the King's Theatre, Haymarket, he attended twenty-two performances out of a possible forty-four; in 1715–16 he attended seventeen times out of a possible twenty-nine; and in 1716–17 thirteen or fourteen times out of a possible twenty-five. In the 1725–6 season, George went to the opera twenty-eight times, and in the 1726–27 season, twenty-nine times, including Handel's opera *Admeto* on nineteen occasions.[7] He also liked concerts, the Italian comedy, and masquerades; the last indeed enjoyed a vogue in London during his reign. George's annual subscription to the Royal Academy of Opera, founded in 1719–20, was £1,000.

Handel also produced and conducted the coronation anthems for George II and Caroline's coronation in 1727, and in 1743 celebrated the king's victory in Germany over a French army by writing the *Dettingen Te Deum*, which was performed later that year at St James's Palace. The *Music for the Royal Fireworks* followed in 1749 to celebrate the Peace of Aix-la-Chapelle of the previous year. George II, however, was not a conspicuous patron of the arts, although he was their subject, not only in music, poetry and paintings, but also in statuary, for example Henry Cheere's statue of him in the grounds of Hartwell House. Queen Caroline was far better read.

As a patron, George's eldest son, Frederick, Prince of Wales (1707–51), was much more important: he was a significant supporter of music, literature and landscape gardening, and an important and discerning patron of the Rococo style. Frederick was painted in 1733 by Philip Mercier, playing music with his sisters Anne and Caroline, while another sister, Amelia, listened with a volume of Milton in her lap: he indeed played the bass viol and, as shown in the painting, the cello. From the mid-1730s, Frederick took an active political role in opposition to his father and the latter's support for the Walpole ministry. This included the Prince's patronage of the Lincoln's Inn Fields theatre as a rival to George II's theatrical politics. Frederick displayed his 'rebellion' by supporting (according to some, co-writing) opposition plays put on in this theatre. Thus, at this juncture, theatre was as much charged with Hanoverian dynastic disputes as with party politics. The recipients of Frederick's patronage included the Anglo-Scot James Thomson, who received an annual pension of £100 and contributed to the Masque *Alfred* (1740), providing the words for 'Rule Britannia'. *Alfred*, which David Mallet wrote jointly with Thomson, was not alone among the literature of exalted Patriotism inspired by Frederick's opposition to the Walpole ministry.[8] There was also David Mallet's tragedy *Mustapha*, Thomson's *Edward and Eleonora* (1739), which was not performed due to censorship, Henry Brooke's play *Gustavus Vasa: The Deliverer of his Country* (1739, also forbidden by the Lord Chamberlain), and Richard Glover's epic *Leonidas*, its theme drawn from Classical Sparta. History thus provided the basis for tales of rousing patriotism, as writers strove to recreate the impact of Addison's *Cato*, but with the added promise of rebirth through a new monarch, the future Frederick I. In *Alfred*, the hermit predicted:

> the virtue,
> The great, the glorious passions that will fire
> Distant posterity when guardian laws
> Are by the patriot, in the glowing senate,
> Won from corruption.

This represented a very different role from that earlier taken by Frederick, whose active love life had been the subject of James Miller's *Vanelia: or The Amours of the Great* (1732), the text of an unperformed opera that went through at least six editions. The diversity of princely activities was amply shown by Frederick, whose roles included the hunting of animals, the subject of group pictures by John Wootton in 1729 and 1734, as well as being seen as a supporter for the creation of an academy for the arts, a project brought to fruition under his son and successor, George III.

Frederick's premature death in 1751 cut short the hopes that had been focused on him, and left a generation gap, although it led to John Delap's lacklustre *Marcellus, a Monody* (1751). Instead, royal patronage in mid century was focused on George II, who was not a major patron. His second son, the militaristic William, Duke of Cumberland, was scarcely going to take on his brother Frederick's role, although he did provide an important topic for a branch of culture that is too easily forgotten: military themes, not least the painting of commanders and battles.[9] John Wootton produced paintings of the Duke with the battles of Dettingen and Culloden in the background, while Cumberland at Culloden was in part the inspiration for Handel's oratorio *Judas Maccabeus* (1747). Viscount Tyrconnel celebrated Culloden by purchasing a rare lead bust of Cumberland by Henry Cheere, who was also responsible for an equestrian statue of the Duke in Cavendish Square. Thomas Newcomb chipped in with *Two Odes to His Royal Highness the Duke of Cumberland* (1746).

More generally, the celebration of martial prowess and success was an important theme of the arts that is underrated today, but that was understandably important, not least because Britain was at war for much of the period, with European powers in 1702–13, 1718–20, 1739–48, 1756–63, 1778–83 and 1793–1802, as well as with non-European powers and peoples in Asia and North America. Aside from paintings of military heroes, for example Reynolds' portraits of Lord Heathfield at Gibraltar and of Colonel Tarleton (a villain in American eyes), and of military reviews, such as William Beechey's of *George III Reviewing the Troops* (1793), a key stage in the implausible iconography of the Prince of Wales as a military hero, there were martial portraits, martial music and celebratory verse. This included Joseph Addison's *The Campaign* (1704) – heroic couplets celebrating victory at Blenheim, and George Farquhar's epic poem *Barcellona* (1707) about the capture of Barcelona two years earlier, while Newcomb contributed *Vindicta Britannica: An Ode on the Royal Navy, inscribed to the King* (1759) and *On the Success of the British Arms: A Congratulatory Ode Addressed to His Majesty* (1763). The contentious nature of politics could, however, extend to the celebration of victory. Addison's *The Campaign* was countered by the Tory John Philips' *Blenheim* (1705) which was dedicated to Robert Harley, a prominent Tory.

There was also an important genre of naval scenes: of warships, royal dockyards and battles. Dominic Serres, one of the founding members of the Royal Academy and Marine Painter to George III, exhibited 105 works at the Academy, many of them scenes of imperial triumph, such as *The Siege at Fort Royal, Martinique* (1769). Victories were also staged. The audience at Drury Lane on 1 January 1785 were promised a new comedy, *The Natural Son*, a pantomime, *Harlequin Junior*, and, as a conclusion, *The Repulse of the Spaniards before the Rock of Gibraltar*, an episode during the recent War of American Independence. Victories were also celebrated with monuments, such as the Quebec monuments celebrating the battle that had led to the capture of the city in 1759, for example the one at Studley Royal at which a cannon was fired annually on the anniversary of the battle, and another at Stowe.

Cumberland's role serves as a reminder that royal patronage stemmed not simply from monarchs and their heirs, but also from other members of the royal family. At Hampton Court, when Cumberland reached the age of ten, a set of rooms was converted for his use by William Kent, including a columned alcove for his bed. Royal patronage could also extend to mistresses, as with Henrietta, Countess of Suffolk, the mistress of George II as Prince of Wales, who was given £11,500 by George in 1724 to build and furnish an appropriate house, the result being the Palladian-style Marble Hill House, whose garden was designed by Charles Bridgeman.

George III grew up into a rich cultural heritage. Aside from the influence from his father, Frederick, his mother, Augusta of Saxe-Gotha, was a patron of the architect Sir William Chambers (1726–96), who taught the young Prince architectural drawings, and who was employed by Augusta to adorn the gardens of her house at Kew. In 1757–62, he erected a number of buildings there in oriental or Classical styles that had a great impact.[10]

George III had varied cultural interests, especially in art and music. He acquired the important art collection of Joseph Smith and was a keen supporter of the artistic world, being a key patron of Chambers and Thomas Gainsborough (1727–88). Culture was linked to patriotism in the foundation of the Royal Academy in 1768, and George's support, not least his knighting in 1769 of the Academy's President, Joshua Reynolds, was an important part of the sponsoring of British culture. In turn it enhanced monarchy, a pattern that can be traced back to Sir James Thornhill's celebration of the new dynasty in paint at Greenwich. Making available the royal apartments in Somerset House for the Academy from 1771 (the Royal Society and the Society of Antiquaries followed), George continued his interest in the Royal Academy into the 1800s. This was part of a more general pattern in eighteenth-century European monarchy. The Danish Royal Academy of Art was founded by Frederick V in 1754. In 1786, Gustavus III of Sweden both reorganised the Academy of Letters, established in 1753, and founded a Swedish Academy devoted to Swedish language and literature, himself selecting the first members.

George III's support for what became the national library housed in the British Museum was crucial. Painters he favoured included

Gainsborough, who painted numerous royal portraits in the early 1780s, Paul Sandby and Benjamin West. The patronage of Gainsborough was in part a reflection of Reynolds' links with the opposition round the Prince of Wales. George's patronage was also artistically bold as Gainsborough's sparing use of paint was less fashionable than Reynolds' habit of slapping it on. Sandby (1725–1809), a master of the watercolour, who made numerous drawings of Windsor where he lived, was, like his brother Thomas (1721–1798), one of the thirty-four original members of the Royal Academy nominated by George. He also taught Queen Charlotte. Thomas Sandby, Deputy Ranger of Windsor Great Park, was made Joint Architect of His Majesty's Works in 1777, following with the Master Carpentership in 1780.

Born in Pennsylvania, Benjamin West (1738–1820) came to England in 1763, acquired a reputation as a history painter and was commissioned by George, who admired his *Agrippina*, to paint *The Departure of Regulus from Rome*. George then became an active patron, nominating West to the Royal Academy, appointing him Historical Painter to the King in 1772 and Surveyor of the Royal Pictures in 1790. As an historical painter, West responded to the serious crisis of the late 1770s – not only the American War of Independence but also rising discontent in Ireland and the Franco-Spanish invasion attempt of 1779 – by depicting crucial victories from the past – *The Battle of the Boyne* and the *Destruction of the French Fleet at La Hogue*, events that had occurred in 1690 and 1692. Exhibited at the Royal Academy in 1780, these paintings greatly increased West's popularity. His *Edward III Crossing the Somme* (1788) showed how successful past monarchs could be portrayed in a dramatic (and colourful) fashion, which reflected glory on their current successor. George also employed West to decorate St George's Hall, Windsor, with eight pictures from the life of Edward III and to produce thirty-six pictures (twenty-eight were executed) on the progress of revealed religion for the royal oratory. By 1801, West, who in 1792 succeeded Reynolds as the second President of the Royal Academy, had produced sixty-four pictures and other designs for George, who had paid him £34,187.[11] West's career and the reputation of history painting also, however, reflected the extent to which the English elite were not guided by crown and court.

George III also took a keen interest in music, playing the flute, harpsichord and pianoforte, collecting music, and being a great enthusiast for Handel's oratorios. George played a conspicuous role in the concerts held at Westminster Abbey in 1784 to celebrate the centenary of the composer's birth. Aside from attending those concerts, he also supported the King's Concerts held in London, while he visited Worcester in 1788 for the Three Choirs Festival in the cathedral, and, for the festival, added his own private band to the orchestra. The festival brought together many of George's concerns, as it was intended for the relief of the widows and orphans of the clergy, and included a cathedral service. On 6 August, George heard the *Coronation Anthem*, the overture from *Esther*, and the *Dettingen Te Deum*, the last a reference to his grandfather's brave service to the nation, and all by Handel. On 7 August, there was more sacred music by Handel, and on 8 August the *Messiah* and later a 'miscellaneous concert', a typical festival programme. George was also a frequent visitor to the theatre, including three times in less than a month in Cheltenham in 1788, as well as often on his summer stays in Weymouth.

Although not a builder on the scale of his son George IV, in large part because he believed in restraining expenditure, George III was very interested in architecture and an important patron.[12] Once he had purchased Buckingham House in 1762 (which was called Queen's House and later Buckingham Palace), George had it considerably altered by Chambers and also furnished as a London palace, not least in order to house his growing library. The fashionable character of the decoration was later matched by the work at Windsor Castle carried out by James Wyatt, from 1796 Surveyor General and Comptroller of the Office of Works, who was George's favourite architect after Chambers. The castle saw much building and decoration in the then fashionable Gothick style, with George spending over £133,000 from his privy purse: his patronage helped make Gothick the national style and one conspicuously proper for major buildings. Windsor, which had been neglected under George II, was the setting for royal ceremonials. St George's Chapel was restored and remodelled as part of George's revival of the cult of the Garter, an important aspect of Windsor's role as a setting for exemplary kingship.

Other expenditure included a castellated palace at Kew, designed by Wyatt in Gothick style, on the site of Richmond Lodge, but never finished and pulled down in 1828. Hampton Court was neglected, becoming grace and favour apartments, rather than a royal residence. In Richmond Park, George III replaced the ornamental landscaping, carried out under George II and Queen Caroline, by the contemporary natural look popularised by Capability Brown. The formal gardens of Mary II and Anne at Kensington Palace was similarly replaced by lawn.

The landed elite, however, played a greater role in artistic patronage than the monarchy. Sir John Vanbrugh (1664–1726) built new palaces for the Duke of Marlborough and the Earl of Carlisle, not for George I; indeed, the ideas he produced for Kensington Palace were thought too grandiose. English culture in the period is particularly noted for its gardens, but although George I was keen on re-landscaping the grounds of Kensington Palace, and both Charles Bridgeman and William Kent worked on the project, the royal family did not play a central role in the development of the distinctive British landscape. George II was an active patron of the German enamellist C. F. Zincke, but this form was scarcely central to British culture.

Aside from architecture and gardens, the history of theatre and music during this period revealed the declining significance of royal patronage. Handel's livelihood came to depend on the commercial success of his works on the London stage. Mozart, in 1764, and Haydn, in 1791 and 1794, came to London in search of the same success. The major forces in artistic patronage were the landed elite and the middling orders, not the monarchy. 'Taste' came from outside the royal court, although George IV (Prince Regent 1811–20, King 1820–30) would have liked to spend enough to challenge this, while, earlier, Frederick, Prince of Wales's sponsorship of the Rococo was important. It was indicative of the cultural importance of the public stage that George Lillo's *The London Merchant* (1731) made his name as a playwright, while the court masque he wrote in 1733 for the marriage of Anne, the Princess Royal, with William IV of Orange was unperformed because of the postponement of the marriage and therefore made no impact. Nevertheless, court ceremonies did provide important occasions for patronage and performance. Maurice Greene, who became Master of the King's Band of Music in 1735, wrote an anthem for the marriage of Princess Anne, which finally took place in 1734, and for that of her brother Frederick in 1736. There was no equivalent to the situation in Madrid, where actors were expected to perform at court at a moment's notice,[13] nor in Vienna where the theatres in mid-century were royal property. Designed for opera, the Teatro Regio opened in Turin in 1740 by Charles Emmanuel III was reserved for the court and privileged individuals. The relatively smaller role of royal patronage in Britain ensured that artistic life did not suffer during royal absences or periods of mourning as it did in most Continental capitals.

It was not only the current royal family that played a role in national culture. Their predecessors were also important, although their images were not sold in the same way that prints of the portraits of current rulers were. Past English monarchs featured frequently in the plots of plays, sometimes in a very far-fetched fashion. In Delarivier Manley's *Lucius: The First Christian King of Britain* (1717), a tale of love and war, Queen Rosalinda, the female lead, is instrumental in the conversion of Lucius to Christianity. The actor Thomas Hull's leading success as a playwright was the tragedy *Henry the Second: or The Fall of Rosamond*, first staged in 1773. Four editions of the play appeared the following year. Fictional accounts of monarchy did not have to be history plays, and yet could be popular, as with Robert Dodsley's successful play *The King and the Miller of Mansfield* (1737), in which John Cockle, the miller, entertains unwittingly a lost monarch.

Despite the grandeur sought by George IV, and the scale and style of the royal court, the Hanoverians presided over an embourgeoisment of British culture. *The London Merchant*, which represented a major change in tragedy, in that it was written in a prose idiom and given a bourgeois setting and values, was a moral counterpart to William Hogarth's satires and the novels of Samuel Richardson and later Jane Austen. If morality was increasingly prescribed and indulgence proscribed in many works – Richardson's first novel *Pamela* (1740) being a very popular work on the prudence of virtue and the virtue of prudence – this, however, represented not so much a bourgeois reaction against aristocratic and royal culture, as a shift in sensibility that was common to both. The architectural equivalent in the remodelling of stately homes was the transformation of the hall into the saloon, as at Poltimore.[14] For every decadent aristocrat depicted on the stage in the second half of the eighteenth century, there were several royal or aristocratic heroes.

Nevertheless, the cultural and artistic role of monarchy and monarch had changed. Both were still important, but they were less central to national identity. In part, this was due to political changes. The failure of the Jacobite challenge, which was clear after the defeat of Charles Edward Stuart at Culloden in 1746, ensured less of a need to emphasise the links of dynasty and government, while George III's lack of the martial propensities and achievements of his predecessors was related to a situation in which national glory, and the glorification of achievements, did not focus on the monarch. Indeed, George was the target of satire, not least in caricature prints.[15] Had George III matched the military interests of his relative Frederick II (the Great) of Prussia (r. 1740–86), then the situation might have been different, not least because there would have been political pressure to celebrate (or criticise) royal achievements, while George might have fought himself in the War of American Independence, with disastrous consequences for his reputation.

But more than the character of the monarch was at stake. There was also a broad pattern of socio-political development that affected cultural interests and artistic activity. However much it might have been supported by a monarch, militarism held only limited appeal to the landed order in England, which was one reason why, numerically, the Scottish and Anglo-Irish elites were over-represented in the senior ranks of the army. More generally, the English elite was not necessarily going to be guided in cultural and artistic matters by the crown and the royal court, and just as the development of architectural and landscape styles clearly reflected this, so it is difficult to see a different pattern of royal patronage affecting the cultural views and artistic interests of the elite. The image of the crown was also affected by a demystification of monarchy.

The limited role of the crown was even more apparent in face of the expanding wealth and influence of urban society, especially of mercantile and professional elements. Demographic and economic expansion from mid-century greatly underwrote this expansion, accentuating social fluidity, and creating new challenges as to how best monarch and monarchy could respond to expectations about appropriate leadership. The cultural patronage with which George III was associated, particularly the foundation of the Royal Academy, was a successful response to a changing political culture, being patriotic, public and institutional, and it was a different response from what his predecessors had felt necessary.[16] An informed paternalism seemed appropriate and necessary; the ruler as patriarch was no longer so feasible, and this was made readily apparent in the 1780s with the public drama of tensions between George and his sons. There was also to be an equivocal response to George, Prince of Wales's patronage and leadership of taste. The aristocracy and the middling orders did not look for aestheticism in their monarch, especially when it was combined with loose morals and extravagance.

3

The Aristocracy

It is usually fine grass and beautiful: above this verdure, which continues the existing slopes of the hills, stand mature trees distributed in masses; they are massed so as to reveal views, a view of a picturesque bell-tower, an attractive village, etc. The woods hide anything that could offend the eye, where the landscape is disagreeable. A bridge, or a pagoda, or a little temple, may be built in order to arrange a view; when the hills don't slope together smoothly enough, a junction is arranged entirely at whim: if necessary, the whole hill can be moved. Above all, one does not forget to bring all the streams to a confluence and turn them into a river, the course of which seems so natural that one could believe it had always been there; and one creates islands, pleasant places; in short, nothing is forgotten. In a well-tended garden there is sometimes not an ugly weed to be seen in the entire vista, which is immense. That is what the English mean by 'a park'.

François de La Rochefoucauld, 1784.[1]

For many today, the most striking cultural legacy of the period are its stately houses and gardens. Over the last seven years, the most frequently visited National Trust properties included, among eighteenth-century sites, Fountains Abbey and Studley Royal, which contain Georgian water gardens; the grounds at Stourhead, a masterpiece of Georgian landscape gardening with a lake especially prominent; and Claremont and Killerton, both of which have impressive grounds. Other houses and grounds have become better known as a result of film and television. The television version of Evelyn Waugh's novel *Brideshead Revisited* brought many more visitors to Castle Howard. Two Georgian properties, Saltram in Devon and Mompesson House in Salisbury, were both extensively used for the film of Jane Austen's novel *Sense and Sensibility*, while Lyme Park in Cheshire appeared in the BBC version of her novel *Pride and Prejudice*.

The landowners responsible for these buildings and grounds were, other than the monarchs, the most influential individual patrons of the century, and were particularly important in that the emphasis on continuity of ownership in the same family encouraged commitment to individual properties. Furthermore, the environments landowners created and sustained helped mould the imaginative world of the age. Novels, plays and paintings used stately homes and parks, as well as the urban playgrounds of the social elite, especially the West End of London and Bath, as settings that became normative through their reiteration.

Most wealth was still tied up in land, although land was more profitable alongside other forms of property such as mineral rights. The relationship between capital and income greatly favoured the former – as, in general, was true of English history until the economic growth of the nineteenth century – and the ability to create income without capital was limited. Both imperial expansion and industrialisation were to increase greatly the possibilities for self-advancement in the nineteenth century. In some cases, however, these processes had led to massive wealth earlier: in the eighteenth century seen with those who made their money in India or the West Indies, such as William Beckford who purchased the large estate of Fonthill in 1745 and Robert Clive, the conqueror of Bengal, who became an aristocratic landowner; and by such manufacturers as Josiah Wedgwood and Samuel Crompton.

Some of this wealth found its way into new houses and parks. Sir Francis Child, a goldsmith and banker who came from a clothier family in Devizes, became Lord Mayor of London in 1698, and in 1713 was able to purchase the Osterley estate on which Osterley Park was built, while his grandson, Francis, spent £17,700 in 1757 buying Upton as a hunting seat. Francis also commissioned Robert Adam to redecorate the interior of Osterley House, which he did with great and often colourful and theatrical attention to detail, not least in the Etruscan Dressing Room. Sir Richard Child, another banker, later 1st Earl Tylney, had Wanstead House built in 1714–20 (it was demolished in 1822), while another banker, Henry Hoare, was responsible for building Stourhead. Making his money from naval prize money, Admiral Lord Anson was a childless self-made man who left his fortune to his elder brother, Thomas, who used the money at Shugborough to extend the house greatly in the 1740s and the late 1760s, and to develop the park.

These figures, however, were still uncommon in the period, and there

was considerable anxiety about new money and the resulting social
mobility. Indeed, throughout the century new money proved a frequent
target for satirists, who were apt to associate it among both men and
women with personal vulgarity and a lack of artistic taste, as well as of
style and sensitivity. Attitudes towards wealth were moral and paternal-
istic, not economic. These attitudes were an obvious way to denote
moral character and social acceptability and value. Correct behaviour
could be outlined by focusing on the vulgarity of the opposite, and harmony was presented as resting on moderation in display and in
accepting the responsibilities of wealth.[2] Indeed, the virtues and values
summarised as sensibility were frequently contrasted with the commer-
cialism and crassness of new money. Land itself represented more than
capital and income. It was the source of honour and status in a way that
commerce could not be. Sir Daniel Fleming wrote that a gentleman who
sold an acre of land sold an ounce of honour.

There was particular suspicion about the wealth produced by 'nabobs'
who had made their money in India, a source associated by critics with
corruption and, less precisely, with a sense of unEnglishness in which
the role of different values played a major role. These men indeed made
their mark. In 1746, Henry Talbot, an East India merchant, bought and
remodelled Vintage House near Dorking, one of the many stately homes
now demolished. 'Nabobs', however, were exceptional. It was the stability of the landed order, especially at the upper levels, that was striking.
In 1400–1660 there had been considerable disruption due to the aristocratic feuds and dynastic discontinuities of the fifteenth century, the
Reformation and the Civil Wars, but thereafter there was more continuity, at least at the elite level, although, lower down, the enclosure of
land brought major social change reflected in particular in the decline
of the yeoman class into peasantry. This stability had important political, social and cultural consequences, and helped strengthen the
hierarchical nature of social assumptions.[3]

The artistic role of the landed elite was particularly pronounced in
their goals for their own environment, their houses and grounds. Aristocrats no longer lived in fortified mansions, and this was not only true
of England. In April 1746, as the Jacobite rising was extinguished, a Scottish peer, Lord Glenorchy, wrote to his daughter regretting that, like so
many landowners, he had weakened his house in modernising it:

> I have often repented taking out the iron bars from the windows and sash-
> ing them, and taking away a great iron door, and weakening the house as

to resistance by adding modern wings to it. If it had remained in the old castle way as it was before, I might have slept very sound in it, for their whole army could not have taken it without cannon.[4]

Yet, this was a short-term panic, and, as they had stopped doing in England in the sixteenth century, Scottish landowners now modelled their houses with scant thought of defence. Instead the emphasis, seen with the walling of estates and gatehouses, was on regulating access to property and in particular preventing poaching and the departure of deer. For the protection of their houses from criminals, landlords could rely on their numerous servants. Fortification was reduced to fantasy, as in fortified walls, for example at Castle Howard, garden follies and mock Gothick castles.

Social stability was linked with culture. Architecture, landscape gardening and portraiture promoted stability by emphasising the power and immutability of the elite leadership of society. Stately homes such as Blenheim, Castle Howard, Stowe and Wentworth Woodhouse were monuments of ostentation that dominated the countryside, both visually and socially. In a typical gesture of decorative aggrandisement, Ralph, 1st Duke of Montagu had his coat of arms and family tree carved on his staircase at Boughton House to promote the idea of an unchanging family succession. Ostentation no longer had the crude correlation with power of the medieval or Tudor nobility: it now entailed a more subtle social authority to which influence over taste contributed.

Newly-established families similarly asserted their position. The banker Henry Hoare marked the transition stemming from his purchase of the Stourton estate in 1717, and the foundation of a new landed dynasty, by pulling down the old Stourton House and calling in the fashionable Scottish-born architect Colen Campbell (d. 1729) to build a Palladian house at Stourhead in 1720–24.

Whatever their scale, the stately homes and their landscaped parkland were a testimony to wealth, confidence, the income generated by rising demand for crops after the sustained population growth that started in the 1740s, the profits stemming from agricultural improvement, the benefits of mineral rights (as at Gibside), and greater political and social stability. The French Revolutionary Wars that began in 1793 brought yet further profits from agricultural rental income, encouraging the 4th Earl of Bristol (also Bishop of Derry) to begin work at Ickworth in 1795. Costs, nevertheless, were high and the expense of building could be ruinous, contributing to the serious debts affecting many landowners.

The cost of building, decorating and supporting the magnificent house and establishment at Canons proved too much and the house and contents were auctioned and dismantled for building material soon after the death in 1744 of its creator, James, 1st Duke of Chandos: Canons had been praised by Pope, while Handel had worked there for Chandos. In Cornwall, Samuel Kempe of Penryn died in 1728 having sold off much of his wife's estate but with the large house he projected incomplete. Capability Brown's remodelling of the late seventeenth-century parkland at Castle Ashby, begun in 1761 when he received £50 for the plan, was brought to an end in 1774 when Spencer, 8th Earl of Northampton went bankrupt.[5]

Expensive houses and landscaping, however, seemed necessary in order to establish and sustain status, with which style was closely interwoven. The 3rd Earl of Carlisle spent £78,000 on Castle Howard between starting work on it in 1700 and his own death in 1738; as he lacked sufficient money, the house was still not completed at the time of his death. Between 1746 and 1763, John, 4th Duke of Bedford spent £84,000 rebuilding Woburn Abbey, including adding a west front designed by Henry Flitcroft, but that did not suffice as a south front by Henry Holland was to follow toward the close of the century. Meanwhile, £90,000 had been spent from the 1720s until 1762 building Holkham House, begun by Thomas Coke, who designed it, taking advice from William Kent. £100,000 went on rebuilding Audley End, including the addition of Robert Adam interiors. Between 1660 and 1760, 389 new country houses and villas were built in England, more towards the end of that period, when agricultural profits were higher, than earlier.[6]

These stately homes were also new. Although they proclaimed hierarchy, longevity and status, they also reflected a concern to be up-to-date. The latter indeed was an affirmation of the currency of their status.[7] This rejection of the past was dramatised when, as often, older mansions were replaced or rebuilt. Rebuilding reflected the extent to which Classical designs came to inform English architecture, an aspect of a redefinition of taste and style that reordered fashion and acceptability. In the 1690s and 1700s, William Blathwayt had his Tudor house at Dyrham Park totally transformed, the east front being the responsibility of William Talman, the Comptroller of the Royal Works. A serious fire at Wilton House in 1705 led to a rebuilding in which the Tudor Great Hall was replaced with a rectangular Classical-style Great Hall. In the 1720s, the Tudor Lyme Park was transformed by the Venetian architect Giacomo Leoni; he also built Clandon Park to replace an earlier Tudor house. Leoni was also concerned to propagate his ideas, being responsible in 1716 for an English edition of the first book of Palladio's *Quattro libri*. The medieval Studley Royal House, damaged by fire in 1716, was greatly altered for William Aislabie in the 1760s, acquiring the fashionable Classical façade, while in the interior, plasterwork from Giuseppe Cortese was commissioned. The Vyne, a sixteenth- and seventeenth- century house, was much altered by John Chute between 1754 and 1776, especially with the Staircase Hall, a masterly Palladian interior, that was both elegant and practical. The Tudor Dunham Massey was rebuilt in 1758 for George, 2nd Earl of Warrington, and in 1761 the Tudor Osterley Park was remodelled by Robert Adam. From 1761, Adam also remodelled Syon House for the Duke of Northumberland, producing a series of five new state rooms inside the Jacobean house, in order to provide an appropriate setting for both entertaining and statuary. Other Tudor houses, such as Killerton and Wallington, were also rebuilt;[8] Hintlesham Hall gaining a Palladian front, a colonnade, stucco and sashes.

Sometimes, the rebuilding took far longer than intended. John Hervey, 1st Earl of Bristol, demolished the Tudor manor house at Ickworth in the early years of the century, intending to build a more impressive dwelling commensurate with his promotion to the peerage (1703), and in it (1714), and received plans from Talman and Vanbrugh, but none was started until the 4th Earl began the current Ickworth in 1795: meanwhile, a farmhouse, Ickworth Lodge, served as a temporary residence.

While landed estates might suggest continuity, the stately homes of the aristocracy, like the new enclosures on their estates designed to increase agricultural effectiveness, reflected change. Whether new or rebuilt, the model for stately homes was of a harmonious unity, which generally required large-scale building, and not the incoherence of a tacked-on extension. Nevertheless, in addition and very often, some work was necessary for reasons of repair. The steady pressure of the elements, particularly rain and frost damage, exacerbated sometimes by the consequences of poor construction, ensured that repair was a major theme of the architecture and building of the period, although it is one that is apt to be neglected. After a report by the architect John James in 1730 had revealed serious problems at Ham House, there were major works that included the complete rebuilding of the bays and the replacement of all the sash windows. The collapse in 1771 of the Great Hall roof at Castle Ashby (where Samuel Richardson had written much of his novel *Sir Charles Grandison*), led to the employment of a local architect, John Johnson, to rebuild the hall.

Repairs, however, did not bring reputation. Major figures and those who wished to seem major proclaimed their prominence with new or greatly rebuilt mansions, such as the Earl of Hardwicke's at Wimpole, Sir George Lyttelton's at Hagley Hall, and Thomas, 2nd Lord Onslow's Clandon Park. Competition between families was important to this process. Ralph, 2nd Lord Verney rebuilt much of Claydon House in order to rival Earl Temple's work at nearby Stowe, while in West Norfolk, Sir Robert Walpole's Houghton rivalled Viscount Townshend's Raynham.

Architecture was also seen as an appropriate interest for members of the landed elite, and many took a role in the design of works. Architectural expertise was not seen as compromising gentility. A sketch for new decorative work for the Long Gallery at Wentworth Woodhouse has been attributed to the 2nd Marquess of Rockingham. Elite interest in architecture was indicated in Hogarth's group portrait, *Holland House Group*, in which Henry Fox, later Lord Holland, is showing John, Lord Hervey an architectural plan.

Lesser houses reflected the motifs and styles of greater works, and there was a variety of the latter on offer. To a certain extent, styles succeeded each other, but there was also a considerable degree of overlap. Sir John Vanbrugh (1664–1726), a leading exponent of the English Baroque, as well as being a playwright of note, displayed at the Duke of Marlborough's seat at Blenheim, the Earl of Carlisle's at Castle Howard, and Admiral Delaval's at Seaton Delaval, a degree of spatial enterprise similar to the architects of princely palaces on the Continent. The emphasis was on scale, and the houses looked powerful: Castle Howard, which Vanbrugh gained the commission to build in 1699, was the first private house in England to be built with a dome, and its hall is seventy feet high. The initial plan for the saloon at Blenheim included niches containing ten-foot-high Italian statues representing the Virtues. Although the planning of Castle Howard and Blenheim may have been Vanbrugh's, the execution, supervision and detailing, however, were Nicholas Hawksmoor's. Vanbrugh also provided Baroque details within houses, such as the screen to the main staircase at Audley End, and pioneered informally laid out gardens and parks.[9] He was not alone in building Baroque stately homes. Work by other architects included Boughton House in the late seventeenth century, and in the new century Beningbrough, the 1720s work on Wentworth Woodhouse, and the east façade of Wentworth Castle.

In contrast to the heaviness of Vanbrugh's architecture, Colen Campbell was influenced by Antonio Palladio and Inigo Jones, as was his principal patron, Lord Burlington, who was responsible for Chiswick House.[10] The degree to which Burlington's Palladianism was an important revival or a continuation of the work of Jones is controversial,[11] but both Burlington and Campbell sought to encourage what they saw as a distinctly British style in contrast to the Baroque of Wren, Vanbrugh and Hawksmoor, which was presented as less purely Classical, and thus less worthy of emulation. Campbell's works included Wanstead House, Mereworth and Stourhead, and he also designed Houghton for Sir Robert Walpole.[12]

Campbell's design for Houghton (which owed much to James Gibbs' initial scheme) was executed by Walpole's protégé Thomas Ripley, and the scale and decoration were grandiloquent, as befitted the leading minister of the age. The Stone Hall and the saloon on the *piano nobile* were grand and magnificent, the former being a cube with forty foot dimensions. As in a royal palace, the state rooms were designed to impress, and Walpole used Houghton for entertaining, most prominently in November 1731 when he was visited by Duke Francis Stephen of Lorraine who was to become husband of Maria Theresa of Austria and the Holy Roman Emperor, Francis I. Indicating the numbers that great houses were designed to entertain and impress, the party also included the Dukes of Devonshire, Grafton, Newcastle and Richmond, the Earls of Albemarle, Burlington, Essex and Scarborough, and Lords Baltimore, Delawar, Herbert, Lovell and Malpas. Pope, a critic of Walpole, had little time for Ripley, and used his architecture as a way to lambast his patron:

> Heaven visits with a taste the wealthy fool,
> And needs no rod but Ripley with his rule.

In 1772, Letitia Proctor thought the 'outside of the house ... too heavy to be pleasing'.[13] Yet, under Sir Robert, Houghton, on which he reportedly spent over £200,000, had fulfilled its function as a symbol and display of ministerial greatness.

Palladianism continued to be important in the second half of the century, with new houses such as Basildon Park built in 1776 by John Carr of York for an Indian 'nabob' Sir Francis Sykes, and Buckland House. Other houses were rebuilt in Palladian style. Euston, the Suffolk seat of the Dukes of Grafton, was remodelled by Matthew Brettingham, formerly assistant to William Kent, with the French-style work of the previous remodelling in the 1660s replaced by the new Palladianism. At Castle Howard, Sir Thomas Robinson, the brother-in-law of the 4th Earl of Carlisle, sought to complete the house, but, as he preferred the Palladian style to that of Vanbrugh, his west wing, built between 1753 and 1759, did not harmonise with the work of the latter, and indeed he destroyed some of it and planned to do so to more.

The standard Palladian repertoire was seen when William Lemon had the architect Thomas Edwards complete Carclew in the 1750s: a grand granite portico was added to the central block, and colonnades and loggias on either side contributed to the contemporary desire for an impression of proportion. The tightly controlled symmetry of Palladianism was an architectural language that worked at a number of scales, and outer symmetry lent itself to the symmetry of interior layout and rooms. An emphasis on symmetry resulted in criticism of buildings that lacked it, such as Castle Howard, which had different types of column on the north and south fronts. The repetition of facades, niches and arches could, however, be wearing as well as symmetrical.

The Palladian style was disseminated by emulation and also through publications.[14] Thus, James Paine (1725–1789) published *Plans, etc., of Noblemen and Gentlemen's Residences Executed in Various Counties, and Also of Stabling, Bridges, Public and Private Temples, and Other Garden Buildings* (2 vols, 1767–83). The 175 plates testified to the activity of the period. Paine, who in 1771 became President of the Society of Artists of Great Britain, found wealth and status through his career as an architect, becoming Sheriff for Surrey. Palladio's influence was freely acknowledged and efforts were made to make it more accessible. William Pain's *The Builder's Pocket Treasure: or Palladio Delineated and explained* (1763) appeared in several editions, as did his *The British Palladio: or Builder's General Assistant* (1785). There was also a vogue for Palladianism in Ireland until about 1760: Sir Edward Lovett Pearce was responsible for Castletown, while Francis Bindon worked on Russborough House.

Alongside Palladianism, there was also a continuing interest in the

Gothick style, which influenced both domestic and ecclesiastical architecture. William Kent employed a Tudor Gothick style for the
clock-tower at Hampton Court, while the castellations of Gothick were
also seen in follies, such as that designed by Vanbrugh for Claremont.
Gothick became more fashionable (and more intellectually respectable)
from the 1740s, as an English reaction against Italian-inspired Classicism, and also as a way of matching the Jacobite and Catholic threat by
transmuting both the threat and the former style into an acceptable
aesthetic interest. Alnwick Castle was remodelled in a Gothick fashion
from 1750, and Henrietta Howard, Countess of Oxford, rebuilt Welbeck
Abbey in this style from 1752. In 1742, the first English book on Gothick
architecture appeared, Batty Langley's *Ancient Architecture Restored and
Improved by a Great Variety of Grand and Useful Designs, Entirely
New in the Gothick Mode for Ornamenting of Buildings and Gardens*.
Horace Walpole's Gothick suburban villa at Twickenham, Strawberry
Hill, and Donnington Grove, a villa designed by his friend John Chute,
were unusual in being new houses, as, in Wales, was Sir John Lloyd's
Peterwell, and Thomas Johnes's Hafod in the 1780s. The Gothick,
however, was largely used for rebuilding, as at Arbury Hall, where
Sir Roger Newdigate between 1748 and 1775 added Gothick details to
mark the house's monastic origins, and at The Vyne, where the Tudor
chapel was given a Gothick antechapel by Chute, who also designed the
Tomb Chamber.[15]

This chamber testified to the commemoration of family that was so
important in many houses, especially in portraiture. It was a setting for
a monument to John's most distinguished ancestor, Chaloner Chute,
who had purchased the estate in 1653, commissioned important work on
the house, and served as Speaker of the House of Commons. The monument by Thomas Carter the Younger is one of the most impressive
pieces of English sculpture of the period: a life-size Chaloner, looking
like a Romantic hero, reclines atop a straw mattress, itself atop a sarcophagus incorporating coats of arms and with fluted Ionic columns;
the heraldic devices are very much subordinate to the founder. Carter
produced many other funerary monuments to mark the passing of the
members of elite, and to commemorate their glory.

The Gothick was also seen in such interior details as bookcases, for
example at Strawberry Hill. Bookcases in Gothick style were also
installed in the library at Sherborne Castle as part of the remodelling of
the interior of the Tudor house by the young Edward, 6th Lord Digby

in 1757–58. This remodelling included the adding of panelled doors and white marble fireplaces. The house would have become much lighter as diamond-pane leaded panes were replaced by sash windows. An extension to the house built in 1787 to provide more guest and staff accommodation was given three pointed Gothick arches in the centre to make it seem historic. Two years later, there was the accolade of a visit by George III.

Aside from Gothick, there was also what has been termed Elizabethan Revival, seen in Capability Brown's additions to Corsham Court in Wiltshire in the 1760s and the new west front at Montacute in 1786–87. This indicated that the Tudor style was not seen as totally unacceptable. The same was true of the Jacobean style. The Strand façade of Northumberland House in London, which was demolished in 1874, was Jacobean in style to match existing parts of the building, while at Blickling, under John, 2nd Earl of Buckinghamshire, who took a close interest in the remodelling, the Jacobean character of the house was retained during extensive work from the 1760s.

The popularity of Gothick was important to the development of the picturesque style (see pp. 66, 207–8), but Gothick was not seen as a style equal to Classicism until the work of architects such as James Wyatt (1746–1813) at the close of the century. As an instructive indication of the varied nature of influences (and, more specifically, of the growing importance of public buildings as opposed to stately homes), Wyatt's earlier reputation as a Neo-Classical architect had been made not by a country house but by his designs for the Pantheon in Oxford Street, London, an assembly room completed in 1772. Influenced greatly by a trip to Italy in the 1760s, Wyatt's Neo-Classical work included Heaton Hall near Manchester, which he extensively rebuilt for the coal-rich Sir Thomas Egerton in 1772, providing a grand staircase leading to a pillared landing. Fourteen years later, Wyatt created a Neo-Classical mausoleum for the wealthy Lincolnshire landowner, Charles Pelham, in order to house a monument to his wife Sophia who had died young. Wyatt's elder brother Samuel (1737–1807), who had served as Clerk of Works under Robert Adam at Kedleston, was a leading Neo-Classical architect who brought simplicity and unity to his buildings, such as the remodelling and enlarging of Shugborough between 1790 and 1798.[16]

The Neo-Classical style was particularly appropriate for the smaller and more compact houses increasingly in favour with patrons in the closing decades of the century. Very few large houses were built in this period, in part because the major landowning families were already well catered for. There was new wealth, some of it ennobled, but the preference was now not for the great show houses, Baroque or Palladian, of earlier in the century, but, instead, for less grandiose houses that were decorated to very high standards and comfortable. In this respect, there was in these Neo-Classical houses a strong resonance from the Adam decorative ethos, and the emphasis was on private elegance not public show. The latter was more clearly the characteristic of buildings in towns, such as the Pantheon, that served public functions. Not all new country houses were small however. Attingham Park, with its massive entrance front, the portico having particularly high Ionic columns, designed by George Steuart in 1782, was an appropriate tribute to the wealth of the Hill family and matched and furthered the social ambition that led to their getting a peerage. Ickworth with its dramatic oval rotunda was begun for the Earl of Bristol in 1795.[17]

The variety of styles on offer ensured that there was no one result of borrowing. Instead, the consequences were often distinctive in character, and this was also true of the reshaping of houses. Thus Haldon House, begun in about 1735 by Sir George Chudleigh, borrowed from Buckingham House in London the pavilions connected to the main blocks by quadrant links. The house was enlarged later in the century by Sir Robert Palk. The sense of appropriate appearance led to the covering of brick by stucco at Haldon House and elsewhere in order to give an impression of a freestone structure.[18]

The stately homes that were built had to be decorated and furnished. This led to a massive amount of patronage ranging from frescoes to furniture. In August 1717, Robert Walpole's account book recorded £86 was 'paid to Mr [Jonathan] Richardson painter for drawing your Honors and Sir Charles Turner and brothers pictures', and the following April £13 was 'paid for two pictures at Mr Graffier's auction'.[19] Samuel Carpenter, a Yorkshire mason, received £84 10s. in 1705 for carving the ornate capitals in the Hall at Castle Howard, while the carpenter's bill for the decoration of the saloon at Wallington in 1741 was £56 17s. and 10d. and the plasterer's £44 19s. and 4d. At Blickling Hall, Joseph Pickford was paid £192 13s. and 5d. in the mid-1740s for the Sienna marble fireplace in the Long Gallery, while, in 1778, John Ivory was paid 100 guineas for the 'statuary Sienna chimneypiece' in the Peter the Great Room.

Styles in ornamentation varied. At Houghton, the decoration was a riot in gilt and stucco, with an ample use of expensive woods, including much mahogany, for extensive and ornate wood-carving, much of it by James Richards, Master Sculptor and Carver in Wood to the King. Pillars, pilasters, capitals, friezes, marble (or scagliola – imitation marble) overmantels, dramatic chimney-pieces, brackets, impressive staircases and lavish tapestries contributed to a heady sense of opulence at the greatest houses such as Houghton and Castle Howard.

This contrasted with the less opulent taste that subsequently tended to prevail, with a more general shift of sensibility away from Baroque decoration towards first lighter Rococo themes, as with the work of James Paine, or of the plasterer Pietro Francini, for example at Northumberland House, Lumley Castle and Wallington, and then a quieter Neo-Classicism. Subtler might be a better word than quieter for the work of Joseph Rose, Adam's stuccoist; seen for example at Claydon House and Heaton Hall, it has an arresting elegance. Furthermore, there was a mingling of tastes. Alterations at Easton Neston in mid-century included a Palladian chimney-piece in the Great Hall, and Rococo panels.[20]

Setting a less ornate tone for furniture, Thomas Chippendale (1718–1779) from Yorkshire, who became one of the leading furniture makers in mid-century London, dedicated his book of designs, *The Gentleman and Cabinet Maker's Director* (1754), to Hugh, Earl of Northumberland. Publication brought this work to the attention of an elite readership, and new editions appeared in 1759 and 1762.[21] Patronage was also a means to establish, in the public mind, the unassailability of the 'taste' and position of the Earl, who was concerned about his social position. Only an in-law of the Percys, he had obtained the title by a curious creation, and much of his behaviour was aimed at striking the pose of a 'real' nobleman – he employed more flambards to light the route of his carriage than royalty. An arriviste patron, the Earl (Duke of Northumberland from 1766) had Alnwick Castle extensively decorated with coats of arms of the Percys and related families.

A lighter, less ornamental and simpler style than that of Chippendale was developed subsequently by Hepplewhite and Sheraton. Thomas Sheraton (1751–1806) from Stockton, established himself in London in about 1790 and began publication of a series of manuals of furniture design. Thanks to such books of designs, fixtures, fittings and furniture became more standardised, and London fashions had a national scope. Thomas Bromwich (d. 1787), a noted metropolitan cabinet and paper-hangings maker, was commissioned to produce a *trompe l'oeil* wallpaper scheme for changes to the Long Gallery at Wentworth Woodhouse. Longcase clocks were another important form of decorative art.[22]

Aside from furniture, the new houses required large numbers of books for the libraries which became an established feature, and this helps explain the numerous book subscriptions by members of the elite. The development of the country house library made the country house a repository of (urban) Classical culture in the midst of the country, and diffused that culture to its estates and environs; as well as being a repository of power. Pride in lineage was also indicated by the armorial devices employed on bookcases and in bookplates.[23] Conversely, libraries were necessary for the books people acquired and, crucially, wished to retain. The importance of display was also reflected in the showy silver and china receptacles used for punch, tea and other purposes.

Numerous portraits were also needed for the large spaces created in the public rooms, especially the grand, often two-storied entrance halls, as at Seaton Delaval, Beningborough and Blenheim. Many members of the elite were keen collectors of paintings. Aristocratic recreations were an important theme in these paintings, particularly horses and hunting, as in the works of George Stubbs (1724–1806); unsurprisingly, he presented his patrons with attractive images of appropriate behaviour rather than the grittier reality of the confusion of hunting and sporting occasions. This was an aspect of the use of both to underline social status. Hunting scenes were also outdoor conversation pieces that showed their subjects in the right company.[24] Foreign painters who came to England, such as Peter Tillemans, who arrived from Antwerp in 1708, responded to the demand for such works. There was also a literature of hunting, prominent among which was William Somerville's lengthy poem, *The Chase* (1735).

Hunting scenes were hung in the main entrance hall of country houses such as Althorp; an aspect of the tendency to hang particular kinds of paintings in certain rooms, that was a product of the growing differentiation of room use and designation. Still lives were hung in the dining room to remind people of food. Hunting scenes were also a form of portraiture. In the Little Dining Room at Stourhead, John Wootton's hunting scene showed Henry and Benjamin Hoare with horses and hounds. This acted as a centre-piece for a series of smaller portraits of members of the family.

Wootton not only painted hunting scenes but was also noted as a painter of dogs and horses. His *Dancing Dogs* (1759) was painted for Sir Walter Calverley Blackett, who bred Bedlington terriers. Growing interest in pets was an aspect of a wealthier society that did not need to continue the former largely (although far from invariably) utilitarian attitude towards animals. In her portrait by William Beechey, Queen Charlotte is shown in a sylvan setting not only with two dogs at her feet but also carrying a third. Interest in pets was not only recorded on canvas. In Francis Coventry's *The History of Pompey the Little: or The Life and Adventures of a Lap-Dog* (1751), the perspective was that of the dog as he was passed between owners. Satirising prominent members of London society, this popular work was written by the vicar of Edgware.

Wootton's paintings were also popular with Robert Walpole and five which belonged to him were engraved for the print-publisher John Boydell's *Houghton Gallery*. Walpole had Wootton paint him in a hunting outfit. Walpole also patronized the young Samuel Scott, a marine painter and drawer of waterfront scenes, a genre somewhat overshadowed by landscape painting but one that found more favour in urban milieux and from mercantile patrons. Seascapes were less common in the houses of the landed elite, even though some drew part of their wealth from investment in trade. It was more common to display paintings of houses and grounds, which reflected pride of ownership as well as the enjoyment offered by viewing such works.[25] Henry, Earl of Pembroke commissioned Richard Wilson in 1750 to paint a set of paintings of Wilton House. This was also true of aristocrats' London houses, so that Canaletto painted *The Thames and the City of London from Richmond House* in about 1747 for the Duke of Richmond, portraying a vista dominated by St Paul's Cathedral.

In country houses, the Classical interests of patrons and artists combined in the depiction of Classical landscapes and stories, the heroes of ancient Rome being suitable companions for the portraits of modern aristocrats. There was also so much space to fill, not least because of the fashion for paintings in overdoors and overmantels. At Petworth, the Duke of Somerset invited artists and craftsmen to 'design' pieces for particular places and spaces in the house. The Lowthers patronised Mathias Read (1669–1747), a Londoner who in 1690 settled in Whitehaven, which the Lowthers were developing as a port. Read painted many of the Cumbrian country houses for their owners and was also one of the first native painters of English landscape, painting Cumbrian mountains and skies. In doing so he became the only notable pre-Picturesque painter of the

Lake District.[26] Patrons varied in the degree of favour they showed foreign and English works, but, thanks to an increasingly self-conscious cultural patriotism, the latter became relatively more popular in the closing decades of the eighteenth century, helping to drive up their price, which further ensured their fashionability.

Portraits were particularly important, providing an exemplary background for socialising. They and other paintings also recorded family glory. At Knole, in the Great Hall, there hangs Wootton's painting of *The First Duke of Dorset Returning to Dover Castle after Taking the Oath as Lord Warden of the Cinque Ports*, painted immediately after the event in January 1728 and sumptuously framed with family devices atop the frame. Wootton was also responsible for an equestrian portrait of the Duke. It displayed his prominence not only because he is pictured in rich clothes and colours and wearing the riband and star of the Garter, but also because he appears in front of a triumphal arch bearing the ducal arms. The painting is still at Knole. The 3rd Duke paid Reynolds 150 guineas in 1769 for a full-length portrait that also still hangs there. At Blickling Hall, John, 2nd Earl of Buckinghamshire's success in becoming Lord Lieutenant of Ireland was recorded when Gainsborough painted him in his robes of office. Providing sitters with individuality was not to be obtained at the cost of their status and reputation. Pride in duty, which defended aristocratic privilege, was also seen in works such as the painting by Thomas Phillips of Hugh, Earl Percy (later 3rd Duke of Northumberland) in the commanding officer's uniform of the Percy Tenantry Volunteers, a painting that still hangs at Alnwick. The rich clothes of swagger portraits, such as Reynolds of James, 7th Earl of Lauderdale, painted in 1759–61 underlined their wealth and status.

Similarly, furniture, porcelain and decorations frequently bore crests and other motifs that both proclaimed ownership and linked the family with taste. At Wallington, the Rococo silver basket in the dining room made by John Jacobs of London in 1750 bears the arms of Calverley and Blackett and the Calverley crest, celebrating the union of Calverley and Blackett lines, while the Owl House, a garden pavilion built in the 1760s, has the Calverley crest above its pediment. At Osterley Park, built for Sir Francis Child, the frieze in the Gallery incorporates marigolds, the symbol of Child's Bank. The Hobart bulls are displayed in the plasterwork in Blickling Hall. Similarly, political loyalties and values could be displayed in interior plasterwork.

The need to show paintings led to particular requirements in interior design (and in some cases, such as Northumberland House and Alnwick Castle, the addition of a picture gallery). This was even more the case with collections of marble statuary which was very much acquired to be seen and thus to display the exemplary 'virtue' of the owner. A loggia was used at the Earl of Pomfret's house at Easton Neston to house his acquisitions from the Earl of Arundel's collection, while William Weddell had a sculpture gallery built at Newby Hall (c. 1767), with Robert Adam working on the designs and pedestals . In the grounds of Ince Blundell Hall, Henry Blundell displayed his collection of nearly six hundred pieces, including many sculptures, in a garden temple and a Pantheon he had built.[27] Thomas, 2nd Lord Berwick had Attingham Park rebuilt to display the paintings and statues he acquired in Italy in 1792–94. The Outer Library, also called the Museum, housed part of his sculpture collection, and the giant pilasters struck a clear Classical theme.

Aside from displaying taste through patronage, for example through design and collecting, it was also important to create spaces within which refined socialising could occur, as that also showed taste and supported status. Within houses, it was necessary to find spaces for dining, dancing, music and cards; and this was accompanied by a process of differentiation by room.[28] Closets were intended for private reflection, anterooms for gathering before meals, and so on. Corridors enabled functions and people to be kept separate. This differentiation created particular decorative requirements. Robert Adam, in his *Works in Architecture* (1772) described eating rooms as:

> apartments of conversation, in which we are to pass a great deal of our time. This renders it desirable to have them fitted up with elegance and splendour, but in a style different from that of other apartments. Instead of being hung with damask, tapestry etc they are always finished with stucco, and adorned with statues and paintings, that they may not retain the smell of the victuals.

The arrangement of rooms in stately houses reflected what were held to be the separate needs of men and women, as well as the creation of spaces where they could be harmoniously together. Drawing rooms served in particular to provide appropriate settings for female sociability.

Music was a major requirement for the stately homes of the period. Many, such as Southside House, sported music rooms, and some of these, for example Heaton, included organs. Music-making, both communal and private, was an important activity in such households. So also were amateur theatricals. These were major aspects of the socialising that was central to genteel living, both in town and in the country. For example, amateur theatricals were a regular feature of life at Holland House in London in the early 1760s.[29] At Blenheim, theatricals were held after John, the 1st Duke's strokes as an amusement for him. Bishop Hoadly, who attended, wrote the prologue to *All for Love* that was recited at an entertainment in 1718.[30] Later in the century, Edward Nares, a Fellow of Merton College, Oxford, took an active part in the private theatricals at Blenheim, but he pushed his connection too far, for the Duke and Duchess refused to allow him to marry their third daughter, Lady Charlotte Spencer, and in 1797 he eloped with her. A friend from the days of the Blenheim theatricals, Robert Jenkinson, later Earl of Liverpool, was to become Prime Minister and in 1813 appointed Nares Regius Professor of Modern History at Oxford.

Styles of architecture and decoration were national, and this emerges clearly from considering the work of individual architects. The Scot Robert Adam (1728–1792) rebuilt or redesigned many stately homes in or nearby London – Syon House and Northumberland House for the Duke of Northumberland, Kenwood for the Earl of Mansfield, Lansdowne House for the Marquess of Lansdowne, Osterley, Hatchlands Park, and Luton Hoo. He also worked further afield including at Bowood for the Marquess of Lansdowne, Culzean, Croome Court, Harewood House, Kedleston, Mellerstain, Saltram, Shardeloes and Ugbrooke.[31] There was no regional pattern. The importance of shared values was also seen in the extent to which Whigs and Tories built in a similar fashion.[32]

The same was true of landscape gardening. Closely linked to wealthy landed patronage, this flourished in England and was also influential on the Continent where a vogue developed for the 'English Garden'. The style was adopted more readily because it was partly modeled on a truly cosmopolitan source, the Classics, specifically imagined Virgilian landscapes mediated through the paintings of Claude Lorrain and Poussin. Landscape gardening represented an Anglicisation of Classical notions of rural harmony, retreat and beauty, as well as what was understood as nature tamed by taste and reason.

Garden design has been seen as a means for the 'construction of cultural values',[33] but the attempt to find a political cause and context for these developments has to be handled with care. Although the rejection of conventional formalism can be seen as a defiance of constraint, and thus continental absolutism, the style was seen across the political spectrum. Tories and Whigs embraced these trends, although differences can be noted, for example with the sculptural lessons about the need for true Whiggery seen in the grounds of Viscount Cobham's seat at Stowe. Later in the century, John Carr of York, a committed Whig and a member of the Rockingham Club, clearly used his connections with the Marquess of Rockingham, a leading Whig, and his circle to obtain commissions in Yorkshire, although this did not prevent him from also working for Tories.[34]

Gardens in the early decades of the period, for example Stansted Park in Sussex, were created and continued in the formal geometric patterns that characterised continental designs. They were an opportunity for ostentation and display, and there was a clear segregation between gardens and the surrounding estate. Many gardens of the period maintained earlier layouts. For example, a drawing by Margaret Weld of 1721 reveals that Lulworth Castle still retained its sixteenth-century formal gardens, with their extensive parterres, the statuary at the centre, and with neatly-regimented and clipped trees in formal lines and blocs. Others reflected newly-fashionable geometric layouts. Formal gardens of the period include the Dutch-style water area at Westbury Court, the French-style creation at Dunham Massey, and Charles Bridgeman's masterpiece of the geometric at Eastbury.[35]

A key figure was Henry Wise (1653–1738), who was superintendent of the royal gardens to William III, Anne and George I, and a protégé of George London, who had in turn been influenced by André Le Nôtre (1613–1700), the French gardener employed by Charles II. London and Wise, described by Joseph Addison in the *Spectator* of 6 September 1712 as 'the heroic poets' of gardening (an instructive comparison from another genre), worked in accord with French and Dutch influences, although they were not slavish emulators and, instead, showed an ability to respond to the possibilities of particular sites. Aside from their work on the royal gardens, especially Hampton Court and Kensington, the partners were responsible for some of the leading gardens of the period, including Wanstead and Melbourne. The gardens of the latter were remodelled between 1704 and 1711, with Wise's plan including a water feature and other fashionable aspects of the formal garden.

Dutch and French influences were very much seen in the use of water in many gardens, but also contributed to a more general favouring of geometric layouts. The water features themselves were straight-edged and part of the geometric pattern. 'Canals' or long straight-edged ponds appeared in many grounds, for example Ickworth in the 1700s. Charles Bridgeman introduced an important innovation, the 'ha-ha' (a term first used in 1712), a ditch, sunk from view, to create a boundary between garden and parkland that did not interrupt the prospect but did prevent animals from entering the garden. In contrast to the short horizons of the Dutch style, this contributed to the stress on long vistas, joining house to park.

The common theme was symmetrical formality. At Chiswick, the grounds included straight alleys converging on a round-point.[36] The aerial perspective plan for Castle Howard in *Vitruvius Britannicus* included two obelisks and a temple-style structure in the grounds; in the event one obelisk was erected, as was a Temple of the Four Winds designed by Vanbrugh, and a Mausoleum designed by Hawksmoor. At Osterley Park, formal gardens were near the house, and the grounds were laid out in a formal plan that imitated Hampton Court, with tree-lined avenues radiating from a double semicircle of trees to the east of the house, as well as plenty of water: canals to two sides of the house and an oval basin on another.

At Studley Royal, John Aislabie laid out an impressive 150-acre geometric water garden including a canal, ponds, a series of cascades leading to a lake, and formal walks and vistas. The cost was great: one hundred men were needed for the heavy manual work, which included, in the mid 1730s, the cutting of the Serpentine Tunnel through a hill. The garden was enhanced by buildings designed to catch and direct the gaze, and thus enhance the vistas. These included Temples of Fame and Piety, a Banqueting House (intended as a orangery and probably designed by Colen Campbell), and an Octagon Tower, the last, built in the mid 1730s, a Gothick building designed to provide vistas. Statuary served the same purpose and was erected in the 1730s. The themes were Classical: statues of Hercules and Antaeus, Bacchus, Galen, Priapus, Pan, the Wrestlers, and the Dying Gladiator, the last a much-copied work, with one copy at Houghton. Both buildings and statuary increased the cost of developing and maintaining grounds, and also contributed to their architectural and painterly qualities. Similarly, at Hartwell House, where the gardens were transformed in the 1730s, they were enhanced with buildings, some by James Gibbs, and statues, including a round Gothic tower, a stepped pyramid and an arcaded pavilion.

Geometric patterns in grounds and in their relationship with houses became less important in the early eighteenth century as part of a rethinking of both. The crucial figure was William Kent (1684–1748), an architect who developed and decorated parks including at Stowe, Chiswick, Claremont and Rousham in order to provide a newly appropriate setting for buildings. He had spent ten years in Italy mostly in and near Rome and offered a type of Italianate naturalism as a model for English landscape gardens. In place of what was seen as French rigidity, Kent offered an energy, variety, and staginess that drew on Italian models, while also trying to work in an English context.[37] Kent used the 'ha-ha', while sunken fences were employed to conceal the limits of properties and to meld them into the surrounding countryside. In his *The History of the Modern Taste in Gardening* (1780), Horace Walpole was in no doubt about his role:

> At that moment appeared Kent, painter enough to taste the charms of landscape, bold and opinionative enough to dare and to dictate, and born with a genius to strike out a great system from the twilight of imperfect essays. He leaped the fence, and saw that all nature was a garden. He felt the delicious contrast of hill and valley changing imperceptibly into each other, tasted the beauty of the gentle swell, or concave scoop, and remarked how loose groves crowned an easy eminence with happy ornament, and while they called in the distant view between their graceful stems, removed and extended the perspective by delusive comparison.
>
> Thus the pencil of his imagination bestowed all the arts of landscape on the scenes he handled. The great principles on which he worked were perspective, and light and shade. Groups of trees broke too uniform or too extensive a lawn; evergreens and woods were opposed to the glare of the champain, and where the view was less fortunate, or so much exposed as to be beheld at once, he blotted out some parts by thick shades, to divide it into variety, or to make the richest scene more enchanting by reserving it to a farther advance of the spectator's step. Thus selecting favourite objects, and veiling deformities by screens of plantation, sometimes allowing the rudest waste to add its foil to the richest theatre, he realized the compositions of the greatest masters in painting. Where objects were wanting to animate his horizon, his taste as an architect could bestow immediate termination. His buildings, his seats, his temples, were more

the works of his pencil than of his compasses. We owe the restoration of Greece and the diffusion of architecture to his skill in landscape.

But of all the beauties he added to the face of this beautiful country, none surpassed his management of water. Adieu to canals, circular basons, and cascades tumbling down marble steps, that last absurd magnificence of Italian and French villas. The forced elevation of cataracts was no more. The gentle stream was taught to serpentize seemingly at its pleasure, and where discontinued by different levels, its course appeared to be concealed by thickets properly interspersed, and glittered again at a distance where it might be supposed naturally to arrive. Its borders were smoothed, but preserved their waving irregularity. A few trees scattered here and there on its edges sprinkled the tame bank that accompanied its maeanders, and when it disappeared among the hills, shades descending from the heights leaned towards its progress, and framed the distant point of light under which it was lost, as it turned aside to either hand of the blue horizon.

Thus dealing in none but the colours of nature, and catching its most favourable features, men saw a new creation opening before their eyes. The living landscape was chastened or polished, not transformed. Freedom was given to the forms of trees; they extended their branches unrestricted, and where any eminent oak, or master beech had escaped maiming and survived the forest, bush and bramble was removed, and all its honours were restored to distinguish and shade the plain. Where the united plumage of an ancient wood extended wide its undulating canopy, and stood venerable in its darkness, Kent thinned the foremost ranks, and left but so many detached and scattered trees, as softened the approach of gloom and blended a chequered light with the thus lengthened shadows of the remaining columns.

Influential as Kent was to be, it is important not to exaggerate the extent to which new ideas were adopted. At Stowe, one of the most influential parks of the period, although Kent's work had an impact from the 1730s, Bridgeman's formal central axis with its geometric pond remained until the second half of the century.

Trained under Kent, Lancelot 'Capability' Brown (1716–1783) rejected the rigid formality associated with geometric continental models, contriving a setting that appeared natural, but was, nevertheless, carefully designed for effect. His deliberately asymmetrical landscapes of serpentine lakes, sweeping lawns, gentle hills, copses on the brow of hitherto bare hills, and scattered groups of newly-planted trees swiftly established a fashion. The straight lines of existing ponds and walls were rounded off, a device that, by softening them, made them appear more natural.

Brown's reputation was noted by François de La Rochefoucauld, a French aristocrat visiting England in 1784:

> Many people believe that the 'English gardens' are made without artistic skill or knowledge, that taste alone presides, and that, in consequence, they can do the job themselves, for everyone thinks he has 'taste', all because no one can properly define what 'taste' is. The proof that it is only by dint of artistic skill and of working at it that one can make a passable imitation of nature is that, since England came into existence, only one man has been reckoned capable of 'landscape gardening'. He died three years ago, and was called Mr Brown. He is famous all over this kingdom. It is said that he had so sure and swift an eye for landscape, that after an hour on horseback he conceived the design for an entire park, and that after that, half-a-day was enough for him to mark it out on the ground. One must believe that it is impossible to draw up a plan for the English garden on paper – in the abstract: everything is determined by the particulars of the surrounding landscape, and the different view-points indicate what tree-screens will be necessary.[38]

Having made his reputation at Croome, Brown laid out or remodelled the grounds at about 180 houses, including Ashridge, Audley End, Benham, Berrington Hall, Blenheim, Branches, Braidlands, Chatsworth, Claremont, Euston, Eywood, Harewood, Heveningham, Ickworth, Ingestre, Kew, Kirtlington, Madingley, Nuneham Courtenay, Petworth, Redgrave, Sheffield Park, Trentham and Wimpole, as well as Burton Pynsent for Pitt the Elder, contributing to the increase in the number of landscaped parks in the second half of the century.[39]

The impact could be dramatic. At Charlecote Park, Brown redesigned the grounds, removing the water gardens, and changing the course of the River Hele so that it tumbled into the Avon within sight of the house. The destruction of earlier formal elements was a major aspect of Brown's work. At Bowood, the avenues and ornamental lake were replaced by Brown in the 1760s with a sinuous lake created by damming two streams, and the ground from the house was levelled to sweep down to the lake. At Sherborne Castle, the formal gardens established in the early years of the century by Robert Digby, with terraces and geometric water features and groves of trees, were swept aside in 1753 by Brown. In two years, he provided an up-to-date landscape garden including a substantial lake, as well as cascade. The vista was enhanced, as beyond the new lake were the ruins of the medieval Sherborne Castle. These were enhanced in 1755–56 with a mock-ruined tower and a crenellated wall, deliberately planted with ivy. Such ruins corresponded to the imaginary ones conjured up in much of the poetry of the period. Similarly, William Aislabie enhanced the Studley Royal estate by purchasing the neighbouring ruins of Fountains Abbey in 1767.

Brown's work at Sherborne in the mid 1750s was complemented in 1765 when the walled formal garden on the east side of the house was destroyed to make way for the East Lawn (around which a ha-ha was built) opening up views. Visiting Sherborne Castle in 1776, Brown laid out the Castle Yard, while the formal terraces north of the house that Alexander Pope had praised in 1724 were smoothed out. The lakeside garden was also set out by Brown and planted with trees, shrubs and flowers. The grounds were also enhanced by buildings at once utilitarian and aesthetic: the Dairy, built in 1756 in Gothick style, the substantial Orangery in 1779–81 and the Ice House in 1780. At Petworth, where Brown landscaped the park between 1752 and 1765, the 'natural' style included the creation of a large lake in front of the house.

Brown's parks complemented the rebuilding of seats. Thus, the Clifford seat at Ugbrooke was rebuilt by Robert Adam from 1763 to 1766: aside from work on the exterior, he extensively redecorated the interior; and the park, with its two lakes, was given its present form by Brown in the 1770s. His work was celebrated in *A Poem on Ugbrooke* by Father Joseph Reeve, a Clifford family chaplain:

> To shade the hill, to scoop and swell the green,
> To break with wild diversities the scene
> To model with the genius of the place
> Each artless feature, each spontaneous grace.

Just as Henry Wise had been able to purchase an estate and mansion and had died wealthy, Brown's efforts brought him substantial wealth; having begun work as a kitchen gardener, he became High Sheriff of Huntingdonshire. Such mobility was an index of the profitability and reputation of landscaping, and the relationship between landscaper and client was not a simple one of supplier and patron. The fashion for the new style was such that grounds that were not reworked were regarded as deficient, while terrain that did not lend itself to such reworking was deplored. Letitia Proctor regretted the absence of a lake at Houghton and, revisiting it in 1772, thought the park 'too flat to be beautiful'.[40] Indeed flat parks, as at Shugborough, created particular problems for an aesthetics that had moved to favour the prospects born of slopes.

The more famous gardeners were emulated by a host of others, such as William Emes at Wimpole, as well as Richard Woods at Buckland and Hengrave. At Saltram, where the Parkers extensively rebuilt the Tudor house to produce a splendid exterior, with excellent Adam interiors in which a number of their friend Joshua Reynolds's paintings hang, the park, created in the early 1740s, was also developed in Brown's style by a Mr Richmond from 1769. An orangery was built between 1773 and 1775, and a chapel, a garden bower and a battlemented octagon were also constructed in the park. At Attingham Park, Thomas Legatt laid out the park for Noel Hill between 1769 and 1772, planting trees and creating a slope. At Raby Castle, Thomas White altered the park for Gilbert, 2nd Lord Barnard; the moat was drained later in the century.

The details of what was added throws considerable light on contemporary interests and tastes. At Osterley Park, an unknown designer was responsible for major changes between 1760 and 1790 . In place of the formal ponds and canals, three long lakes created the appearance of a river curving round the house. Lawns and pasture with clumps of trees replaced the formal garden, and the planting – about three thousand trees – was extensive. The grounds were enhanced with buildings designed to provide interest for those strolling in them. These included a 'tea room', which was really a summer house, a pine house, a windmill and temporary structures, including a flower stage and another summer house. A menagerie with rare birds, including from the Orient, and boating on the lake added to the interest. Lakes for boating, ponds for fishing and menageries, as at Bowood, Hartwell and Castle Ashby, were aspects of the recreations offered in many parks. At Osterley, a rustic stone bridge contributed to the painterly quality of the landscape. Similarly, at Wallington, Sir Walter Calverley Blackett had the park enhanced by damming the Wansbeck to create the feature of a more impressive river and then having a bridge designed by James Paine built across it: aside from the view of river and bridge down the slope from the house, this gave an impressive prospect of the house coming into view from the bridge.

The painterly quality of landscape was referred to by the popular travel writer William Gilpin in 1798 when he wrote of 'that kind of beauty which would look well in a picture'. This helped ensure that even grounds that did not change greatly, such as Knole, were enhanced by buildings designed to lend picturesque interest: in Knole's case fake ruins, built in the 1760s, and a Gothick Bird House built in about 1761.

Similarly, a folly tower was built on Conigar Hall in the grounds of Dunster Castle, and another on St Michael's Hill on the Montacute estate in 1760. Other parks that had not changed for a while were eventually brought into line with new ideas. At Dyrham Park, at the close of the century, Charles Harcourt-Master replaced the formal Dutch water garden of the 1690s with a classic park with picturesque clumps of trees, while Humphry Repton was paid for advice in 1801 and 1803.

Kent and Brown's system was criticised for the formalism it retained by Sir Uvedale Price (1747–1829), who argued in his *An Essay on the Picturesque* (1794) in favour of a wilder, less regular and smooth, and more natural and 'picturesque', beauty that would accord with 'all the principles of landscape painting'. Price was supported by Richard Payne Knight in *The Landscape: A Didactic Poem* (1794). Their arguments influenced Humphry Repton (1752–1818), who transformed about 220 gardens, and developed Brown's ideas in accordance with the concept of the 'picturesque'. This stressed the individual character of each landscape and the need to retain it, while making improvements to remove what were judged blemishes and obstructions, and to open up vistas, as at Attingham Park; he also added a weir there to maintain the water level in the upper reaches of the River Tern so that a cascade could then enhance the landscape. At Antony House, Repton swept away the formal parterres. Alongside his naturalistic preference, Repton was also prepared to see flower gardens close to houses as an aspect of an acceptable formality.

Many grounds were worked on by more than one designer. At Euston, Brown followed on from Kent, while Claremont and Stowe evolved from Bridgeman through Kent to Brown and Repton. At Stowe, where Brown remodelled the grounds in 1780, the boundaries of woodland and the shapes of lakes were rounded, and some of the geometric bodies of water near the house were removed. At Bowood, Brown's work was enhanced in the mid 1780s by a 'picturesque' landscape designed by Charles Hamilton including a cascade, grottoes and a hermit's cave.

Friendships and family links aided transitions and provided continuity. At Blickling, the 1st Earl in the early decades of the century rearranged the grounds to provide an imposing vista that closed with a Doric temple on a large terrace. In the 1760s, however, his son replaced the geometric woodland layout with a more fluid network of serpentine paths. At Broadlands, Brown landscaped the park for Viscount

Palmerston between 1766 and 1780, while his son-in-law, Henry Holland, redesigned the entrance hall between 1788 and 1792. At Studley Royal, the formalism of John Aislabie's work was superseded, from 1742, by his son William's interest in the newly-fashionable picturesque style. This involved not the destruction of his father's work but the landscaping of the garden below the lake where the River Skell flows down a narrow gorge. William enhanced the rocky cliffs of this area with eye-catchers, including a belvedere, a Chinese pavilion that was an early example of *chinoiserie*, and the 'Devil's Chimney', a building possibly inspired by a tomb near Rome, and by planting beech woods designed to tower over the valley. William Aislabie sought similar effects at the garden he created at Hackfall on the River Ure in 1749–68. He also incorporated Fountains Abbey into his Studley Royal estate, in accordance with the fashion of the period: instead of a formal approach to the abbey, there was the De Grey Walk, a sweep of grass with woods also ensuring a natural frame, while on the estate, a Gothick alcove known as Anne Boleyn's Seat provided a picturesque view of the abbey. In addition to the canal gardens, major changes were made to the deer park at Studley Royal. John Aislabie had laid out seven large intersecting avenues designed to focus on features of the estate such as a distant prospect of Ripon Minster. Under the influence of Brown and others, however, the park at Studley Royal became less formal and the avenues were replaced in favour of an apparently unplanned space: 'parkland', that is pasture with impressive specimens of trees, such as oaks and beeches.

Other grounds were similarly changed. At Belton House, the park went through a series of transformations. Sir John Brownlow, the builder of the house, created, judging from the plate in *Vitruvius Britannicus*, a state-of-the-art landscape at the same time from 1685, with formal parterres, symmetrical patterns of walks, some centred on *rond points*, ponds with straight boundaries, plentiful statues, topiary trees and an obelisk; all enclosed within a five-mile wall. Under his nephew, Viscount Tyrconnel, the grounds were extensively remodelled in mid century with the creation of a wilderness, including a cascade and picturesque ruins. In 1778, the 1st Lord Brownlow hired William Emes to remodel the grounds further. The last of the parterres was replaced, while the formal late seventeenth-century planting was thinned out in order to make the woods appear naturalistic rather than geometric. At Ham House, the seventeenth-century parterres were replaced by a large lawn with clumps of trees.

Many landowners displayed a close personal interest in the landscaping of their own and friends' parks, a fashionable and expensive pastime. Prominent examples included Burlington at Chiswick, Robert Digby at Sherborne Castle, Lord Cobham at Stowe, George Bowes at Gibside, the 5th Lord Byron at Newstead, John and William Aislabie at Studley Royal, Thomas Anson at Shugborough, John Chute at The Vyne, Charles Hamilton at Painshill,[41] and Thomas Jones at Hafod, which was landscaped in the 'picturesque' style by 'Warwick' Smith. Many parks reflected the role of the owner, and both they and local landscape gardeners were influenced by the general pattern of the period. Chute removed most of the formal garden features at The Vyne. Influential gentlemen amateur landscape gardeners included William Mason and Sanderson Miller. William Pitt the Elder shared this hobby, possibly because it was relaxing, gave him a sense of control, and created a social ambience of shared pastimes. Interested in laying out grounds, he played a role in works at Encombe, Hagley, Shenstone, Stowe, West Wickham and Wotton. At South Lodge in Enfield Chase, where he held the lease from 1747 until 1753, Pitt added a temple dedicated to Pan and a garden pyramid. In contrast, the landscaping of the Hell-Fire Club's grotto at Medmenham Abbey had more sinister overtones. Other landlords took a more distant role. From 1759 to 1768, the 3rd Duke of Bridgewater, famous as the 'Canal Duke', employed Henry Holland to work on his seat at Ashridge, and Brown to landscape the park.

Although the established narrative of the English landscape garden is clear, it is necessary to note that not all grounds looked like Brown parkscapes. In part, there were issues of detailed topography and landownership, but stylistic preferences also played a role. At Shugborough, where the flat landscape ensured that architectural elements, trees and water would play a greater part in establishing shape than slopes, Thomas Anson in the 1740s and 1750s provided a layout that has been described as Rococo. This was a reference not so much to the serpentine walks as to the delicate structures erected to help shape the grounds. Several had Chinese themes, in honour of Thomas's brother, Admiral George Anson, who, in sailing round the world, had visited Canton in 1743: the Chinese House, the pagoda, and two *chinoiserie* bridges. A *chinoiserie* bridge was also added at The Vyne in the 1750s, and there was another at Painshill. The childless Admiral Anson died in 1762 leaving a fortune to his brother Thomas who pressed on to transform the park at

Shugborough. Rather than turning to Brown, he hired James 'Athenian' Stuart to recreate a vision of Classical Greece. Stuart had carefully surveyed the Classical ruins of Athens while there in 1751–53, and in 1762 published the first volume of his *The Antiquities of Athens*.[42] Anson wanted Stuart to breathe new life into his careful illustrations, and he responded by designing a series of structures including a copy of the Choragic Monument of Lysicrates – a monumental plinth to support a bronze tripod, as well as the Tower of the Winds, which included an upstairs banqueting room. Stuart also provided a copy of the Arch of Hadrian at Athens, which, when completed in 1764 served to commemorate Admiral and Lady Anson. Far from the sea, in Staffordshire, the upper stage of the arch holds marble sarcophagi topped by busts of them and flanking a naval trophy. The landscape thus marked both family and national triumph. Stuart also reconstructed the orangery. With its colonnade façade and an apse with a coffered semi-dome, this was intended to display a section of Thomas Anson's sculpture collection. Anna Seward in her 1767 poem on Shugborough wrote of:

> Where the stately colonnade extends
> Its pillar'd length, to shade the sculptured forms
> Of demigods or heroes, and protect
> From the cold northern blast each tender plant ...
> Here while we breathe perfume, the ravished eye
> Surveys the miracles of Grecian art.

The admiral's wealth was crucial at Shugborough, but, in many cases, agricultural profits were more important. The enclosure movement of the period provided opportunities for the creation of new parks as land ownership was reorganised and land use altered. Elsewhere existing deerparks were reshaped, although there was not always continuity from deerparks to parkland. What parkland did reflect was agrarian wealth and power, and the nature of a society in which private owners could do as they chose, and chose to do what was regarded as appropriate to the taste they wished to display.

Parks were characteristic of areas with large estates, for example west Suffolk, and not of those where there were numerous smaller landlords. Areas with large estates were frequently those of relatively low land value, whereas the most fertile regions were densely populated and did not lend themselves as readily to the emparkment of land round great houses, as woodland and less valuable land did. As a result, the detailed geography of parkland varied greatly. In Cheshire, for example, parks were common in the north-central and eastern regions of the county, but not in the west. In much of England, the pattern of estates did not alter greatly during the century. In Oxfordshire, the Churchill estate centred on Blenheim could be created only because there was a royal manor – Woodstock – to use. Smaller parks, however, could be created on more modest sites. Charles Hamilton, the far-from-wealthy four-teenth child of the 6th Earl of Abercorn, used about 300 acres centred on a sandy hillside sloping to the River Mole to create Painshill.

Status was both reflected and reinforced by parks. Although park landscape was not without economic value, sheep serving as more than natural lawnmowers, the labour required to excavate basins for artificial hills or to create hills was considerable. Lakes had to be dug out by hand, and the lining of their base and sides with clay to prevent leakage was labour-intensive and took a long time. The movement of huge, living trees was also very difficult.

As a result of such efforts, major expense was incurred, and most parks did not repay their cost. Nevertheless, wood from parkland had considerable value, providing fuel for industry and timber for construc-tion. The Leicestershire parson and planter William Hanbury insisted that planting trees was a gentleman's patriotic duty, publishing an *Essay on Planting, and a Scheme for Making it Conducive to the Glory of God and the Advantage of Society* in 1758. Planting trees reflected the elite's sense of permanence: it was worth planting for the benefit of your distant descendants.

New developments in horticulture, especially imports, mainly from North America, greatly extended the range of possible trees, shrubs and flowers that could be planted, while Classical texts provided inspiration for the layout of parks. Newly-introduced plants included the rhodo-dendron in 1736, the magnolia grandiflora in 1737, the camellia in 1739, buddleia in 1774, the fuschia in 1788, the strelitzia in the 1780s and the dahlia in 1798. William, 4th Earl of Rochford returned to England from Italy in 1755 with a cutting of Lombardy poplar, the first planted in England. The cultivation of imported plants was a sign of taste and status, as was the stocking of ponds and menageries with different fish and animals. They attracted interest, reflected affluent discrimination, and were related to the rise of observational science and the collecting of specimens as leisure activities.

Landscape gardening also reflected and created a new aesthetic that was interested in nature, albeit an altered nature that reflected and enhanced aesthetic judgments, enabling those who viewed and perambulated the landscape to display their own worth and, with it, that of nature. In her poetic account of an English country house, *Crumble Hall*, Mary Leapor, a kitchen maid, wrote of climbing up to the roof to view the 'beauteous order' of a landscaped park. Visiting Torbay in 1793, John Swete claimed that the influences of Kent and Brown enabled society to 'escape from the darkness of prejudice and trace the path of nature without the aid of geometric art'.[43]

The new fashion entailed stylistic conventions and derived from artistic models, for example the presentation of the landscapes of Roman Italy in the paintings of Claude Lorrain influencing the banker Henry Hoare when he laid out the gardens at Stourhead which he inherited in 1741: gardens were planned as an English realisation of the Classical landscapes depicted by Lorrain, and, more generally, as an Anglicisation of Classical notions of rural peace and beauty. In 1736, there was much laughter in the House of Commons when John, Viscount Tyrconnel, MP for Grantham, announced that he loved peace as much as the pictures of Lorrain.[44] Visiting Hagley in September 1753, Horace Walpole noted 'there is such a pretty well under a wood, like the Samaritan woman's in a picture of Nicolò Poussin'.

Alongside the appeal of the interpreted Classical physical (and mental) landscape came that of a pastoralism. This was seen with the poetry of William Shenstone (1714–1763), who was unusual in being a landowner as well as a poet, and a landowner who himself enhanced his landscape. His role in this was celebrated by his friend, Richard Jago, a clergyman, in his poem *Edge-Hill* (1767):

> so lib'rally their crystal urns
> The Naiads pour'd, enchanted with his spells;
> And pleas'd to see their ever-flowing streams
> Led by his hand, in many a mazy line.

The impact of these Classical notions was also seen in English landscape painting. Richard Wilson, who visited Okehampton Castle in 1771, soon after painted a Romantic vision of the hilltop castle ruins silhouetted against the evening sky. Wilson was not concerned with architectural detail. Instead, he sought to depict an atmosphere at once calm, entrancing, melancholic and picturesque. Landscape gardeners sought similar effects to those who provide painterly landscapes.

With the coining of the phrases landscape design and landscape gardener, there was a self-conscious character to the development that emphasised the significance of contemporary developments and that reflected the shift from the park as a place to hunt to the park as landscape: as a source for, and site of contemplation. There was an active shaping of new designation, aesthetic and usage as parks ceased to be defined by the presence of deer, or as looking as though they should be. Hunting in fact continued to be a leisure activity in the new parks, as did shooting, and there was much expenditure throughout the century on stables, kennels and hunting lodges, often on an elaborate scale. Stables such as those at Kedleston were elegant as well as utilitarian.[45] Aside from his massive spending on the stables at Houghton, Walpole also spent very heavily – allegedly £14,000 – on Old Lodge, his hunting lodge in Richmond New Park. The architectural effort devoted to such works has been underrated.

The social status of hunting was established by the Game Laws. The Game Act of 1671 gave the exclusive right to hunt game to freeholders worth £100 a year or leaseholders worth £150 a year. This substantial landed property qualification restricted the sport to wealthy landed gentry. There was supplementary legislation in 1707, 1771 and 1773. Such Acts were supported by gamekeepers and mantraps, and both the legislation and its defence helped to make clear the nature of hierarchy and power in the rural community. From the late 1770s, game preserves were protected by spring guns and mantraps. Hunting was not only restricted by legislation: keeping horses was expensive. The nature of hunting was also affected by the reorganisation of rural space and control encapsulated in the enclosure movement. Fox-hunting became immensely popular in the second half of the century, and many great landlords had their own private packs, while others were maintained by subscription. Tree planting in the open country was often undertaken to provide cover for the fox.

Alongside the continued interest in hunting, the elite entertainment parks now provided was presented in a more aesthetic fashion than hitherto. This was an aspect of the role of cultural patronage in defining not only taste but status. In the grounds, temples and prospects provided sites for sociability, also enhancing the circuit for visitors created within most parks. Ornamental buildings created landscape compositions, attracting the viewer and then centring the scene. Many landscapes were enhanced by buildings that referred directly to the

Classical world. An obelisk was erected in the gardens of Chiswick House by 1733, while Burlington also erected a column carrying a statue of the Venus de Medici. Kent was responsible for the Temple of British Worthies at Stowe: portrait busts of fourteen worthies selected to make political points, but, as a joke, with a tribute to the virtues of a dog at the back. The imitation Temple of Theseus (or Hephaestus) designed for the grounds of Hagley Hall by James 'Athenian' Stuart in 1758, was the first copy of a Greek Doric-style temple. Others, such as the one at Bowood, provided opportunities for strollers to rest and talk. Robert Adam designed a large pedimented Doric orangery for Osterley Park in 1763–64, and this complemented the Doric temple with Rococo interior plasterwork already in place. In the grounds at Painshill:

> stands a large Doric building, called the temple of Bacchus, with a fine portico in the front, a rich *alto relievo* in the pediment, and on each side a range of pilasters: within, it is decorated with many antique busts, and a noble statue of the god in the centre; the room has none of that solemnity which is often affectedly ascribed to the character, but without being gaudy is full of light, of ornament, and splendor; the situation is on a brow, which commands an agreeable prospect.[46]

Parks were also embellished with grottoes, follies, shell houses, columns and Classical statues. The column and statue of liberty at Gibside, erected in 1750–57, a Roman Doric column higher than Nelson's Column, is topped by a twelve foot high originally gilt statue of liberty carved by Christopher Richardson in 1756–57 dressed in Classical drapery and carrying the cap of liberty and the staff of maintenance. Daniel Garrett, who began the column, had already built a smaller column bearing a copy of the Apollo Belvedere for Hugh Smithson at Stanwick Hall.[47] Commenting in 1762 on Stourhead, the grounds of which had been enhanced with Classical features, Lord Lyttelton revealed a sense of confident cultural competitiveness:

> The Pantheon [by Flitcroft] is finished, and is an abode worthy of all the deities in Olympius ... I think I never saw the Graces of Sculpture and all the power of that divine art before I saw them there. I would have every Frenchman that comes to England be brought to this place, not only that he may see the perfection of our taste, but to show him that we have citizens who have a truer politeness in their manners, and a nobler elegance in their minds than any count or duke in France.[48]

At Stourhead, Henry Hoare dammed the springs of the River Stour to create a large lake around which he placed temples and grottoes in order to provide appropriate vistas. Flitcroft also designed the Temple of Flora at Stourhead, and the grounds included a Temple of Apollo and a Rustic Cottage.

Mausoleums, for example at Castle Howard or the one designed by Robert Adam at Bowood, added further interest to parkland. The potentially eclectic nature of garden buildings was seen at Wallington, where a Chinese House (Rococo *chinoiserie*) shaped the estate with a Portico House, as well as with Rothley Castle, a Gothick folly, and, sub-sequently, Codjah's Crag, another pretend fortification designed to lend interest to a prospect. Painshill included a life-size statue of *The Rape of the Sabine Women* as well as a Gothick pavilion, a Turkish-style can-vas tent, a grotto, a mock ruin of a Roman mausoleum, a Gothick tower and a Chinese bridge.

The new fashion in landscaping was less rigid and formal than its predecessor, and this permitted a more personal response by visitors to the tamed natural environment that was presented, a direction that led towards the more personal response to nature that was to be such a major theme in Romanticism.[49] In both fiction and on canvas, foreign landscapes were increasingly presented in light of the English style as it became more defined. In Samuel Johnson's *History of Rasselas, Prince of Abyssinia* (1759), the travellers come across the grounds of a wealthy individual and find nature harmoniously tamed:

> The shrubs were diligently cut away to open walks where the shades were darkest; the boughs of opposite trees were artificially interwoven; seats of flowery turf were raised in vacant spaces, and a rivulet that wantoned along the side of a winding path had its banks sometimes opened into small basins, and its stream sometimes obstructed by little mounds of stone heaped together to increase its murmurs.[50]

English landscape gardening was indeed increasingly admired and copied abroad. In Russia, English experts created and looked after Catherine the Great's parks. When Thomas Jefferson visited England in 1786 he was particularly interested in seeing gardens. The following year, he wrote 'The gardening in that country is the article in which it excels all the earth. I mean their pleasure-gardening. This, indeed, went far beyond my ideas'. He noted his impressions in 'Memorandums made on a Tour to Some of the Gardens in England, Described by Whately in his Book on Gardening', a reference to Thomas Whately's *Observations on Modern Gardening* (1770), which was a prominent example of the copious literature about landscape gardening. Jefferson used Whately as guide and inspiration, walking over the gardens he visited with the book in hand. He toured the gardens with John Adams, visiting, among others, Stowe, Claremont, Painshill, Hagley and Blenheim.[51] The influence of the visit can be seen in Jefferson's landscaping of his grounds at Monticello in Virginia.

In Ireland, Scotland and Wales, although there were specific influences and characteristics, the landed elite, nevertheless, increasingly responded to and shaped the same cultural impulses as their English counterparts. Their patronage of distinctive cultural traditions, such as bardic poetry, declined, and these traditions suffered accordingly. Roderick Morison (*c.*1656–*c.*1714) was the last famous bardic harper of Gaelic Scotland. Highland dancing, however, was being renewed by 1780. As the Welsh gentry increasingly intermarried with their English counterparts, while a greater number of heirs were educated in England, so English cultural norms had a growing appeal in Wales. This was seen in both architecture and landscape gardening. In Wales, new houses, such as Nanteos for the Powells, and enhancements, such as the stately rooms at Chirk Castle for the Myddletons and the ballroom at Powis Castle for the Herberts, were produced in what were established British aristocratic styles. This was also true of the gardens. William Emes advised Philip Yorke at Erddig between 1767 and 1789, creating hanging gardens and 'natural' clumps of trees. He was also responsible for the landscaping at Chirk and Powis. One of the leading Welsh painters of the period, Thomas Jones (1745–1803), a country gentleman as well as a painter of Welsh scenery, studied at Oxford, and from 1762 lived for many years in London, following the style of his teacher Richard Wilson. There was a similar process of Anglicization of Scottish landowners.

Across the British Isles, the role of wealthy landowners as patrons and leaders of fashion ensured that they played a crucial role in the artistic world. Due to the availability and impact of capital and to the significance of show in an age of greatly expanding ranges of commodities, display was a major part of the nature of patronage, and the conspicuous consumption and display of culture emphasised social status. Major stately homes, such as Blenheim, Castle Howard, Chatsworth, Houghton and Stourhead, open to respectable looking visitors, acted as display models for architectural, artistic and landscape styles, while it was not only great houses and gardens that were accessible to visitors. Over 2,300 people visited Wilton in 1776.[52] Guidebooks for the most notable were published from mid century. Richard Cowdray, the house steward, published *A Description of the Pictures, Statues, Bustoes, Basso-Relievos and Other Curiosities at the Earl of Pembroke's House at Wilton* (1751), and this was only one of six different guides to Wilton published between 1750 and 1800.

Kedleston was always open to the public and perhaps the most admired: in about 1759, Sir Nathaniel Curzon had the house there built in about 1700 demolished and replaced by a mansion in which Robert Adam embellished the established Palladian plan with Roman motifs, making the Marble Hall seem like a Classical atrium,[53] an example of the appeal of Classical models. Such architectural models also were felt to lend themselves to Classical and Classical-style decoration, such as statuary. At Kedleston, hall and saloon were modelled on the atrium and vestibulum of a Roman palace, although, visiting it in 1774, Johnson thought the house 'ill contrived' and that the marble pillars in the Hall took up too much room. Revisiting Kedleston with James Boswell in September 1777, Johnson was shown the house by a housekeeper who had a printed list of the many pictures. Visiting stately homes was one means of lessening the gap between the culture of the elite and that of other ranks, although admission was not equally open to all. Holkham Hall was open every day bar Sunday to the quality, but only on Tuesdays to others.

Another means by which the gap was lessened was the contribution of the less affluent gentry. They provided an important way in which new styles, whether in clothes or portraits, buildings or gardens, were disseminated. If less affluent gentry could not emulate the patronage of the elite, they were still of considerable importance in rural regions, and in aggregate terms sometimes more significant, although their influence has received insufficient scholarly attention, not least because they could not afford to patronise major artists. At the same time, contrasts can be drawn between the 'alien architectural intrusions' favoured by the elite and the more accessible works of the gentry.[54] In Berkshire in the early decades of the century, much of the building was undertaken by gentry families favouring solid, four square houses, such as Ardington House built in 1719–20, all probably designed by local builders, such as Thomas Strong and William Townesend, influenced by Wren and Vanbrugh.[55] In the north east of England, Daniel Garrett, who had been a man of business in Lord Burlington's household, played a comparable role in the 1740s and 1750s, providing Palladianism for houses such as Fenham for William Ord, Nunwick for Lancelot Allgood, and the south front of Blagdon for Sir Matthew White. Houses built or rebuilt for the less affluent gentry looked toward not only more impressive seats but also the less grand farmhouses of a wider segment of the rural population; similarly parks looked towards paddocks. La Rochefoucauld noted:

> Gentlemen who are not wealthy enough to have parks have what they call lawns, a small area of land round their houses, with bordered walks, beautiful turf and a small clump of trees, all kept in extremely neat order. They themselves design these garden walks. It's everything they need for the surroundings of the house, to give them an air of ownership and to walk in for half an hour after dinner.[56]

Outside towns, villas were built, particularly toward the close of the century. These drew on the same architectural and garden languages as gentry homes. In contrast, however, those manor houses that were not improved risked becoming farmhouses, an aspect of a serious fall in status.

Some of the gentry were writers, but this was not a large group. Hildebrand Jacob (1693–1739), the son and son-in-law of baronets, published his collected works in 1735. He subsequently added more poetry, as well as three plays in addition to *The Fatal Constancy*, the tragedy he had published in 1723. A younger son, Edward Jerningham (1727–1812), was a convert from Catholicism, and an active but much criticised poet. He took up popular themes in *Elegy, written among the Ruins of an Abbey* (1765) and *Yarico to Inkle* (1766). John, Lord Hervey wrote *Agrippina*, a Classical play. Frederick, 5th Earl of Carlisle fancied himself as a poet and tragedian, although his ward, the poet George, Lord Byron, disparaged his plays and verse.

An emphasis on stately homes and grounds suggests an elite that was withdrawn from the bulk of the population, and that was true to a considerable extent.[57] Intellectually and aesthetically, references to the oligarchical elite of republican Rome provided a cultural and political resonance that served to define what appeared to be their modern descendants, not least in comparison to others.[58] At the physical level, much work was devoted to gates and associated lodges that segregated the world of the landed elite; and these features indeed recorded changes in architectural style. This withdrawal, like the power of the landed elite itself, has left other evidence, but it tends to be patchy and at times ambiguous or contradictory, and to need 'reading' carefully. Other aspects of the impact of the landed elite have also left only limited evidence. Whitegates Cottage on the Gunby Hall Estate in Lincolnshire is a small thatched home built in about 1770 to provide accommodation for estate workers. Its mud and stud walling was very different to the red-brick panelled Gunby Hall, and it would also have been colder, darker and wetter as a dwelling. Such contrasts can be all too rarely glimpsed as much estate building does not survive, although, as part of the reorganization of much of the countryside, such building was extensive. In Northumberland, Sir Walter Calverley Blackett not only rebuilt his rural seat at Wallington but also used the architect Daniel Garrett to draw up plans for the estate cottages built in the village of Cambo and for the chapel there.

The reorganisation of much of the countryside through enclosure reflected both the power and the aesthetic of the age. Enclosing landowners alarmed much of the rural population, creating wide disruption of traditional rights and expectations. The utilitarian straight lines that were employed for field boundaries and roads, as rural land use was altered, contrasted greatly with the serpentine patterns for woods and rivers seen as desirable for 'natural' landscapes in parkland. These straight roads were seen as magnificent by commentators such as Arthur Young who applauded what they saw as economic modernisation. The demolition of villages to provide parkland was a more vivid instance of the same process, which also affected 'public space' in the shape of the routes of canals and roads. The route of the London-Portsmouth canal was altered to allow improvement of the grounds at Claremont, while, in 1779–80, the London-Holyhead road was moved away from another stately home, Attingham.

The ability of the elite to define the terms of its relationship with the rest of society was not restricted to their landed estates. It was also seen in towns, especially in the West End of London, as well as in spa towns, and in the genteel quarters of other towns. The turnpiking of roads made it easier to visit towns, from both the countryside and from other towns, and was celebrated for bringing speed and certainty to travel. By 1770, when there were 15,000 miles of turnpikes in England, most of it was within a dozen miles of one, although in his play *She Stoops to Conquer* (1773) Oliver Goldsmith wrote of a rural journey 'it is a damned long, dark, boggy, dirty, dangerous way', a fit prelude to the misperception of identity that provides the key plot device. Travel was also made faster by the cross-breeding of fast Arab horses to pull coaches, while improvements in comfort came from the replacement of leather straps by steel coach springs, and from the introduction of elliptical springs. Increasingly, the elite spent the Season in London,[59] socialising with each other from townhouses they owned or rented. These houses were decorated to provide appropriate settings for luxurious life and elegant entertaining,[60] such as the drawing room for Northumberland House designed by Robert Adam in the early 1770s. The new houses in which the elite lived helped differentiate the genteel areas of cities from where the bulk of the population, including the merchants, lived. Garden squares, which brought the devices of parkland into the city, contributed to the same effect.

The presence of the elite can also be seen in publicly available works, for example the subscription lists printed in many books and in major published scores, such as those of Handel. Such lists were headed by the elite in order of social hierarchy. The newspaper advertisements for the Handel concerts at Westminster Abbey in 1791, for instance, were headed:

> By command and under the patronage of their Majesties; and under the direction of the
> Earl of Uxbridge, Honorary President (of the Royal Society of Musicians)
> Honorary Vice Presidents –
>> Duke of Leeds
>> Earl of Exeter
>> Earl of Sandwich
>> Viscount Fitzwilliam
>> Lord Grey de Wilton
>> Joah Bates Esq.

Bates was the expert. A Yorkshire-born musician who had become a fellow of King's College Cambridge and a protégé of the Earl of Sandwich, Bates became conductor to the Concerts of Ancient Music in 1776 and played a major role in launching the Handel concerts. In terms of the social hierarchy, however, he came below the other vice presidents. The style had been set by the 1784 Handel commemoration.

The expansion of the middling orders ensured, nevertheless, that elite activity was less central to the cultural world than hitherto. Elite values and models remained important across society, but others were also of value. Furthermore, considerable play was made of contrasts between these values and the actual conduct of members of the elite. This served not to deny the values nor the models, but to suggest a measure of hypocrisy on the part of members of the elite, as well as the extent to which appropriate values were not solely displayed by its members. In the listing of 'Names of the Principal Persons' in the novel *Sir Charles Grandison* (1753–4), Richardson listed the men and women by their moral worth rather than their rank. In his novel *Joseph Andrews* (1742), the contrast was important to the plot and explicitly mentioned by Henry Fielding. He enters a caveat about judging groups. At the same time, in 'Matter prefatory in praise of biography', the first chapter of book three of the novel, Fielding indicates the true quality of patronage, but then continues to deadly effect:

> as in most of our particular characters we mean not to lash individuals, but all of the like sort, so, in our general descriptions we mean not universals, but would be understood with many exceptions: for instance, in our description of high people we cannot be intended to include such as, whilst they are an honour to their high rank, by a well-guided condescension make their superiority as easy as possible to those whom fortune chiefly hath placed below them. Of this number I could name a peer no less elevated by nature than by fortune who, whilst he wears the noblest ensigns of honour on his person, bears the truest stamp of dignity on his mind, adorned with greatness, enriched with knowledge, and embellished with genius. I have seen this man relieve with generosity while he hath conversed with freedom, and be to the same person a patron and a companion ... By those high people, therefore, whom I have described, I mean a set of wretches, who, while they are a disgrace to their ancestors, whose honours and fortunes they inherit (or perhaps a greater to their mother, for such degeneracy is scarce credible), have the insolence to treat those with disregard who are at least equal to the founders of their own splendour. It is, I fancy, impossible to conceive a spectacle more worthy of our indignation than that of a fellow who is not only a blot in the escutcheon of a great family but a scandal to the human species, maintaining a supercilious behaviour to men who are an honour to their nature and a disgrace to their fortune.

Patronage issues brought the mismatch of rank and nobility abruptly home to many writers. This encouraged a critique of the values of polite society, as when Fielding wrote that the lascivious Lady Booby was 'perfectly polite, nor had any vice inconsistent with good breeding'. His plots, like those of many other works, frequently revolved around issues of inheritance, and this was a device, appropriate for both comedy and tragedy, that struck a resonance across society and indeed genres, play-ing a major role in the first Gothic novel, Horace Walpole's *The Castle of Otranto*. The travails of a rightful inheritance, however much depicted in landed society, also echoed at all levels. This was also seen in the lead-ing work of Fielding's younger sister, Sarah, her novel *The Adventures of David Simple* (1744), in which David has been disinherited by his younger brother's use of a forged will, while the friends he makes, Cyn-thia, Camilla and Valentine, have also been harshly treated, the last two due to a dishonest stepmother. In Tobias Smollett's novel *The Adven-tures of Roderick Random* (1748), Roderick's father has been disinherited.

Henry Fielding's condemnation of false values was directed across the range of society. In his mock-heroic novel *The History of the Life of the Late Mr Jonathan Wild the Great* (1743), Fielding offered an ironic account of false greatness aimed not only at the criminal but also, for example, against great conquerors, Alexander the Great being among those condemned:

> When I consider whole nations extirpated only to bring tears into the eyes of a GREAT MAN, that he hath no more nations to extirpate, then indeed I am almost inclined to wish that nature had spared us this her MASTER-PIECE, and that no GREAT MAN had ever been born into the world.

The parallel of false greatness and crime had also been drawn by St Augustine, and Alexander was a figure represented critically by a num-ber of eighteenth-century writers, including Christopher Smart in 1751.[61] Fielding offered a telling piece on the subject, one that proclaimed his moral concerns and his ironic, but deeply-felt, hostility to human evil. A sense of social division was also present: 'the plowman, the shepherd, the weaver, the builder, and the soldier, work not for themselves but others; they are contented with a poor pittance (the labourer's hire)'. In contrast, 'the GREAT' enjoyed 'the fruits of their labours'.

At the same time, a sense of social inclusion was expressed in cultural institutions and in the language and symbolism of Patriotism. The Soci-ety for the Encouragement of Arts, Manufactures and Commerce (now the Royal Society of Arts) was instituted in 1754 by a group of 'noble-men, clergy, gentlemen, and merchants', and its achievements were celebrated in *Arts, Manufactures, and Commerce: A Poem* (1769) by George Cockings, a porter and subsequently Registrar to the Society:

> I sing the generous plan (the worthy cause)
> From whence a noble elevation rose:

> The public good; the manufacturer's gain;
> (Who now attempts no useful scheme in vain)
> Arts, commerce, and our cultivated lands,
> The base whereon the superstructure stands.

This inclusiveness was helped by the extent to which, whatever the apparent distinction between aristocratic mores and the politeness and gentility of the middling orders, there was in practice considerable overlap.

4

Religion

The ridiculous notion of witches and witchcraft still prevails amongst the lower sort of people.

Reading Mercury, 15 March 1773.

The thronging streets of the capital were under the shadow of an architectural masterpiece that was both new and built for the glory of God. Christopher Wren's St Paul's Cathedral was a triumph of architectural accomplishment – one of the first domes erected in England – and also a statement of the importance of religion. As such the dome had to be prominent, and therefore high and large. The cathedral, much of which was built in the 1700s, combined Classical and Christian roots with mathematical and artistic ability.[1] It borrowed the style of church architecture of Baroque Rome, but did so to the glory of the Church of England.

At a superficial glance, the eighteenth century may not appear a particularly religious age. Eighteenth-century urban building – Bath and the West End of London – is not generally recalled for its churches, no more than the English painters of the period are remembered for religious works. As a result of interpretations that developed in the nineteenth century, the eighteenth century is generally seen as a period of enlightenment, indeed as the Age of Enlightenment, and, prior to the Evangelicalism toward the close of the period, signs of faith are mistakenly ascribed to superstitious conservatism or irrational religious enthusiasm. Though such inaccurate views are not found in most scholarly works, they are still widely held, and the role of faith is underrated not least in cultural and artistic matters.

In fact, the religious life of the country overlapped significantly with its cultural life and was also important in the development of the Enlightenment, which took place within, rather than against, Protestantism. Religious writers indeed thought knowledge a potent weapon against atheism and deism. Furthermore, the image of England as a 'polite' society is never more misleading than when it is taken to imply secularism. Instead, the Church of England was the guardian of faith, morals and social order, and its position an expression of them; or so it was represented.[2] The churches were important patrons of cultural activity, and religion continued to be a major theme of the arts. What was judged immoral or sacrilegious in lay culture could be condemned. There was uneasiness, for example, about obscenity in the novel *Tristram Shandy* (1760–67), although the author, Laurence Sterne, was a cleric, and when he published *The Sermons of Mr Yorick* (1760) there were complaints that he had entitled them after the clergyman in the novel, which was held to mock the church.

There was particularly strong criticism of the alleged profanity and immorality of the stage, for example by the non-juror cleric Jeremy Collier in his pamphlet *A Short View of the Immorality and Profaneness of the English Stage* (1698). Such agitation led in February 1699 to government pressure on London playhouses, and to William Congreve and John Vanbrugh making some alterations in their plays. The shift from Restoration comedy to sentimental drama was a long process and had a variety of causes, but criticism of immorality was one of them. Not only drama was criticised. In 1712, the Society for Promoting Christian Knowledge asked Collier to write a pamphlet discouraging the teaching of lewd songs and the composing of music to profane ballads. John Gay's *The Beggar's Opera* (1728) was condemned for immorality by both Thomas Herring, later Archbishop of first York and then Canterbury, and the painter William Hogarth. The influential clerical writer William Law (a non-juring apologist) denounced the stage, while the Bishop of London was opposed to masquerades.[3] Edward Young stopped writing plays when he took religious orders, and in 1753 brought out his earlier unpublished tragedy *The Brothers* only in order to give the profits to the Society for the Propagation of the Gospel. James Miller, however, both took holy orders and wrote plays. Criticism of the stage linked England to Scotland and the Continent. The Spanish clergy was able to restrict the spread of the theatre outside Madrid, plays being banned in Granada in 1706 and Seville in 1731. Many European theatres were closed during Lent and on Sundays and days decreed for prayer. Hostility to the theatre was not limited to Catholic Europe. The Scottish church effectively prevented the setting up of provincial theatres in Scotland before 1750.

In England, criticism was stronger amongst Dissenters and

Methodists who offered an alternative to secular culture, just as many of the German Pietists were critical of both theatre and secular literature. The strong Methodist attacks on the theatre, indeed, led Samuel Foote to satirise the prominent Methodist preacher George Whitefield as Shift in his play *The Minor* (1760), not least by linking his arguments with seduction. In 1766 John Wesley, the most prominent Methodist, who two years earlier had praised the conversion of Birmingham's first theatre into a Methodist chapel, criticised the building of the new theatre in Bristol. In practice many plays took their support for conventional morality sufficiently far to conjure up divine intervention. In the last scene of Nicholas Rowe's *The Tragedy of Jane Shore* (1714), a melodramatic episode of violence and redemption with elements of a secular sermon, Shore asks Heaven to show mercy on his adulterous wife. Redeemed, she dies, asking for divine mercy.

Whatever their views on theatre, the churches showed more favour for other arts, especially music, as important means for the glorification of God. Fear of accusations of crypto-Catholicism, nevertheless, led Frederick Cornwallis, Archbishop of Canterbury and Richard Terrick, Bishop of London in 1773 to block attempts by the Dean of St Paul's Cathedral to commission religious paintings for the interior of the cathedral. The five painters in mind were James Barry, Giovanni-Battista Cipriani, Nathaniel Dance, Joshua Reynolds, and Benjamin West. Reynolds wrote before the scheme was blocked:

> We are upon a scheme at present to adorn St Pauls Church with pictures, five of us, and I fear there is not more qualified for this purpose, have agreed each to give a large picture, they are so poor that we must give the pictures for they have but the interest of £30,000 to keep that great building in repair which is not near sufficient for the purpose. All those whose consent is necessary have freely given it. We think this will be a means of introducing a general fashion for churches to have altar pieces, and that St Pauls will lead the fashion in pictures as St James's does for dress. It will certainly be in vain to make historical painters if there is no means found out for employing them. After we have done this we propose to extend our scheme to have the future monuments erected there instead of Westminster Abbey, the size of the figures and places for them so as to be an ornament to the building to be under the inspection of the Academy.[4]

Reynolds' second-biggest fee was for the oil sketch for the *Nativity* designed for the large west window of New College, Oxford, for which he received 1200 guineas from the Duke of Rutland. His designs were used by Thomas Jervais when he made the paintings on glass. Religious art, however, was far more common in Catholic Europe.

In general, church patronage of art in England was less fulsome than that for music and popular prayer books. The enjoyment of religious art was suspicious to most divines, but much depended on the subject matter, and there were some important private clerical collections. Furthermore, there were opportunities to produce religious art for other institutions and individuals. Although religion was not his main inspiration, William Hogarth painted *Christ Healing the Lame Man at the Pool of Bethesda* and *The Good Samaritan* for St Bartholomew's Hospital in London. Hogarth also took inspiration from Milton, producing a sketch of *Satan, Sin and Death* based on their meeting at the Gates of Hell in *Paradise Lost*. Major painters mostly did not devote much attention to explicitly religious themes. Gainsborough's *Rocky Landscape with Hagar and Ishmael* (*c.* 1788) was his only original overtly religious composition. Its dark tonalities have been seen as a product of the influence of Murillo; but, in general, Spanish painters had only a limited impact on their British counterparts. This was due not so much to their Catholicism as to the greater interest shown in Italian and Dutch art. In an important instance of the role of religion in aesthetics, Gainsborough himself has been seen in his landscapes as responding to Dutch theology. Churches often featured at the focal point of the eyeline of his landscapes.[5] In 1800, Benjamin West painted *Joshua passing the River Jordan with the Ark of the Covenant*. Not one of his better works, it provides a somewhat crude Baroque impression while employing a Neo-Classical style and depicting a Romantic sky.

The construction and decoration of churches and chapels involved much activity, although far less than over the nineteenth century. The population rose greatly from the 1740s, but the episcopal and parochial organisation of England did not alter, so there was relatively little call for new construction. When the Commission for Building Fifty New Churches in London and Westminster, established in 1711, was abolished in 1758 owing to the inadequacy of its principal source of funds, the coal duty, it had authorised the construction of only twelve churches. Yet there was important building during the century. New churches included Thomas Archer's Baroque St Philip's in Birmingham (1711–24), and St Michael's (1734–42) and St James's in Bath (1768–69), All Saints, Gainsborough (1736–48), Holy Cross, Daventry (1752–58), and St Paul's in Liverpool (1765–69). Others were planned but never begun or finished.

In addition, many churches were rebuilt, for example in Bristol St Nicholas's in the 1760s and St Thomas's in 1790. All Saints, Newcastle was rebuilt by David Stephenson between 1786 and 1796 with an oval body. Furthermore, the pressure of the elements, particularly rain, put continuous strain on the fabric of churches, ensuring that frequent repairs were necessary. At the start of the century, in the Northamptonshire parish of Upper Boddington, the roof was repaired at the rate of a bay a year for four years. The plastering was mended, the Creed was put up, and the windows repaired, the vicar, Edward Maynard recording: it 'not being half glazed, gave them new glazing … I made it at last a lightsome, decent church which was before a most squalid rueful place'.[6] Entry for light was very much in line with the values of the period. The congregation was expected to follow the service, and darkness and gloom were seen as functionally and aesthetically undesirable and as aspects of a past that was redundant. The essence of most Georgian church refurbishment was the seating, box pews and galleries, offering facilities for hearing the word.

Repairing or altering a church, an often-underestimated feature of the period, could indeed be the most significant artistic event in a parish during the century. For towns, the academic focus is generally on the developments discussed in chapter nine – enhancements of the secular urban fabric – but this underrates the amount of activity devoted to the ecclesiastical fabric, and the importance of churches and other ecclesiastical buildings for the cultural life of communities. Worcester, for example, had ten parish churches. During the century, several were substantially altered. Far from this process clashing with that of secular enhancement, there was a common purpose of improvement. In architectural terms, this led to a remodelling of churches in the 'modern taste' that matched the use of Classical themes in secular work. St Martin's, Worcester, for example, gained a Classical balustrade for the tower with urns at each corner. In the 1730s, St Nicholas's and All Saints were rebuilt with Baroque influences, including mighty pilasters, while St Swithin's displayed a Palladian theme, like St John's, Gloucester, which was also rebuilt in the 1730s. Ecclesiastical architecture was not restricted to places for worship. In Newcastle, Sir Walter Calverley Blackett provided a library to St Nicholas's Church in 1736, the building carrying the Palladian style into the city centre.

The careers of several architects reflected this activity. Nicholas Hawksmoor (1661–1736) was responsible for several of the London churches and for the west towers of Westminster Abbey. Thomas Archer (d. 1743), a pupil of Vanburgh, was responsible for St. Philip's, Birmingham (1711–19) and St John's, Westminster, which was consecrated in 1728. James Gibbs (1682–1754), an Aberdonian and a Catholic who studied in Rome and settled in London, was responsible for important non-ecclesiastical work in Cambridge and Oxford, including the Radcliffe Library in Oxford, but also for St Mary-le-Strand, St Peter's Vere Street, St George-in-the-East, and St Martin's-in-the-Fields (1721–26) in London, and All Saints, Derby.[7] Henry Flitcroft (1697–1769), a protégé of Burlington, became Comptroller of the Works and helped on Wentworth House for the Marquess of Rockingham and Woburn Abbey for the Duke of Bedford. He was also responsible for the new church of St Giles-in-the-Fields in London (1731–34), which cost £10,000, as well as for the church of St Olave in Southwark (1737–39), which cost £5000, and that of St John at Hampstead, and for rebuilding the church at Wimpole.

Architects noted for their work in other fields still found time for ecclesiastical commissions. In London, George Dance the Elder was responsible for St. Botolph's Aldgate, St. Luke's Old Street, and St. Leonard's, Shoreditch. Robert, later Sir Robert, Taylor was responsible for Long Ditton church in Surrey in 1776, and for the Bishop of Ely's London house about then. He also carried out work on Ely Cathedral. Robert Adam was responsible for Croome d'Abitot in Worcestershire for Lord Coventry.

Plans for churchbuilding, extension and alteration also provided opportunities for controversy, as well as for other activities. Laying the foundations for a new church in Honiton, built within the town, led in 1743 to a procession begun by the 'town musick' and, at the close of the ceremony, to the singing of the *Jubilate*. The newspaper report in the *London Evening Post* of 12 February 1743 included a poem, possibly by the rector, Charles Bertie, an uncommon example of provincial poetry in the London press:

> When Salem's house (the pride of all the Earth)
> By flames destroyed, was doomed a second birth;
> The aged eyes with briny tears beheld
> Its bounds confined, and ancient glory veiled.
> A kinder fate, All Hallows, thee befalls,
> Which totterest but to rise with nobler walls;
> Firm on its base the sacred pile shall stand,
> And brave the assaults of time's devouring hand.

So the bright Phoenix, when with age oppressed,
Pines and expires within his spicy nest;
But strait it does with brighter plumes return,
And blooms with endless vigour in the urn.

The decoration and furniture of churches were also important.[8] Demand for church silver, for example communion cups, was valuable to silversmiths. In 1741, William Kent, best known today for his land-scape gardening, designed a pulpit and choir furniture for York Minster and a choir screen for Gloucester Cathedral. At a more humble level, £15 was spent in 1785 in erecting a gallery at All Saints' Church, Trull, in Somerset; this greatly assisted the musical life of the church, as it could be used by the singers and the church musicians, whose instruments included a violin, bass and tenor viols, and an hautboy.[9]

Many improvements were linked to the enhancement of the musical life of communities. Thus William Lemon, the leading merchant and smelter in mid-century Cornwall, gave a new organ to his parish church of St Mary's Truro, and also paid most of the cost of a new peal of bells for the tower of Kenwyn Church, before joining in the ringing.[10] The installation in 1789 of an organ at the newly-built St John's, Portsea, and the appointment that year of Stephen Sibly as the first organist, has been seen as a major event in the development of Portsmouth's musical life. Yet, this involved Sibly focusing on lay opportunities. From an active church-based musical background – he had been a chorister in Salisbury – Sibly became a key figure in local concert life, not least as a performer – of piano and violin – as well as leader of the local amateur ensemble.[11]

For a society that took death seriously and treated it publicly (although decreasingly so), much effort was put into funerary monu-ments. Some sculptors, such as Henry Cheere, made their name that way. He was responsible for several monuments in Westminster Abbey. In his early career as a sculptor, Robert Taylor was also responsible for monuments in Westminster Abbey. John Flaxman (1755–1826) deco-rated grand tombs and monuments for Chichester and Winchester Cathedrals.[12] Such monuments recorded changing styles. Sir Isaac New-ton's, erected in Westminster Abbey in 1727, was a Baroque work including attendant cherubs, whereas Flaxman sought a Neo-Classical tone.

As a sign of a changing society, such monuments were matched by the development in the press of the practice of funerary verses. Whereas monuments were permanent but (unless reproduced visually) only seen by spectators, such verses were more ephemeral, but permitted a response at once personal and read by a large public. Furthermore, as a reflection of a literary culture, such verses could be far longer than the inscriptions on monuments. The *Reading Mercury and Oxford Gazette* of 14 May 1770 printed a forty-eight line obituary poem for Charles Godwyn, a fellow of Balliol, full of references to nature and beginning

> Where blooming osiers spread their new-born shade
> Responsive to the ringdove's distant moan,
> And kiss the wave that slumbers in the glade,
> I wind my pensive way, unseen, unknown.

A less literary note was struck in *Swinney's Birmingham and Stafford Chronicle* of 22 December 1791, the poem, *On the Death of Mr Stephen Chatterton*, beginning:

> For manly spirit, and for judgment sound,
> His equal is but seldom to be found.

Religious art and music were determined by the elite, but also enjoyed by the congregations. They were at once elite and mass culture. Religion also provided themes for music, while the cathedrals and larger parish churches provided training and employment for many musicians: they could afford to employ a professional musician as an organist and the latter provided training. Aside from the music appropriate for the liturgical year, there was also music for special occasions.[13] The young William Shield, leader of the orchestra at Scarborough theatre, composed an anthem (now lost) for the consecration of St John's Church, Sunderland in 1769. He himself had been trained by Charles Avison, organist of St Nicholas, Newcastle, part of the process by which the leading musicians also held office as church organists and, as such, played a key role in musical life, especially, but not only, in the provinces.

In his *An Essay on Criticism* (1711), Alexander Pope noted:

> As some to church repair,
> Not for the doctrine, but the music there.

Henry Purcell, organist of Westminster Abbey in 1680–95, and the composer of a large number of anthems, mostly written for the Chapel Royal, had a considerable influence on the next generation of English musicians, although it was superseded in terms of style by that of

Handel. William Croft (1678–1727), organist of the Chapel Royal, wrote music for plays at Drury Lane as well as anthems for state ceremonies and thanksgiving services. John Weldon (1676–1736), another successful composer of both sacred and secular music, was organist of New College, Oxford and later of the Chapel Royal, St Bride's Fleet Street, and St Martin's-in-the-Fields. Maurice Greene (1696–1755), the son of a London vicar, was educated by Richard Brind, the organist of St Paul's Cathedral, whom he succeeded in 1718 after being organist of two other London churches; in 1727 he also became organist and composer to the Chapel Royal, and, eight years later, Master of the King's Band of Music as well. Noted as an organist, his works included numerous anthems, as well as *The Song of Deborah and Barak* (1732), the first oratorio by a native-born Englishman, though not called such by Greene and two other oratorios, *Jephtha* (1737) and (the now lost) *The Force of Truth* (1744). Very much a Handelian, William Hayes (1706–1777) had been organist at St Mary's Shrewsbury, Worcester Cathedral and Magdalen College, Oxford, before becoming Professor of Music at Oxford in 1742. In addition to a good deal of sacred music, Hayes also composed a great many songs, cantatas, concertos and convivial vocal music. Some of this activity tends to be ignored by the focus on George Frideric (popularly spelt Frederick) Handel, although his influence can be readily traced in such careers.

Handel's oratorios, including *Esther* (1732), *Deborah* (1733), *Athalia* (1733), *Saul* (1739), *Israel in Egypt* (1739), *Messiah* (1741), *Samson* (1743), *Joseph and his Brethren* (1744), *Belshazzar* (1745), *Judas Maccabaeus* (1747), *Joshua* (1748), *Solomon* (1749), *Susanna* (1749), *Theodora* (1750) and *Jephtha* (1752), helped to offer an Anglicised choral version of Biblical history, also locating modern Britain in terms that provided an attractive parallel to the echoes of Rome offered by Classical references. The oratorio texts pressed the need for national unity and the moral value of art.[14] In Italy, oratorio was a substitute for opera with a religious rationale – opera was banned during Lent in Catholic countries. In Britain, in contrast, oratorio worked because its religious rationale could be made commercially attractive. Handel's *Samson* was performed eight times in its first season, a considerable triumph. The Reverend Arthur Bedford of Bristol complained that organists played the tunes from oratorios in churches as a way of drumming up private students and commissions. Audience reception was crucial as oratorio was not always commercially successful, as Handel found out with *Theodora*

(1750) and Thomas Arne discovered with *The Death of Abel* (1755), written for Dublin, and *Judith* (1761).

Church music was not separate from the lay tradition, as an advertisement in 1776 illustrated:

> By subscription. At the Church in Newport, on Wednesday the 10th of April 1776 will be performed the most admired pieces in the oratorio of *Messiah* ... and at the townhall in the evening will be a concert of vocal and instrumental music, consisting of select pieces, and favourite songs by the most eminent masters ... After which will be a ball.[15]

This was the standard format for Three Choirs festivals: oratorio in the morning, and secular concert in the evening, followed by a ball.

It was also a great age of hymns and metrical psalm settings by masters such as John Byrom, William Cowper, John Newton, Christopher Smart, Isaac Watts and Charles Wesley. Wesley alone wrote over 10,000 hymns.[16] Hymns and psalm settings offered clear and attractive expressions of religious tenets and messages, and sought to direct the consciences of the audiences, although it was not easy to express often troubling religious ideas, especially about sin, in terms of the aesthetics of the period. This was not the sole problem. In the *Olney Hymns* (1779), Cowper and Newton reflected with their evangelical fervour the vitality of an active tradition of hymn writing seeking new topics and voices and attempting to provide hymns applicable to the congregation, rather than more exalted odes. There was also the need to reconcile individual experience and expression with the communal dimension provided by the congregation.[17] Hymns, carols and psalm settings linked England to other countries, although the amount of borrowing was limited.

The continued popularity of the Three Choirs Festival, the meetings of the cathedral choirs of Gloucester, Hereford and Worcester, is one legacy of the period,[18] and also a testimony to the collective and sociable nature of an important cultural strand. The Festival technically began in 1724 when it rotated between the three cathedrals, but in 1719 there were advertisements for choral events and in Worcester a festival before 1709. At the 1749 meeting, William Hughes, a canon of Worcester Cathedral, preached 'On the Efficacy and Importance of Music'. He published both this and *Remarks upon Church Music, to which are Added Several Observations on Mr Handel's Oratorios* (Worcester, 1763). The popularity of religious music was spread by publications, for example John Brown's *The Cure of Saul: A Sacred Ode. As ... Performed at … Covent Garden. Set to Select Airs … from Handel* (1763). William Boyce's three-volume collection of *Cathedral Music* (1760–73) was the first-ever historical anthology of a particular area of the repertory.

Religious literature was also of importance. Although the percentage of works published in London on religious and theological topics declined, this was as part of a greatly-expanding publishing world. Striking the right tone could be difficult. Joseph Johnson, the Unitarian publisher of the 1785 first edition of William Cowper's poems, persuaded Cowper to remove John Newton's preface on the grounds that it was overly solemn and Evangelical, and thus likely to depress sales. Popular religious works, such as William Law's *A Serious Call to a Devout and Holy Life, adapted to the State and Condition of All Orders of Christians* (1728), nevertheless sold incredibly well, and older works, such as John Bunyan's *Pilgrim's Progress*, appeared in new editions. 4590 individuals subscribed to the sermons of John Conybeare, Bishop of Bristol, which were published in 1757 for the benefit of his children, and there were over 2500 subscribers to Edward Miller's *The Psalms of David* (1790): Miller was organist of Doncaster parish church. The frequent printing of new editions of the Bible was matched by changes in taste, not least an emphasis on private reading that led both to smaller-style Bibles and to the printing of notes that assisted understanding.[19] This lessened the intermediary role of clerics. Printers competed for the right to publish Bibles as they sold so well.

Devotional verse and religious poetry were also popular. Thomas Newcomb, a cleric, published in 1723 his longest work *The Last Judgment of Men and Angels: A Poem in Twelve Books, after the Manner of Milton*. In part, such works appeared in response to the liturgical year. *The Crucifixion*, a poem by T. L. O'Beirne, a Catholic who later became an Anglican convert and a Church of Ireland bishop, was published on Good Friday 1776. Other poems were less specific to a particular moment. *The Screech-Owl: A Moral Fable*, printed in *Swinney's Birmingham and Stafford Chronicle* on 9 May 1776 included Sabbath observance as a topic.

The comparisons made in much religious literature appear far-fetched but reflected the extent to which morality was presented in Christian terms. *Brice's Weekly Journal* of 16 February 1728 included two such pieces. A poem by 'Philo-animarum' began:

> In companies the merchants do combine,
> Let scattered Christians their example mind;

> By factors, merchants drive great trades abroad,
> Saints trade in Heaven, though here be their abode.
> From small to great estates some merchants rise,
> And so might Christians, if they would be wise.

'D.S.', in contrast, provided *A Meditation upon a Broom-Stick* including the remark 'Surely mortal man is a broom-stick', and a comparison accordingly.

Sermons and traits were a major branch of literature, those of the Bangorian Controversy of 1716–20 being printed in their thousands, while the printing of charity sermons became common. Translations of and commentaries on the Psalms abounded, and some novels, such as those of the staunch Anglican Samuel Richardson, can be seen in part as Christian fables. More controversially, Daniel Defoe's novels such as *Moll Flanders* (1722) and *Colonel Jack* (1722) have been presented as at least in part allegorical religious narratives.[20] The standard device in much drama and fiction – resolution towards the close by an almost-providential good fortune – was readily reconcilable with the narrative themes of a religious culture that emphasised quasi-providential action: frequently through the repentance of the sinful. Redemption was common to both. There was a particular devotional literature for children, as in Anna Barbauld's very successful *Hymns in Prose for Children* (1781), and a Nonconformist tradition of devotional literature for the young. The religious press was especially active in the second half of the century, notably with the *Christian's Magazine* founded in 1760, and with John Wesley's *Arminian Magazine* established in 1778.[21]

The variety of religious culture was one of its most impressive features. Alongside the popularity of music and hymns, there was bell-ringing. The variety of religious artefacts ranged from funeral rings and gloves to inexpensive prints of popular clerics. Few manufacturers or businesses could have been independent of a religious element in their trade.

Clerics played an important role not only in religious but also in secular culture. The most significant was Jonathan Swift (1667–1745). Born in Dublin and educated at Trinity College, Dublin, Swift was an example of the importance in English culture of individuals from Ireland, Scotland and Wales. Coming to prominence with *A Tale of a Tub* and *The Battle of the Books* (1704), Swift was a Anglican cleric who commented on religious topics, as in his satirical pamphlet *An Argument Against Abolishing Christianity* (1711). He took a major role in politics as a Tory, supporting the Harley ministry, for which he wrote a number of polemical works, including the pamphlet *The Conduct of the Allies* (1711), an attack on Whig views on foreign policy, and a journal the *Examiner* (1710–11), and later opposed Sir Robert Walpole. The adversarial nature of the public sphere, one also seen in the politics of literary criticism, ensured that Swift's *Conduct of the Allies* was in turn countered by *A Defence of the Allies and the Late Ministry: or Remarks on the Tories New Idol. Being a Detection of the ... Frauds ... in 'The Conduct of the Allies'* (1712). More seriously, the Whig ascendancy from 1714 meant that Swift never became a bishop. He wrote a number of powerful satirical works, including *A Modest Proposal for Preventing the Children of the Poor from Being a Burden to their Parents or Country* (1729), a masterpiece of directed anger, works in defence of Irish interests, such as the *Drapier Letters* (1724), and his best-known work, *Gulliver's Travels* (1726), a wide-ranging satire written in the form of a travelogue.

Many writers of the period were clerics, although their approach varied greatly. Although some clerics wrote exclusively on devotional and ecclesiastical topics, others ranged more widely. James Miller, the son of a rector who eventually succeeded his father, in the meantime had brought out a number of political pamphlets and a series of comedies including *The Coffee-House* (1737) in order to supplement his income. Edward Cobden (1684–1768), who became Archdeacon of London and President of Sion College, published a collection of poetry in 1748 for the benefit of his former curate's widow, and in 1756 added *A Poem Sacred to the Memory of Queen Anne for her Bounty to the Clergy*. Prior to being ordained in 1741, John Dyer (*c.* 1700–58) had studied painting and written *Grongar Hill* (1727), a poem relishing rural scenery. Once a Lincolnshire cleric, Dyer brought out *The Fleece* (1757), leading a critical Dr Johnson to ask 'How can a man write poetically of serges and druggets?' Among clerical writers, the harsh social observation of George Crabbe was very different to the personal melancholia of William Bowles's sonnets or the robust patriotism of the latter's poem *The Battle of the Nile* (1799). Lawrence Sterne included one of his own sermons in his novel *Tristram Shandy* (1760–67), and also in the novel presented religious tension, with the Catholic Dr. Slop interrupting the reading of the sermon.

Clerics were particularly well suited to take advantage of the shift from Augustan values and interests to the more introspective concern with melancholy, the soul and graveyards seen with works such as

Edward Young's poem *Night Thoughts* (1742–46) and Thomas Gray's *Elegy Written in a Country Churchyard* (1751). Young (1683–1765) himself also came to the church late, becoming rector of Welwyn in 1730. Already a poet and playwright, he added a patriotic ode, *The Foreign Address* (1735), before writing a far more prominent, influential and lengthy work of poetry *The Complaint, or Night Thoughts on Life, Death and Immortality* (1742–46) (generally known as *Night Thoughts*). This called for faith and virtue and included a vision of the Day of Judgement and an invocation to God. Young subsequently wrote *The Centaur Not Fabulous* (1755), a similar work in prose, and *Resignation* (1762), a melancholic poem that reflected the gloom of his last years. John Wesley testified to the appeal of *Night Thoughts* in 1770, writing that it 'contains many strokes of the most sublime poetry and is full of those pathetic strokes of nature and passion which touch the heart in the most tender and affecting manner'.[22]

Among other multi-talented clerics, William Mason (1724–97), was a poet, playwright, garden designer, writer of music, and editor and biographer of Gray, while Charles Jenner (1736–74) was a poet, on both sacred and secular themes, from *The Destruction of Nineveh* to *Two Ecologues*, as well as a novelist, his *The Placid Man: or Memoirs of Sir Charles Beville* (1770) being successful, and a playwright, writing the sentimental comedy *The Man of Family* (1771). James Hurdis, while curate of Burwash, published a popular volume of poems, *The Village Curate* (1788), and, five years later, he was appointed Professor of Poetry at Oxford. Clerics did not restrict themselves to prose, poetry and plays. John Pixell, then vicar of Edgbaston, published *A Collection of Songs* in 1759, while the Rev. William Felton (1715–69) published no fewer than five sets of organ concertos between 1744 and 1760. There was also an honourable tradition of clerics as antiquarians and county historians.

Many female writers were the daughters or wives of clergy. The dramatist Mary Pix, for example, was daughter of the vicar of Nettlebed, while Jenny Warton, a poet, essayist and novelist, was daughter of Thomas Warton, formerly Professor of Poetry at Oxford and, at the time of her birth, vicar of Basingstoke. Elizabeth Singer, the daughter of a Nonconformist minister, married Thomas Rowe, another Nonconformist minister in 1710. Already a noted devotional poet with a particular individual and introspective voice, she was best known as the author of the much-reprinted *Friendship in Death, in Twenty Letters from the Dead to the Living* (1728), a sequence of exemplary novellas, followed by her *Letters Moral and Entertaining* (1729–33). Praised by Dr Johnson, her leading works were translated into French and German, but her worthiness has now sunk into disfavour.[23] Several of the daughters of the church devoted some of their fiction to its activities, Anne Plumptre publishing a three-volume novel *The Rector's Son* (1798).

Clerics and churches also provided topics for painters and other artists. Large numbers of portraits appeared, with artists trying to endow a commonplace form with individuality, as in Hogarth's portrait of Bishop Benjamin Hoadly. The first drawing to be shown by J. M. W. Turner at the Royal Academy was of the Archbishop of Canterbury's palace at Lambeth.

Writers were ready to participate in disputes over the role of religion in English society. There was a widespread critique of religious enthusiasm, which was seen as responsible in part for the political divisions of the seventeenth century (although such enthusiasm was not the same as Puritanism), and also as the product of cant or delusion. Colley Cibber's play *The Non-Juror* (1717) was a popular version of Molière's *Tartuffe* that, in its attack on Anglicans who refused to accept the ecclesiastical and political consequences of the Glorious Revolution, struck a chord with Whig audiences. Attacks on Methodism were an obvious sequel. A critique of enthusiasm did not mean, however, support for atheism. Instead, both 'practical' and 'speculative' atheists were generally held up as individuals made rootless and immoral by their lack of values, as in Charles Lamb's poetic attack in *Living Without God in the World* (c. 1798) on those who are 'short-liv'd, short-sighted' with 'dissolute spirits' and 'pride'. In his poem *The Castaway* (1799), William Cowper discussed how the absence of grace brought fear to a fading life. Earlier, in *The Rape of the Lock*, Pope had indicated Belinda's preferences, with the Bibles on her dressing table no distraction to her concern with her appearance.

Alongside the criticism of the irreligious, there was also a language of enthusiasm. The misleading consequences of periodisation are such that spiritual autobiography is generally seen as a seventeenth-century genre, but this is inaccurate. In addition to the accounts of the pious from that period, for example the Seventh Day Baptist Joseph Davis's *Brief Account of ... his Life and Profession* (1707 reprinted 1720), came those of the newly-saved including Methodists. Furthermore, the culture of Nonconformity flourished, not least due to the literary and educational traditions which flourished in and around the Dissenting academics.

Clerics and laity wrote not only about religious topics but also in a language suffused with biblical references. Furthermore, their own lives provided occasion for religious reflection, especially as they came to terms with the fear of their own death and the experience of that of others, particularly family members. The theme of the need for religious resignation was frequently repeated, not only by clerics but also by lay writers, such as the young Mary Leapor dying of measles. The degree of religious sentiment varied, but the need for resignation in the face of ill-health and death joined those who looked to the Bible with others also affected by the Classical legacy. It was a frequent theme in novels, verse and correspondence, and for both men and women, in contrast to the plot lines of many novels which left their female characters overly dependent on the actions of men over whom they had only limited influence.

The prevalence of religious references also affected the attempts to systematise knowledge and literature. In the fourth edition of his *Dictionary of the English Literature*, which appeared in 1773, Samuel Johnson replaced quotations from James Thomson's *The Seasons* and turned, instead, increasingly to John Milton, who was treated as an inspirational voice. The more contentious ecclesiastical debates of the 1770s, and the sense of the Church of England in danger in the face of Dissenters, led Johnson to a more explicitly political and religious approach in which he drew on conservative writers, not least Non-Jurors. Johnson was not alone in responding to flux and challenge by relying on a conservatism defined in religious terms.[24] Unlike many fashionable clerics Johnson did not interpret religion in terms of the obvious purposes of a benign God made manifest through human institutions. His view of the uncertainty of human affairs was a coherent religious, moral, and intellectual position, as well as a reflection of the exclusion of Toryism from power.

Religious themes and morality were offered across a wide range of forms. Although the twentieth-century films of Henry Fielding's novels *Tom Jones* and *Joseph Andrews* present them as jolly romps, with the many twists of the plots being essentially contrivances to move the stories along and to obtain comic effect, there was also, on Fielding's part, an attempt to show the follies of self-serving human searches for control. Instead, he emphasised the role of Providence; not as excuse for an inactive contemplation of divine grace but rather as a counterpart to good human activity that itself reflects the divine plan. Parson Adams is presented in *Joseph Andrews* as an exemplary individual, not least when, oblivious to his own safety, he hastens to the aid of Fanny Adams who is resisting rape. Fanny declares that she had 'put her whole trust in Providence', and Adams sees himself as the means of Providental deliverance. This is at once humourous and deadly serious: the vehicles of divine judgement might be comic, but it alone could save the innocent from malign fate in the shape of unhappy coincidence and the wretched designs of the sinful. Furthermore, the role of Providence alongside the explicit interventions of Fielding as author-narrator demonstrated the need for readers to be cautious in anticipating events, passing judgement and determining the plot, thus instructing them in a humility to match that of the benign characters depicted.

In his *A Journey from This World to the Next* (1743), Fielding drew on Classical models and images to produce a series of stories in which a spirit-narrator introduced the reader to the moral reflections offered by the transmigration of souls: metempsychosis providing a satiric device that enabled Fielding to scour history in order to tilt at the universal ills of selfishness and self-regard, and their focus in the distorting impact of ambition. This is a sermon of true wit, with much narrative and flow to sustain the reiterated attacks on the conceits of power. Seven years later, in the magazine the *Rambler*, Johnson claimed that novels 'are written chiefly to the young, the ignorant, and the idle, to whom they serve as lectures of conduct, and introductions into life', and argued that they must therefore meet high moral standards. Corrective satire was not always religious in language, content or tone, but the essential themes conformed to Christian social teaching. So, more explicitly, did the popular genre of criminal biographies, many of which were written by gaol chaplains.[25]

The moral punchline of novels culminated in plot terms in some of the more untrammelled Gothic novels, especially Matthew Lewis's *The Monk* (1796). This sensational tale of the temptation of a devout young monk to deadly depravity by the emissary of the Devil, was very successful, and was followed by his *The Castle Spectre* (1797), a horror play. The exemplary endings of Gothic works, such as Ann Radcliffe's successful novel *The Mysteries of Udolpho* (1794), reflected the prevalence of a Christian morality that was a characteristic feature of the culture of the period. This morality was rejected by some writers and artists, such as William Blake in his *The Marriage of Heaven and Hell* (1790), *Europe* (1794) and *The Song of Los* (1795), but Blake, although a presence in artisan culture, was more marginal to that of other social groups. For most of the population, whatever dissatisfaction they felt, itself expressed the importance of religion, the church and the clergy. Few believed that they could or should be dispensed with. Disputes and criticism should not distract attention from the symbiotic relationships of faith and reason, church and state, clergy and laity, religion and the people, that played a major role in the cultural context and content of the century.

5

The Middling Orders

> My bookseller informs me, that the bulk of his readers, regarding in a work of this kind the quantity more than the quality, will not be contented without an additional half sheet; and he apprehends that a short dedication will answer the purpose.
>
> But as I have no obligations to any great man or woman in this country, and as I will take care that no production of mine shall want their patronage, I don't know any person whose good offices I so much stood in need of as my bookseller's: Therefore, Mr Vaillant, I think myself obliged to you for the correctness of the press, the beauty of the type, and the goodness of the paper, with which you have decorated this work of, Your humble servant, Samuel Foote.
>
> Dedication to published version of Foote's play
> *The Englishman in Paris* (1753).

In Bernard Mandeville's pamphlet *The Fable of the Bees* (1705) the arts are ended by an insistence on virtue in the beehive, which leads to a situation of no self-indulgence or luxury. As this book remained a disconcerting utopian parable, and no such rule of apian utilitarians was introduced in England, commerce instead provided the wherewithal to translate the interests of a wide section of society into artistic activity.

The patronage of the middling orders was of growing importance in the eighteenth century. Unable individually to provide sustained patronage, they participated through public performances of works and public markets for the arts, and these expanded considerably during the century, helping to provide a public culture that saw itself in terms of openness and reasoned argument,[1] thus forming an equivalent to the English self-image of their own religious culture in the shape of the unique Church of England.

Public culture in the form of the patronage of the middling orders was of varied importance: more for literature than architecture. Although aristocratic patronage was especially evident in music, the private orchestra and choir that the 1st Duke of Chandos kept at Canons in the 1720s and 1730s was expensive and not in accordance with the interests of later aristocratic magnificos. Handel, who worked at Canons composing anthems for the choir, moved to the public market, reinventing himself, from a servant of the rich composing Italian operas, to the nationalistic author of English-language oratorios.

Across the arts, the patronage of the anonymous public was increasingly crucial to performers: singers at the concerts at Vauxhall Gardens in the second half of the century knew that their future engagements depended on the number of encores, while, in 1772, the anger of the audience prevented Charles Macklin from acting Shylock at Covent Garden, and the manager brought order by confirming that Macklin had been discharged. Plays that were damned by audience hissing did not survive their opening nights, while audiences could also be critical about productions of established works. The *Worcester Post-Man* of 28 February 1718 carried a London report noting, 'Last Saturday night, the Tragedy of Cato being acted at the Theatre in Drury-Lane, the audience took disgust at the manner of acting some part, and thereupon committed such disorders by hissing, throwing the sconces ...'

At the same time, it is important to appreciate the degree to which patronage by the middling orders, as by other groups, did not always take place in a public context. Instead, there was also a major domestic theme in cultural patronage and consumption. This was particularly important for women. Within the domestic sphere, women were able to assert independence and self-control, for example in music-making, although this assertiveness was not limited to the domestic sphere.[2] Similarly, religion could be 'consumed' privately by reading sermons and by individual prayer.

The nature and role of the commercial market could lead to concern, which was generally related to perceptions of the political and social situation. Tory writers, such as Jonathan Swift and Alexander Pope, who had a particular political reason to dislike the Hanoverian world, were hostile to the shift in patronage from individual, particularly court, patronage, or subscription editions, to a world moulded by entrepreneurs, its values dissolved in and by money. Whether located in truth or metaphor among the shiftless, turn-a-penny, jobbing writers of London's Grub Street, this process was seen as an unworthy corruption of quality and morality, a pejorative view that captured a cultural and social snobbery latent, if not explicit, in many writers who did not work for Grub Street, and in some who resented doing so. In the 1730s, a time of particularly marked and partisan cultural discontent, when the political rejection of Sir Robert Walpole was linked to a criticism of the state of the arts, both James Thomson and Aaron Hill felt that the arts were in decline and sacrificed to the commercial market-place, that it was necessary to revitalise national culture, and that this would both further and benefit from a wider national regeneration.

Anger with entrepreneurs was often linked to concern about public taste. James Miller's satirical poem *Harlequin Horace: or The Art of Modern Poetry* (1731) criticised John Rich, both theatre manager and a great actor of the part Harlequin, for sacrificing art to the popular wish for buffoonery. The frontispiece to the third edition showed the works of Shakespeare and others trampled while Harlequin and Punchinello kick Apollo, the Greek god linked to the arts. If culture was being commercialised, to the regret of some, the terms of this commercialisation engaged (as well as enraged) writers and others struggling to get their work to market. Writers were left very exposed by the transition from patronage to the market. At the same time, writers and others sought to understand this new market, and also looked at the responses of other artists. There were also more specific criticisms of commercialisation. The art market was presented as fraudulent in William Hogarth's *The Battle of the Pictures* (1745).

The rise of a modern, commercial, urban and, increasingly meritocratic culture, at least in terms of the market, was represented by commentators under the influence of traditional civic humanist ideas as a growth in luxury and effeminacy, and grave concern was expressed about standards.[3] The theme of the enervating threat of luxury to taste and, more seriously, civilisation was a weighty motif of anxiety. It contributed to caricatures of fashion in prints and prose and was reflected in much of the literature of the period. The need to satisfy prevailing tastes indeed affected not only the content of new works, helping lead to the preference for satisfactory plot resolutions, but also the content of earlier works. Shakespeare's plays were 'improved', and *King Lear* appeared in Nahum Tate's version of 1681, with a happy ending in which Cordelia survives and is betrothed to Edgar.

The public culture driven by the purchasing power of the middling orders reflected and sustained a set of commercial practices and agencies that became stronger during the century, and this brought changes to particular activities. Whereas the reproduction of paintings for wealthy collectors had commonly taken the form of having individual copies painted, there was now a considerable increase in their mass reproduction in the form of engravings, for example of the works of Hogarth. This created copyright problems, leading to the Engravers' Copyright Act of 1735, but also provided opportunities for entrepreneurs; even more so because the Act did not stop pirate production. Engravers made available both new and old works, and in quantity. George Vertue (1683–1756) alone engraved more than five hundred portraits. Derby-born John Raphael Smith, who came to London in 1767, became a skilled miniature-painter and engraver, and developed a significant business as a publisher of engravings, making widely available works by Joshua Reynolds and Heinrich Füssli (Henry Fuseli) among others. Print shops displayed such works in windows for public entertainment and 'consumption', and the scale of the latter influenced the form of prints and portraits. About 15,000 satirical prints were published in 1740–1800, with biting caricaturists such as James Gillray (1767–1815) serving the needs of a politically-aware society.[4]

Technology and commerce were linked. 'Pictures' became an important element in print culture during the century and, whilst mezzotinting was invented in the 1640s, it was very much improved after Christopher Wren worked on it. By the early eighteenth century, mezzotinting had speeded up the process of producing large numbers of inexpensive copies from engraved plates. In place of wood prints, there were now fine copper plate prints and cheap mezzotints.

The public sale of paintings, and production for such sales, rather than in response to a specific commission, were far from novel, but there was a considerable expansion of the art market in London and of art publishing. This was important in the development of buying paintings for pleasure rather than because of what they showed, whether portraits or houses. James Christie held his first sale at Pall Mall in 1766. The growth of art dealership and of middlemen, such as the dealer Robert Bragge and the auctioneer Christopher Cock, also led to an enormous market for fakes.[5] These were aspects of the link between exhibition, publicity and artistic production. Developments in London matched those in Paris where the public art market became more active and developed. Whereas, in mid-century, Parisian catalogues for picture sales often begin with a panegyric on the collector or a statement of the pleasures of collecting, later in the century the investment opportunities offered by buying paintings were presented more clearly.[6]

In England, economic expansion and extensive building helped to fuel the art market, as did widespread interest in artistic issues, which extended to a development of printed art criticism. Jonathan Richardson's *Essay on the Theory of Painting* (1715) both advanced art criticism in England and argued that English painters could equal Italian old masters. Aside from this comment on cosmopolitanism, the ethics of 'politeness' affected ideological justifications for art, leading to an emphasis on exemplary taste. The forum for the perception of art also changed: painting increasingly addressed public audiences, at the same time that economic and commercial progress enabled the creation of public spaces and places for the enjoyment of art, such as Vauxhall and Ranelagh Gardens in London, as well as the foundation of clubs and societies. There were also new points of connection between artists and patrons, such as the London Foundling Hospital, established by Thomas Coram in 1739 and in full occupation by 1753. The paintings in its court room depicted religious scenes and were designed to incline the viewers' hearts to charity. Hogarth, who painted Coram's portrait in 1740, glorifying philanthropy and trade, not rank, encouraged artists to present works free to the hospital in order to decorate it, thus ensuring the creation of a substantial permanent collection of contemporary English paintings. In 1760, the Society of Artists staged the first major contemporary art exhibition in London, while the Royal Academy held its first exhibition in 1769. This growth in the public viewing of art followed developments in Paris where the public exhibitions in the Salon Carré of the Louvre palace, known as the Salons, were regularized in 1737 and encouraged artistic criticism and the idea and importance of public taste.

Although many musical productions were still private, the musical world was becoming more public. The opera houses were centres of fashion, and public concerts became more frequent, and not only in London where John Banister's concerts in 1672 were the first such to be advertised. The role of advertising was enhanced by the expansion of the press from the 1690s, and this in turn helped create the sense that music performed for, and paid by, the public was normal. Henry Playford, who succeeded his father as an active publisher of music, in order to broaden his position in the music market founded a tri-weekly concert in 1699 at a coffeehouse where his music could also be sold, and also established clubs for music practice in London and Oxford. In a manner common to the cultural aspirations of the period, Playford used improvement and sociability as mutually-supporting themes:

> The design therefore, as it is for a general diversion, so it is intended for a general instruction, that the persons who give themselves the liberty of an evenings entertainment with their friends, may exchange the expense they shall be at in being sociable, with the knowledge they shall acquire from it.[7]

Although musical activity naturally centred in London, it was by no means confined to the capital. As in the world of the theatre, some provincial towns which nowadays enjoy no live music (other than karaoke in the local pub) had regular instrumental concerts, and could boast their own amateur musical societies, many of which bought, or subscribed to, all the latest productions of the London music publishers. Across the country, people (mostly men) met together regularly to make music (chiefly orchestral). And in some cases, for example with the Academy of Ancient Music, the normal social barriers between the elite and the middling orders were sufficiently relaxed to enable members of both groups to mingle in the common pursuit of music making.[8]

Although there were local variations, in general concerts outside London not only became more frequent but were also held in more appropriate settings. The situation in the early decades was captured in an advertisement carried in *Brice's Weekly Journal* on 22 March 1728:

> For the benefit of Mr Francis Wellington: At the large room, at the Half-Moon, in the High Street, Exon [Exeter], Wednesday April the 3rd (being the Assize Week) will be held a consort of vocal and instrumental music taken from the most celebrated masters. NB. Tickets may be had at Mr Score's bookseller, Moll's coffee-house, Rummer tavern, and at the place of performance, at 2s. 6d.

With time, events became more regular. In 1736, the composer Charles Avison started winter subscription concerts in Newcastle, while the Assembly Rooms, also opened that year, were a popular venue. The Portsea Concert Room was built in 1751. In Hertford, there were subscription concerts in a specially built concert room from 1753 to 1767, and in the 1770s concerts in the new Shire Hall, completed in 1771, which had assembly rooms built for such functions. Although, thanks to its fashionable character, Bath had the richest musical life, it was not alone. *Swinney's Birmingham and Stafford Chronicle*, in its issue of 1 June 1775, advertised both that 'a good band of music' would be provided during the public breakfast in Birmingham, and that the printer took subscriptions for 'The Musical Entertainments'. The issue of 11 April 1776 included an advertisement 'On Wednesday the 1st of May 1776, will be performed at the court-house in Warwick, a concert of vocal and instrumental music, under the direction of Mr Hobbs, organist. After the concert will be a ball'. Inns, however, remained important as locations for concerts in many towns, the Crown Inn in Portsea being used for that end until the early nineteenth century.[9]

The world of music was closely linked to that on the Continent. Mozart visited London in 1764, and Carl Friedrich Abel and Johann Christian Bach launched a successful annual concert series in London in 1775. Johann Salomon, a prominent impresario and violinist, was responsible for organising Haydn's visits to the capital in 1791–92 and 1794 to give very successful public concerts for which he wrote his London symphonies. He also composed his oratorio *The Creation*.[10] Such concerts encouraged and reflected the more frequent performance of popular works.

Looking to German orchestral music proved far less controversial than the taste for Italian opera had proved in the 1720s and 1730s. Criticism of Italian opera led to concern about cultural borrowing, with more specific worries about effeminacy (and allegedly related Catholicism) and the impact on women. This was seen with Francis Lynch's 1737 play *The Independent Patriot*. Dedicated to the Earl of Burlington, whom, the dedication claimed, had travelled 'to improve his mind for the embellishment of his country', the work was an attack on the impact of tourism:

> Happy had it been for themselves, and for their country, if all our travelling youth of condition had followed the example of Your Lordship: Had they, like you, turned their thoughts to the solid and useful, we should not have seen so many of them returning ... only with the weaknesses and vanities of foreigners. Had they, like your Lordship, studied to improve first their own taste, and next that of their country, there would have been no foundation for satyrizing that affected, false, modern, musical taste, which partly gave rise to the following scenes ... The reigning tastes all Italian. Music has engrossed the attention of the whole people: the Duchess and her woman, the Duke and his postilion, are equally infected. The contagion first took root in the shallow noodles of such of our itinerant coxcombs as were incapable of more virtuous impressions.

In the play, the musical Lady Wardle instructs Dulcissa:

> Now my dear, you are naturally well-fashioned and are blessed with a
> taste: Improve it – Travel, Dulcissa – Make the tour of Italy; but set your
> heart most on dear Rome – Oh! Dulcissa! no tongue's able to express the
> charms of dear Italy – The Italians pay us English women an adoration lit-
> tle short of that due to the Deity ... hear the song composed for me by
> my dear Cardinal.

Lady Wardle presents travel as a correction for what she claims are the
deficiencies due to limited education. In the London society, a private
world of elite cultural assumptions, depicted critically by Lynch for the
benefit of his public audience, tourism could be seen as the key to culture, 'taste' was crucial, and 'taste' could only be acquired abroad.
Tourism thus could be presented as distancing the elite from public
cultural assumptions and expressed this distance, or so it could be
suggested:

> Travelling's thrown away upon the tasteless ... Mr Medium, a handsome
> figure of a man, with an uncommon share of sense and learning, they say;
> but for want of taste he's returned from his travels with not one qualifi-
> cation of the gentleman ... I'm indebted to travelling for all that's easy and
> careless in my deportment.

The fop Addle declares 'When I have made the tour of Italy, Gad, you
shall see me taste all over'.[11]

Commerce was not the sole nexus of culture. It was also easy for amateurs to participate in instrumental and vocal music. The popularity of
glee-singing testified to the latter. It was an aspect of the sociable aspect
of culture that is apt to be misunderstood if the emphasis is on the
patronage of the market. Instead, families, friends and neighbours took
part in sociable singing, frequently accompanied by other aspects of
conviviality, especially food and drink. In London in 1793, John Ley
reported to his mother that he had visited relatives in Blackheath:

> monstrous good fun it was, every person in the highest spirits and very
> much pleased, we danced the most riotous dances we could, Sir Roger de
> Coverley, Country Bumpkin etc which on account of the party's being
> select were very pleasant, we had nine couple.[12]

Chamber and solo works intended for amateurs enjoyed considerable
popularity, and instruments, music and manuals were produced accordingly. William Felton (1715–69), a cleric attached to Hereford Cathedral,

1. The Laughing Audience, by William Hogarth (1733).

Sold by H. Overton
without Newgate.

A Merry new Song
Les Chanteurs de Chansons
Catarine & Strada

2. 'A Merry New Song', from *Cryes of the City of London Drawn from Life*, by Marcellus Laroon.

M E S S I A H,

A N

O R A T O R I O.

Set to Muſick by GEORGE-FREDERIC HANDEL, Eſq;.

M A J O R A C A N A M U S.

---

*And without Controverſy, great is the Myſtery of Godli-
neſs : God was manifeſted in the Fleſh, juſtify'd·by the Spirit,
ſeen of Angels, preached among the* Gentiles, *believed on in
the World, received up in Glory.*

*In whom are hid all the Treaſures of Wiſdom and Know-
ledge.*

L O N D O N:

Printed and Sold by THO. WOOD in *Windmill-Court,* near *Weſt-
Smithfield,* and at the THEATRE in *Covent-Garden.* 1743.

[Price One Shilling.]

3. Title-page from the word-book for Handel's London performances of
Messiah (1743).

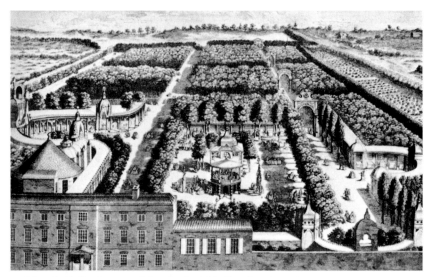

4. Vauxhall Gardens, etching by I. S. Müller (1751).

5. Covent Garden Theatre, a riot during a performance of Thomas Arne's *Artaxerxes*, 1763, engraving by L. Boitard (1763).

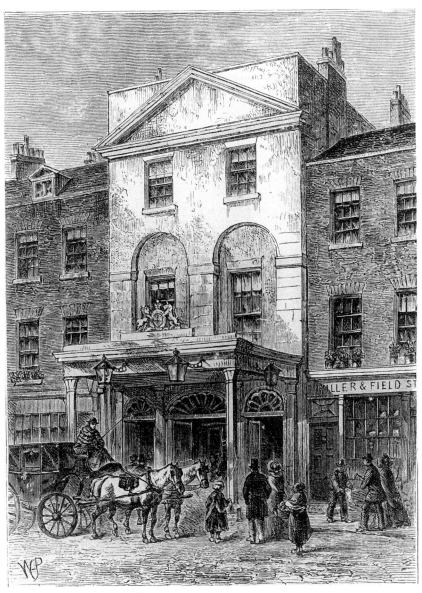

6. Astley's Theatre, London.

HISTORY preserving the Monuments of Antiquity

7. 'History Preserving the Monuments of Antiquity', from Francis Grose, *The Antiquities of England and Wales*, 4 vols (1772–76). (*Special Collections, University of Leicester*)

8. Members of the Society of Dilettanti, by Sir Joshua Reynolds (1777–79).

9. The Bookseller and the Author, by Thomas Rowlandson (1780–84).

10. The Royal Academy exhibition at Somerset House, engraving (1788).

wrote thirty-two keyboard concertos, more than anybody else in Britain, as well as popular practice pieces designed for the amateur market. An idea of the scale of activity can be grasped from the accounts of Thomas Green (1719–1791), a Hertfordshire organist, tuner of musical instruments, and teacher of music. In 1755–65, he tuned about 180 different harpsichords, 115 spinets and forty pianofortes, nearly all within eight miles of Hertford. In 1785, a French visitor commented that music was cultivated 'universally, in London as it is throughout the Kingdom'.[13] Music teachers came to play a major role, while women were often depicted in paintings and fiction as playing music, as Charlotte Raikes was in her portrait by Romney. It was a sign of the moral and cultural disorder in Hogarth's *Marriage à la Mode. The Tête à Tête* (1745) that both violin and music lie neglected on the floor. Orchestras, however, were all male. Children were also shown playing music, as in Thomas Hill's portrait of Garton Orme at his spinet (*c.* 1705–8).

The private world of music provided the demand for an expansion in the publication of music, and the music publishers such as John Walsh sought to catch and mould this demand through newspaper advertising. Music publishing played a major role in fixing a canon by enhancing the reputation of musicians dead or alive. Such publishing greatly benefited Handel's reputation, while Johann Christian Bach's compositions for the newly successful pianoforte became more influential when they appeared as printed sheet music. Maurice Greene producing a *Collection of Lessons* [ie. Pieces] *for the Harpsichord.* These benefited the large numbers who played themselves. Self-improvement was important across English culture, from devotional literature to guides to how to play music or devices to improve artistic skills.

Instruments were displayed and played in the fine rooms constructed in so many houses during the major rehousing of much of the better-off in both town and countryside, and helped to structure family space and activity. New houses also had more furniture, especially chairs, tables, dressers, clocks and looking-glasses, as well as plastered ceilings, curtains and fireplaces. All provided opportunities and employment for craftsmen. Economic expansion, consumerism and material culture were interrelated.[14]

Middle-class patronage was also crucial in the theatre, which developed both in London and elsewhere. Money could be made, to support entrepreneurs, playwrights and actors. By means of a rapid sequence of readily accessible and topical comedies, Henry Fielding was able to make a living from the theatre before the restrictions of the Licensing Act of 1737 changed the situation.[15] Profits encouraged building: purpose-built theatres opened in Bath in 1705, Bristol in 1729 and York in 1734. In Exeter, the upper rooms of the Seven Stars Inn were adapted as a theatre for touring players in 1720 and the first provincial performance of *The Beggar's Opera* followed eight years later. The first purpose-built theatre in the city was opened in 1738.[16] The Orchard Street Theatre at Bath opened in 1750; while the New Street Theatre in Birmingham in 1774, was the fourth in the city but the first to be a longstanding institution; and the first permanent theatre building in Lancaster was constructed in 1781. Some of these theatres were big: the Theatre Royal in Bristol built in 1766 had a capacity of about 1600. Regional circuits developed out of the routes of strolling players, and they increasingly acted in purpose-built playhouses. When, in 1786, the leading theatrical company in East Anglia, the Norwich Comedians or the Duke of Grafton's servants, ceased to tour smaller towns, it was still able to concentrate its attentions on Norwich, King's Lynn, Great Yarmouth, Barnwell (Cambridge), Bury St Edmunds, Colchester and Ipswich.[17]

Virtue was identified with the middling orders in George Lillo's *The London Merchant* (1731), in which a weak apprentice led astray by the evil Sarah Millwood commits murder and then undergoes an exemplary repentance, such that masters sent their apprentices to see it. This popular work represented a major change in tragedy in that it was written in a prose idiom and given a bourgeois setting and values. The plot's central theme was itself based on a popular ballad, *The Young Man's Warning Piece*. Such a work can be seen as a moral counterpart to William Hogarth's satires and Samuel Richardson's novels, but was not unique to England. In Germany, state-supported theatre was used to encourage a 'middling orders' consciousness opposed to indulgence, whether decadent aristocratic mores or popular ignorance and vice. In his dedication, Lillo claimed 'that tragedy is so far from losing its dignity, by being accommodated to the circumstances of the generality of mankind, that it is more truly august in proportion to the extent of its influence'. As Henry Fielding noted in the prologue to Lillo's tragedy *Fatal Curiosity* (1736),

> No fustian hero rages here tonight
> No armies fall, to fix a tyrant's right:

From lower life we draw our scene's distress:
Let not your equals move your pit less.

Earlier, in Nicholas Rowe's *The Tragedy of Jane Shore* (1714), a popular play about Edward IV's mistress, a London merchant acts an honourable part in support of 'the common ties of mankind' in opposition to a vicious nobleman, and when Lord Hastings attacks Dumont, aiming to teach him 'The distance 'twixt a peasant and a prince', he is vanquished. The success of the play helped lead to the development of a genre of what Rowe termed 'She-tragedy'. By providing women with major tragic roles,[18] this genre not only gave opportunities for leading actresses, such as Ann Oldfield who played Jane Shore, but also qualified the practice of presenting women in tragedies as passive heroines, or indeed only as the marginal figures that the dramatisations of Classical stories usually allowed. George I indeed attended Ann Oldfield's benefit performance in 1724, just as he attended benefits for two actresses in 1720.[19]

Tragedy's service to morality was staged against a variety of backgrounds, both historical and contemporary. In Edward Moore's successful play *The Gamester* (1753), the title part is a dupe driven to suicide. Moore's pursuit of morality was also seen in his *Fables for the Female Sex* (1744) and in his plan to dramatise *Clarissa*. Hogarth's painted satires also offered clear moral lessons, depravity depicted from within a Christian view of vice and morality. Thus in *After* (1730–1), the moral disorder of a successful seduction was expressed through dishevelment, and the absence of elegance in the scene drove home the moral lesson. In *The Rake's Progress* (1733–35), the rake ended up insane, presumably a consequence of his contracting syphilis. In the exemplary apprentice sequence of 1747, the idle apprentice was eventually hanged.

The operations of theatres were regulated by the Licensing Act of 1737 which gave the Lord Chamberlain the power to censor plays and made unlicensed theatres illegal. This was probably a response to attacks on the Walpole government on the stage, and was subsequently also employed against other critical works.[20] For example, Charles Macklin's *The Man of the World* was refused a licence until heavily revised, only finally appearing in 1781 with its original title *The True-Born Scotchman* deleted. Written in the 1760s, the play with its protagonist Sir Pertinax McSycophant was an attack on Bute and other Scots favoured by George III. The Act also confirmed the position of the two London theatres with royal patents to stage spoken drama –Drury Lane and the new Covent Garden theatre built in 1732 – and closed down competing playhouses. In 1766, the Haymarket Theatre was also granted the privilege of being licensed to stage plays during the summer when the other two theatres were usually closed. Another Act, in 1752, enabled Justices of the Peace in and near London to license 'places of public entertainment'. Combined with the restrictions on spoken drama, this legislation led places like Sadler's Wells to focus on spectacle, although that could entail what in effect were plays. Nevertheless, attempts to stage clear-cut plays were resisted. John Palmer, a noted actor who was the first Joseph Surface in Sheridan's *The School for Scandal*, opened the Royalty Theatre in East London in 1787, but was obliged to desist in the face of pressure from the existing theatres and the threat of legal action.

Although Hogarth's print *Strolling Actresses in a Barn* (1738) referred to them as assembled 'for the last time of acting before the Act commences', the consequences of the Licensing Act of 1737 were far less severe in practice outside London than in the capital: other theatres could obtain permission – existing ones being licensed under the Act, while new ones could receive special approval – although doing so or seeking to do so made them vulnerable to their opponents. The net result was similar to that of much eighteenth-century legislation and regulation: a world of considerable variety. The Act did not prevent a growth in the theatrical world, with nearly three hundred theatres in the British Isles by 1800. The impact of the Licensing Act was further modified by the Enabling Act of 1788, which allowed Justices of the Peace to issue licenses for performances, but it did contribute to a slackening of theatrical energy, with relatively few new plays staged each season – an average of only three in the decade after the Act. Furthermore, the range of plays on offer in the early 1730s was curtailed, especially with Fielding's abandonment of satirical plays for novels, and also with the loss of tragedies that were politically pointed. Revivals dominated and the new plays of the thirty-five years after the Licensing Act have not found favour with subsequent critics.

Morality was matched by comedy. Whether on the stage, on canvas or on the printed page, the middling orders watched both themselves and caricatures that reflected their anxieties and drives being depicted. The comedies of the Irish playwright Richard Brinsley Sheridan (1751–1816), *The Rivals* (1775), *A Trip to Scarborough* (1777), *The School for Scandal* (1777), and *The Critic* (1779), offered satires on manners that in part captured anxieties over social standing. Mistaken identities played a major role in Sheridan's plays, as they also did in Oliver Goldsmith's successful comedy *She Stoops to Conquer* (1773). Although these mistaken identities were exploited to comic effect and provided much of the situational dynamic of the plots, they also captured a concern about identity, and the dangers that mis-identification could lead to. In *The School for Scandal*, the most frequently produced play of the last quarter of the century, Joseph Surface is menacing in his deceitful self-interest and unctuous hypocrisy, and part of the pleasure of the play derives from seeing him thwarted. *The Rivals* was set in Bath, like the West End of London, a particularly important setting for playwrights and novels.

In comedies, tensions could be defused, and social role-playing could be presented with humorous consequences and no long-term difficulties, thanks to benign fortune. In George Farquhar's *The Beaux' Strategem* (1707) the death of Aimwell's brother ensures that he can indeed be an affluent peer and marry Dorinda without her losing status. Conversely, in some tragedies, news of good fortune arrived too late. Reversals as plot devices also captured both a sense of social fluidity and an underlying set of social rules, although the latter could be variously class or moral in character, or both.

Isaac Jackman, like Sheridan a transplanted Irishman, similarly produced a series of comic works, *Milesian* (1777), *All the World's a Stage* (1777), *The Divorce* (1781) and *Hero and Leander* (1781), although they lacked Sheridan's characterisation and skill with dialogue. *The Divorce*, an operatic farce about a divorce arranged to ensure publicity, presented, like Sheridan's *The Critic*, a sense of a world in which the pressure for artificiality was strong and open to satirical representation as absurd.

Alongside the moral critique of affectation in much of the writing of the period, and the preference for honesty as an aesthetic as well as a moral choice, can be seen the sense of flux and uncertainty that led to a lack of clarity over identity and classification, or, at least, a challenge to them. In this situation of flux, performance was both the condition of mankind, certainly in the social maelstrom of London, and a challenge to appropriate conduct, and to the social categorisation that it was supposed to reflect and sustain. In terms of transgression of norms, the representation of men and women proved as troubling as that of social groups,[21] although, looked at differently, this fluidity provided both plots and also satisfied public interest.

The role of the middling orders has recently been seen as the driving force of eighteenth-century English culture. In this perspective, the forcing house of public demand provided the essential pressure for cultural modernisation and for the definition of taste. This is an account of a conflation of consumerism and the public sphere through which taste is defined, imagination organised and encouraged, and culture developed.[22] Such an assessment is linked to a portrayal of the English Enlightenment as an inclusive movement, sustained by a vibrant and unconstrained world of newspapers, coffee houses, and other public meeting houses.[23]

The problem with this account is that polite consumerism can act as a universal solvent, apparently banishing analytical problems. One relates to the definition of the middling orders and their culture. In practice in much 'middling' culture there was a 'trickle down' effect, in both form and culture, from elite culture. For example, urban growth and prosperity and increasing demand for public buildings such as theatres and libraries did not lend to a distinctive architectural style.[24] Secondly, divisions affected every aspect of life, including such cultural dimensions as music and the patronage of painters, but that is not a theme that is adequately worked out if the emphasis is on consumerism. Social and regional divisions are underplayed in such an emphasis, as much as those derived from politics and religion.

Thirdly, gender has to be considered. As both producers and consumers of culture, women shared in the same cultural world as men, but there were also important differences in access and presentation. Thus, in conversation pieces, the group portraiture that presented relationships, men took the more prominent roles and also commissioned the paintings. In London, instrumental music was largely an all-male profession, although there were women pianists.[25] The situation, nevertheless, was far from constant. For example, in the theatre from the late seventeenth century, actresses took over female roles from actors and this led to a more realistic presentation of women and of gender relationships. Both became more relevant to women playgoers. Plays by female playwrights were also staged. Susannah Centlivre, a not particularly successful actress, was far more popular as a playwright, with social comedies such as *The Busy Body* (1709), *The Wonder! A Woman Keeps a Secret* (1714) and *A Bold Stroke for a Wife* (1718). Mary Beale and Sarah Curtis were examples of women excelling as painters, both in the fiercely commercial world of portraiture. Tilly Kettle (1735–1786), a London portrait painter, who also worked in India from 1770 to 1777, died en route for a second visit.

As with music, painting by women for money, however, was far less common than private performance. The same was true of writing, a sphere greatly illuminated by recent scholarship that has drawn attention to works that have been neglected.[26] In Tobias Smollett's novel *The Adventure of Roderick Random* (1748), his narrator visits the study of Narcissa, a lady whose affection he is pursuing:

> Here I found a thousand scraps of her own poetry, consisting of three, four, ten, twelve, and twenty lines, on an infinity of subjects, which, as whim inspired, she had begun, without constancy or capacity to bring to any degree of composition. But, what was very extraordinary in a female poet, there was not the least mention made of love in any of her performances. I counted fragments of five tragedies, the titles of which were, "The Stern Philosopher – The Double Murder – The Sacrilegious Traitor – The Fall of Lucifer – and The Last Day".

Women writers who published, however, faced difficulties, in part, it has been argued, because they were objects of a cultural anxiety directed at 'empowered' women outside their proper roles and at 'feminised' men led by their emotions. Thus, Eliza Haywood (*c.* 1693–1756), a successful and prolific novelist (and also a playwright and poet), who offered frank discussions of female desire in her *The City Jilt* (1726) and *The Mercenary Lover* (1726), could be seen as a threat. Haywood's *Anti-Pamela* (1740) was less successful than Samuel Richardson's *Pamela* (1741) because it was more disturbing and less didactic, and because Richardson was better able to capitalize on the market for fiction thanks to his authorised role in the print trade.[27] There were also differences in plots. Duty or love was the choice posed by many male writers, but female counterparts were apt to unite the two.

Whatever the difficulties, many women did publish plays, poems and novels, so that in the 1750s and 1760s over 15 per cent of novels were by women,[28] and Haywood herself went on publishing novels until the 1750s. Many female writers, however, are obscure, for example the dramatist Mary Pix (1666–*c.* 1720), whose plays included the comedy *The Beau Defeated* (1700), and Penelope Aubion (*c.* 1679–1731), the author of romantic novels including *The Life and Adventures of the Lady Lucy*. Writers prominent in their day, such as Jane West (1758–1852), have frequently slipped from attention, in part because the canon of major and second-rank works emphasises male writers. The wife of a

farmer, West was an industrious writer, illustrating the widespread tendency to produce across genres with her novels, plays and poems. An
insistent moralist – one of her novels was *The Advantages of Education:
or The History of Maria Williams* (1793) – West was opposed to what she
saw as the troubling radicalism of writers such as Mary Wollstonecraft.
Her politics are further indicated by her *Elegy on Edmund Burke* (1793).

A combination of such values and a somewhat leaden style help
explain why West has slipped from attention, but in her day she was
much published.[29] The fall of women writers from discussion invites
attention to the process by which the canon was constructed and
upheld, and, in particular, to the fate of writers who could not be
defined in terms of Romanticism.[30] In recent decades, the canon has in
turn been revised to take far more note of female writers particularly,
but not only, in this category, and this appropriately matches interest in
female readers, as the two were linked.[31] At present, it is unlikely that
Anne Plumptre's play *Pizarro* (1799), for example, will surpass the play
of the same title and year by Sheridan, but the canon may change further. Hannah More, another critic of Mary Wollstonecraft, who wrote
Percy (1777), one of the most successful plays of the period, as well as
books that greatly outsold those of Jane Austen, has recently made a
return to the spotlight with the first modern biography, and the first to
make full use of her extensive correspondence. Although seeing herself
as a conservative, More envisaged women playing a prominent role.
The implication of her call for female patriotism was that politics in
its broadest sense had to involve women, who were responsible for
protecting the morality of the country.[32]

Most of the world of female private cultural activity is obscure. An
ability to play music, however, was regarded as an important accomplishment, and, particularly from the later eighteenth century, girls'
schools advertised their ability to teach music as well as dancing
and drawing. At Miss Baly's Ladies Boarding School in Warwick in
1790 music was the most expensive item after board and cost £1 1s. per
quarter.[33]

In the tenth issue of the *Spectator*, Joseph Addison expressed the
ambition to be held to have 'brought philosophy out of closets and
libraries ... to dwell in clubs and assemblies, at tea-tables and in coffee-
houses'. These mixed gatherings, especially tea-tables, indeed saw
women discussing literature. Women's diaries and correspondence indicate that they read widely. Mary Wollstonecraft's first surviving letter,

the contents of part of which may have come from an anthology or commonplace book, includes quotations from Pope's *Essay on Criticism*, William King's *The Art of Love*, Dryden's *Aeneis*, and his and Nathaniel Lee's *Oedipus*.[34]

As far as history was concerned, their correspondence reveals that in 1748 Louisa, Countess of Pomfret read the hack-writer James Ralph's *Introductory Review of the Reigns of the Royal Brothers Charles and James* (1744), in 1766 Lady Mary Coke finished a life of the Spanish minister Ripperda and began a history of France while at Bath, and in 1775 Elizabeth Montagu, known as a 'blue stocking' or female intellectual, spent six hours daily reading the 2nd Earl of Hardwicke's *Miscellaneous State Papers from 1501–1726* and Noailles's *Mémoires*. The variety of interests served by reading was indicated by Elizabeth Montagu who, in 1759, suggested most readers want to 'find history a smart libel on former times and persons'.[35] This demand attracted entrepreneurs: in addition to trying to sell to women works not intended specifically for them, there was the publication of works largely or explicitly for that market, such as particular journals or newspapers, for example Eliza Haywood's the *Female Spectator* (1744–46) or, in the provinces, the *Ladies Kentish Journal* and the *Sussex and Kentish Ladies Polite Pocket Journal*. The pre-nuptial settlement drawn up in 1751 by Susannah Hubert, a wealthy Warwickshire widow, reveals that she had £100 worth of books and music.[36]

Women's reading troubled many male commentators;[37] and indeed some did not like them having views, an aspect of a more general concern about the disruptive consequences of female curiosity, a theme often presented in sexual terms.[38] In Fanny Burney's novel *Cecilia* (1782), the opinionated, practical man of business Mr Hobson declares, 'for as to not letting a lady speak, one might as well tell a man in business not to look at the *Daily Advertiser*, why it's morally impossible'. Possibly a different form of uneasiness was reflected by the report in *Berrow's Worcester Journal* on 13 September 1770 of a woman returning from a performance of the Shakespeare Jubilee Ode at Leominster to find her husband embracing their servant.

The assertiveness of some women was presented more sympathetically, Millamant in William Congreve's play *The Way of the World* (1700) appearing impressive when she made it clear that marriage to Mirabell (a man) would only be acceptable under certain conditions. With Congreve's comedy *Love for Love* (1695), this has been taken as an example of John Locke's contract theory in drama. At the same time, in *The Way of the World*, Lady Wishfort's desire for a lover is made to appear ridiculous, while the anger of Mrs Marwood at Mirabell's failure to reciprocate her desire helps provide the malice that drives the malign counter-plot thwarting the benign plot provided by Mirabell's quest for Millamant.

Many men presumably would have preferred their wives to focus on needlework and other traditional activities such as managing the household. Indeed many did, although relatively little needlework survives. In Wallington, however, there are ten panels of needlework done by Julia, Lady Calverley in the 1710s for the drawing room at Esholt Hall, the family seat. Wallington also has a substantial needlework screen worked in 1727 by Lady Calverley. These reflect the influences of the period: the scenes on the screen are from engravings from editions of Virgil's *Georgics* and *Eclogues*, while the designs of the panels were influenced by imported Oriental textiles.

Even biblical and devotional reading were not always considered safe for female readers. Imaginative literature was seen as potentially exacerbating the female imagination, and drama also raised the perils of sensibility in the form of heightened emotion. Reading works about science became increasingly acceptable for women, but, for many commentators with conservative inclinations, science, especially botany, remained problematic. It was less so, however, than fiction and philosophy, both of which led to persistent reading bans on women and girls. Conduct literature, instead, was held to be the best way to shape expectations of womanhood. Too many novels seemed, to anxious parents in the second half of the century, to require glossing from works such as *A Dictionary of Love, Explaining the Language of Gallantry* (1776), and, more generally, to be a drug:

> Madam, a circulating library in a town is an evergreen tree of diabolical knowledge! It blossoms through the year! And depend on it, Mrs. Malaprop, that they who are so fond of handling the leaves, will long for the fruit at last.[39]

The extent to which novels were about courtship, and thus offered women, in particular, models of desirable partners and wooing different from whatever might be sanctioned by parents and guardians, was troubling to the latter, but also sustained the feminisation of the genre by proving particularly attractive to female readers. Marriage for love was endorsed,[40] although, in accord with conventions of sensibility and practicality, it was constrained by an emphasis on propriety and on filial duty. Such marriage was often the concluding episode of a story that was essentially about growing up into society, with a young woman usually serving as the protagonist. In Fanny Burney's first novel, *Evelina: or A Young Lady's Entrance into the World*, Evelina is shown being brought into the world at the age of seventeen, a course which closes when she marries one of her guides, the sage Lord Orville. This process of maturation provided opportunity for exciting but predictable sensibility. A far less benign upbringing, with malevolent guardians and a melodramatic descent to insanity, was presented in Burney's second novel, *Cecilia: or Memoirs of an Heiress* (1782). The third, *Camilla: or A Picture of Youth* (1796), was less unsettling, and more conventional, although the challenges were more marked than those in *Evelina*.[41]

Women were thought especially vulnerable to new philosophical ideas, and the Low Church salons organized by Caroline, Princess of Wales, later Queen Caroline, aroused controversy. The danger to women of reading radical texts was repeatedly imagined in fictional works in terms of sexual transgression leading to illness, breakdown and death. The tendency of women in sentimental novels to lack self-restraint was presented as a sign of heightened nerves and emotions that could also be seen as a lack of maturity. Men were also among the readers, and in Jane Austen's novel *Northanger Abbey* (1818, but begun in 1798), Henry Tilney responded to the suggestion that 'young men despised novels amazingly':

> It is *amazingly*; it may well suggest *amazement* if they do – for they read nearly as many as women. I myself have read hundreds and hundreds. Do not imagine that you can cope with me in a knowledge of Julias and Louisas.

In that novel, Catherine Morland herself was 'left to the luxury of a raised, restless, and frightened imagination over the pages of *Udolph* [Ann Radcliffe's *The Mysteries of Udolpho*], lost from all worldly concerns of dressing and dinner', although she discovers that the abbey of the title is not a setting from the pages of Gothic fiction. Ironically, in *Northanger Abbey*, real life turns out to be worse in some respects than the imagined perils of Gothic fiction.

Heightened nerves were also a commonplace in sentimental plays, with the audience given clear clues, a process mocked in Sheridan's *The*

Critic: 'when a heroine goes mad she always goes into white satin'. In Mary Wollstonecraft's novel *Wrongs of Woman: or Maria* (1798), over-whelmingly a tale of male cruelty and the oppression of women, there is also a reference to the interacting dangers of female sensibility and fiction, as a novel, Rousseau's *La Nouvelle Heloise*, plays a role in an unfortunate love affair.

Concerns were not always expressed about women, but they were fre-quently, as in conduct literature, treated as if minors. There was, indeed, much admonitory judgement on the cultural interests and needs of the young. Joseph Cradock, a man of letters, claimed 'young men are encouraged to take up general history much sooner than they ought. I would have them strongly impressed with moral virtues, before they venture to read so dreadful a detail of crimes and misfortunes'.[42]

Despite, and at times because of, strictures about their reading, many women enjoyed reading, and explicitly commented on its pleasureable-ness; it brought wider prospects. Reading also permitted critical engagement with issues of authority, although that could help accentu-ate the anxiety that reading could give rise to. Where women were to read was an issue. Private libraries were generally seen as male domains, being frequently identified with patriarchal power: women were not there as equals. Libraries were by 1800 painted a 'masculine' colour: dark (Brunswick) green. In novels by women, the male authority and ration-ality figured by the library was likely to have a dark side which became explicit in Gothic fiction. There the ruined library recurs as a symbol for the bankruptcy of male authority and literary culture.

Women, in contrast, favoured subscription and circulating libraries, which were crucial to the 'democratisation' of literature. Women writ-ers were also dependent on them as a reliable market for their writing. The image of libraries dominated by the works of women for female readers, and, more generally, the ubiquity of the female reader as an icon, intensified. Female novel-reading gave women writers a series of potent images to deal with their anxieties about, or even to fight for their rights to, literary authority.[43]

Women were also the key figures in family life and the culture of its sociability, especially music-making. In increasingly focusing on their activities, it is important not to forget the position of children and adolescents, both male and female. They were often presented, as in Hogarth's paintings *A House of Cards* and *A Children's Tea Party* (in which a spaniel upsets the tea table), as in some way both adult and different. Increasingly, children were treated as a distinctive part of society, with products being designed particularly for them. These included types of literature, a genre in which women writers played an important role. Much was didactic and, to modern tastes, wearing: it is difficult to read works like Thomas Day's *The History of Little Jack* (1788) without sharing Oscar Wilde's response to the fate of Little Nell, unless that is one's social circle includes someone suckled as a child by goats; although modern children's fiction is not exactly short of the fantastic. More prosaically, children's history books appeared, such as Richard Johnson's *History of France from the Earliest Period to the Present Time ... Designed for the Use of Young Ladies and Gentlemen* in 1786. Children's literature was a massive publishing phenomenon in the second half of the century.

The depiction of children also became more informal. John Zoffany's picture of *The Blunt Children* (*c.* 1765) is a good instance of the abandonment of the tendency to treat them as young adults. Adults became readier to enjoy seeing children depicted as at play. As a result, children were increasingly painted in groups and interacting, and not simply as adjuncts of their parents. When they appeared with adults in paintings, they could be shown following their own pursuits, as with the vigorously playing boys in Hogarth's group portrait of the Cholmondely family (1732), and also with performances of plays by children.

The middling orders were an increasingly influential tranche of society as a result of their growth in numbers and affluence with economic expansion. Although the effects of enclosures were discussed by poets,[44] the amount of imaginative literature thrown up by the major changes in transport resulting from turnpiking, bridge-building and canal construction was modest, and even less resulted from industrial development. J.F.'s *Song on Obtaining the Birmingham and Worcester Canal Bill*, printed in *Swinney's Birmingham and Stafford Chronicle* of 4 August 1791, held out prospects of gain, but it was not much of an advertisement for the genre. The song began:

> Come now, begin delving, the Bill is obtained,
> The contest was hard, but a conquest is gained;
> Let no time be lost, and to get business done
> Set thousands to work ...

Nevertheless, prominent manufacturers had their portraits painted and Richard Arkwright was happy to have Joseph Wright depict him in 1789–90 alongside cotton-spinning rollers, a mechanism that had brought him wealth. Far more discreetly, George Stubbs' portrait of the Wedgwood family includes a small puff of smoke from a kiln.[45] Industrial sites also attracted painters, most famously the iron smelting at Coalbrookdale, while the new communications infrastructure of the age – canals and new harbours – similarly attracted attention.

Science proved more of an appeal for poets, especially astronomy, with Sir Isaac Newton, whose portrait James Thornhill painted in 1710, being much celebrated. The analysis of the nature of light in his *Opticks* (1704) was not without importance for the idea that art had the objective quality of science. More generally, science became public, fashionable and a matter of cultural status. Museums of natural history were created, societies of enthusiastic amateurs were founded and public scientific lectures became frequent. In Norwich, a Natural History Society was founded in 1746, a Norwich Botanical Society in the 1760s, and two general scientific societies in the 1750s and 1780s. The level of scientific knowledge was rarely profound, and much of the interest was dilettante and restricted to display rather than scientific theory; but this made it easier to make science fashionable. As Joseph Wright's paintings such as *A Philosopher Giving that Lecture on the Orrery, in which a Lamp is put in Place of the Sun* (1766) and *An Experiment on a Bird in the Air Pump* (1786) suggested, it was the phenomena themselves that attracted attention because they appealed to the imagination as well as, or rather than to, the intellect. This was true of star-gazing, mesmerism and electricity.

There was also a fascination with mechanisms. This was seen most obviously with interest in technological developments, the details of which were carefully depicted in drawings of machines, but also with the workings of other phenomena, both natural and artificial. The beautifully-carved automata produced by James Cox, a London goldsmith active from 1749 to 1797, enjoyed considerable favour. *Swinney's Birmingham and Stafford Chronicle*, in its issue of 13 April 1775, printed anonymous lines *On Seeing the Microcosm, Now Exhibiting in the Red Lion Assembly Room*:

> Through all the long records of time,
> Wherever science blessed the clime
> ...
> Here, Things inimate can move,
> And make the ravish'd Fancy rove
> Where, to Amphion's music sound

All nature seem'd to dance around.
Here all Copernicus's pains,
The labour of great Newton's brains,
What puzzled ages – one short view
(Each knowledge of the mind) can shew.
Inigo Jones, with envious eyes
Might see the finished orders rise;
Raphael, outdone, behold, with grief,
The painted figures spring to life.

Astronomy and geology enlarged horizons in space and time. If the first was mathematicised, and thus taken from the sphere of the wonderful, the second provided an idea of the Earth's history as one of great antiquity, marked by major cataclysms, and the strange animals recorded by fossils which attracted increasing attention in the second half of the century. This accorded with an image of the Earth as sublime and full of wonder in Romantic terms. The non-mathematical character of geology was more suitable than astronomy for audiences wanting to be enthralled and entertained, rather than instructed.[46]

The extent to which the growing influence of the middling orders should be presented in terms of the development of a middle-class culture was in part dependent on local cultural situations, as a variety of local cultures existed, each a specific response to the local context and to the resulting experiences. Politics, economics and religion all played a role in this context, but as individuals' experiences shaped the world they made for themselves so this constructed world also affected their assumptions and actions. The shared values and new forms of sociability of the private sphere helped shape identity. Sociability became more exclusive and orderly, with male clubs and mixed assemblies offering settings for behaviour and social consciousness that were very different to alehouses. The culture of gentility therefore encouraged and drew on specific settings, with consequences for social differentiation in terms of behaviour, or, at least, statements about behaviour.[47]

The sense of social distinction in traditional classification was captured by Henry Fielding in his preface to *Joseph Andrews* (1742) when he distinguished comic from tragic romances in terms of characters, manner and language:

a comic romance is a comic epic poem in prose, differing from comedy as the serious epic from tragedy; its action being more extended and comprehensive, containing a much larger circle of incidents, and introducing a greater variety of characters. It differs from the serious romance in its fable and action in this, that as in the one these are grave and solemn, so in the other they are light and ridiculous; it differs in its characters by introducing persons of inferior rank and consequently of inferior manners, whereas the grave romance sets the highest before us; lastly, in its sentiments and diction by preserving the ludicrous instead of the sublime.

In one of Fielding's periodicals the *Covent Garden Journal* (1752), many of the essays were devoted to the cause of good behaviour both against specific abuses, such as gambling and adultery, and against the general problem of selfish and improper conduct, while much of the satire was directed at the abuses of the polite world. 'People of Fashion' were criticised for their behaviour and their attitudes and presented as dangerous role models for tradesmen. This social tension arose in part from the uneasy neighbourhood of the City and the West End.[48]

Genteel manners and sensibility had been prefigured in Restoration comedy, when they were sometimes presented as foppish folly, as well as being the forerunner of politeness. In the eighteenth century, genteel manners and sensibility were extolled as the desirable norm, contributing powerfully not only to the developing idea of the gentleman but also to the extent to which it was not restricted to the landed elite. This form of refinement has been presented as a feminisation of culture at the behest of an ascendant middle class, but in practice the manners of sensibility and the sensibility of manners embraced more than one tranche of society.

At the same time, as the furore over the Earl of Chesterfield's letters to his son published in 1774 indicated, there were problems in defining not only gentility but also how best to pursue it. Much depended, as so often, on the relationship between intent and surface and between truth and form. Frequently reprinted, the letters were attacked as immoral, not least for emphasising how to alter appearances in order to please. The young Thomas Pelham, later 2nd Earl of Chichester, however, felt the advice excellent, and, in a letter that ably reflected the norms of the period, cited with approval the characteristically Classical simile, and the argument for moderation:

He makes religion, morality and knowledge the basis of his fabric; affability, desire of pleasing and attention to outward appearance his superstructure, esteeming them all so many necessary parts to compose perfection; which he illustrates by this beautiful simile continuing the metaphor: 'The Corinthian order (says he) without a Tuscan or solid base

appears as much too light as the simple Tuscan is too heavy'. The generality of people who are ready enough to pass over everything respecting
the more severe part of his reasoning criticise merely upon one circum-
stance instead of the whole – he well knew the passions and foibles of
man; he wrote to a young man and endeavoured to touch the ruling ones
of youth: he excited his vanity, but for what purpose? to give him all
abomination of everything dishonorable and below an honest man; he
knew that vice had too many charms and that every young man must in
some degree sacrifice to Venus; he therefore instructed him how to be virtuous without offending virtue and by making the Graces his friends to
avoid falling a sacrifice to debauchery in his offerings to love. There are
certain temptations that no man can resist, the great art therefore is to
know how when and how far to give way to them; our passions are never
so innocent as when humoured to certain degree. They are never so rebel-
lious as when they meet too much restraint, nor so tyrannical as when we
abandon ourselves entirely to them.[49]

6

Pleasures for the Many

they were so rude and ignorant, so little able to compare the good with the evil of the occupation [being shepherds], and so indistinct in their narratives and descriptions, that very little could be learned from them. But it was evident that their hearts were cankered with discontent; that they considered themselves as condemned to labour for the luxury of the rich, and looked up with stupid malevolence towards those that were placed above them.

The shepherds in Samuel Johnson's
The History of Rasselas, Prince of Abyssinia (1759),
chapter nineteen.

The 'No Dedication' for the 'Apology for Painters' that William Hogarth was working on at the end of his life was dedicated not to 'any man of quality', but 'to every body'.[1] Everybody indeed played a role in culture, both in the narrow sense that many works were intended for an anonymous market rather than for the individual, and in the wider sense that the bulk of the population had a cultural life and formed a part of national culture.

In practice, the anonymous market tended to mean the middling orders described in the previous chapter, and issues of cost and manners ensured that the rest of the population found equal access to specific cultural events and practices impossible. Nevertheless, there was a certain degree of movement across what were very porous social boundaries, so that much that was discussed in the previous chapter about the middling orders is also relevant for this one. Indeed, when writers juxtaposed an elite with the rest, their placing of the middling orders could be ambivalent. They could be part of the world of commerce contrasted with the more gracious and refined (or absurd and self-satisfied) elite, or could be linked with the latter and opposed to the populace. In David Garrick's epilogue to *The Clandestine Marriage*

(1766) an assembly of the quality is joined by the splenetic Miss Crotchet:

> A playhouse, what a place! I must forswear it
>
> ...
>
> Such crowds of city folks! – so rude and pressing!
> And their horse-laughs, so hideously distressing!
> Whene'er we hissed, they frowned and fell a-swaring
>
> ...
>
> In the first act Lord George began to doze,
> And criticized the author – through his nose;
> So loud indeed, that as his lordship snored,
> The pit turned round, and all the brutes encored.

Yet, rather than this being a clear critique aimed at the unacceptable snobbery of the elite, Crotchet admits that some lords approved the author's jokes, and, in the play, a peer is responsible for the benign close of the plot. The behaviour of the audience, both high and low, at public performances was indeed a matter of frequent complaint. *To* —, a poem printed in *Swinney's Birmingham and Stafford Chronicle* on 23 May 1776, included criticism of a concert audience in Bath for not concentrating on the music, especially of a peer who talked during an excellent chorus. In practice, it is difficult to know what really happened or how widespread the problem was.

The social placing of culture in this period relates to what is sometimes presented as a tension between high and popular culture. In practice the latter is a subject that is still largely uncharted and that poses serious conceptual and methodological problems.[2] In John Dyer's *The Fleece* (1757), the operatives winding yarn on 'swiftly-circling engines' are recorded as warbling at their work 'as a choir of larks', but we know little of what they sang. Yet we know that singing was common. It was a free pastime, and surviving songs suggest that courtship was the major theme. This was part of a pattern of display and entertainment that included decorating clothes and hair. Song, like display, was also linked to the annual rhythm of life in a fashion that is now largely lost to view. The most famous reference to this pattern was James Thomson's poem *The Seasons*, which appeared in parts from 1726 with the first complete edition in 1730. The indoor life of *Winter* (1726) contrasted with the varied outdoor activities of the others.

At a less self-conscious level, the same pattern was true of more vernacular celebrations, not least as the rhythms of agrarian life helped determine marriage and thus affected courtship. Indeed Thomson's *Spring* referred to 'the passion of the groves'. Although he meant the courtship of birds, the parallels between animal and human loves were frequently noted, both being seen as desirable. Pastorals both reflected the Classical literary tradition and also permitted an engagement, sometimes fairly direct, with themes of sexuality. If the countryside was seen as a sphere of innocence, this innocence was not divorced from desires presented as natural.[3] The beauty of women was much applauded, as in a poem by Isaac Gumley, a Leicestershire village framework-knitter:

> Of all the Girls that e'er were seen
> To walk the town, or trip the green,
> There's none has such a charming mien
> As lovely Polly Jordan.[4]

The rhythms of agrarian life varied between pastoral and arable areas, and each had their individual note in terms of festivals, songs, and references and allusions in verses. There were numerous love songs and verses in the provincial press, and it would be surprising if those who did not put pen to paper lacked the opportunity to demonstrate their ardour in song and other forms. In his *Philosophical Enquiry into the Origins of Our Ideas of the Sublime and Beautiful* (1757), Edmund Burke claimed that 'the common sort' were 'strongly roused' by ballads and popular songs.

Across the social divides, or rather gradations, there was a common emphasis on love, particularly on courtship. Poems and songs played a role in the latter, as did correspondence, while poems also served to record the emotions of the smitten for their own benefit. In truth, the categories overlapped, as poems written as a confidential journal of emotions could then be passed on. A manuscript volume,

> Being a choice farrago of new Poems. – lately collected from the papers of that wonder-working Genius, S. Simpson of Coventry, Weaver. – piae quo caeteri poetae sordent, and now first copied by himself at his Garret in the High Street. Cum privilegio Apollonis. 10th July 1773.

indicates the nature of at least some unpublished material. The twenty-seven poems written from 1773 and 1776 vary greatly in style – some are ballads or simple lyrical pieces, others are elegiac, fabulous, monodic or epistolary, and reflect a range of emotions, especially the courtship of Sarah Leaper. The sentiments such as: 'Dearest Leaper, best of Friends,/ on whose Joy my Bliss depends' are conventional. As so often in the

period, death intrudes, and that of Simpson's young friend Robert
Laroque in 1773 leads to an expression of grief:

> The solitary shade, the moss grown seat
> Where Man commencing with the Realms above
> Finds his calm seat warm'd with celestial fire
> Sees all his wishes, all his hopes compleat,
> And rapt, in extasy of thought expires.[5]

Generalisations about peasant conservatism and cultural borrowing
from the more prosperous are still too common in discussion of popular culture, while the notion of a battle of cultures rests in part on a
misleadingly sharp differentiation between high and popular culture.
The latter is often presented as being under assault from the moral
didacticism of the secular and ecclesiastical authorities and the middling
orders. It is not only in the artistic sphere that this tension has been discerned and that the analysis of relationships has been coloured by the
use of words and phrases such as oppressive, control and protective
mechanisms. Indeed, the discernment of artistic duality is but part of a
wider sense, or allegation, of cultural control, of different *mentalités*, of
worlds in collision, which has also influenced the assessment of popular
religiosity. New intellectual and artistic fashions and codes of behaviour
are held to have corroded the loyalty of the upper and middling orders
to traditional beliefs and pastimes, and it is claimed that the Scientific
Revolution, the Enlightenment, the cult of sensibility, and Evangelicalism marginalised the common culture and pushed it down the social
scale. Given such an analysis, it is not surprising that attention has been
devoted to the contrast between popular and respectable culture, and
that this is held to have inspired initiatives to 'reform' popular practices.[6] Newspapers of the period indeed attacked such popular practices
as wife-selling, gambling, the shooting of street lamps for fun, boxing,
swearing and cruelty to animals, although all bar wife-selling was also
popular with the aristocracy.

Far from there being contrasting *mentalités*, however, there was a
common culture, albeit one with different styles. A shared currency of
interests, notions and idioms was matched by a mutual interchange of
ideas. Performers and the public sought to investigate and express common problems and emotions, and to make sense of a common world in
a number of different styles and formats. There was noticeable overlap
between the amusements of the 'best people' and the rest at the theatre,

and at such entertainments as public executions, horse racing, cricket, bear baiting, cock fighting and boxing. This artistic interaction can also be seen in music. Far from 'art' and 'folk' music being distinct and antithetical, with folk music being conservative and transmitted almost solely in oral tradition, there was, instead, a considerable interrelationship and change, both thematic and stylistic, although it could be that theatre songs for example were simpler and/or coarser in a more popular forum. If for the bulk of the population, music meant ballads, hymns and primitive instruments, that does not mean that popular music was necessarily unsophisticated or unchanging. Furthermore, broadside ballads were printed in large quantities.

In addition, popular interest in the world of spirits and witches, in elements of white and black magic, was not completely removed from respectable culture. It has been assumed that, due to the Scientific Revolution, belief in the supernatural was now weak. If so, many at all social levels, had not noticed this injunction. Particularly in the early decades of the century, there was much writing about the world of spirits. Furthermore, far from this being seen as necessarily antipathetic to science, and the progressive cause it supposedly presented, spirits and witchcraft were presented as scientifically proven by empirical means and therefore requiring explanation. Different ways to understand the world were believed to run in parallel, testimony through history providing one, theology through revelation and the Bible another, and psychology through the senses a third. The latter could be trained to do so, thus enabling those benefiting from this education to experience what others could not, including the occult. John Beaumont, a Fellow of the Royal Society, published in 1705 his *An Historical, Physiological and Theological Treatise of Spirits, Apparitions, Witchcrafts, and Other Magical Practices: containing an account of the genii or familiar spirits, both good and bad, that are said to attend men in this life, and what sensible perceptions some persons have had of them (particularly the author's own experience for many years). Also of appearances of spirits after death, divine dreams, divinations, second sighted person, &c; likewise the power of witches and the reality of other magical operations, clearly asserted.*[7] Similarly, Newton's mystical and religious views were less incompatible with his physics than they might appear to modern commentators.[8]

Indeed, an emphasis on occult skills as a means to learn the secrets of the universe and nature, while in some respects it may appear a conservative aspect of a superstitious popular culture, could also be found in

Freemasonry, which was a new cult (the Grand Lodge was established in 1717) and form of sociability. Freemasonry was popular among the elite, and the royal family quickly joined the cult. Rosicrucianism also drew on the interest in occult skills. This interest was not so much a defiance of what has been seen as the Enlightenment as a reminder of the variety of strands that composed it. This indeed makes the relationship between English culture and 'the Enlightenment' less clear-cut than is sometimes assumed. For example, the exuberant fantasy horrors of Gothic novels and plays are not so much 'anti-Enlightenment' as aspects of its sub-world or dark side that are reduced in size and to explanation by the interrogative gaze of author, reader and viewer. Gothic literature fiction-alised the process of explication seen among those who wrote on the world of spirits, while, at the same time, drawing on deep-seated beliefs and making them serve the ends of emotion-raising and entertainment.

The idea of a sharp distinction between the culture of the bulk of the population and that of the rest is also misleading because the use of the vernacular allowed a degree of democratisation and inclusion in reli-gion, culture, society and government. Whereas cosmopolitan languages – French, German and Italian – were the languages of the European elites, or at least of much of their culture, in English there was no such divide. In the United Provinces (the modern Netherlands) the major newspapers were published in French, but in England French-language periodicals were few and short-lived, and all major publications were in English.

An emphasis on the vernacular was an aspect of a more pronounced cultural distinctiveness that drew on a strong patriotism frequently expressed in terms of a vigorous rejection of foreign cultural influences. The robust xenophobia of the London populace was made brutally apparent in a series of disturbances, such as those provoked by the arrival of French companies of actors. Aside from the major riot at the Haymarket Theatre on 9 October 1738, further disturbances and tension were provoked in London by similar attempts to introduce foreign actors on subsequent occasions, including in 1739, 1743, 1749 and 1755. In 1777 Philip Yorke feared a riot when plans were laid for a French play in the new theatrical season in London. He regretted this, because he enjoyed the theatre and thought a French play would be of great value to those learning the language, but the latter intention would have been seen as a sinister motive by the crowd.[9]

The overlap of elite and popular entertainment can also be seen in the press. There were different tones in newspaper coverage, but it would be mistaken to think that the popular papers were necessarily only of interest to those who were not members of the elite. On 19 September 1719, the *Weekly Medley* disparaged Nathaniel Mist's the *Weekly Journal: or Saturday's Post* by referring to Mist's 'vast success among the lower class of readers', ie. still the literate; but Mist preferred to regard his popularity as due to tone not to a particular social appeal. In his issue of 6 February 1720, Mist indeed identified a major section of his market in a letter from Timothy Trifle: 'To me it is not one farthing matter, who you are for, what king, what church, what party: it is enough that you write the Journal, where we expect something to please us or displease us, make us laugh, or make us frown'. Certainly, Mist deliberately sought a large popular market, and his course was pursued by inexpensive serial publishers in the 1730s, such as William Rayner and Robert Walker, who ignored copyright and used the metropolitan system of cheap newspapers to publish and advertise their works. These papers were curtailed, however, as a result of legislation and action against street hawkers in 1743, and a major unstamped press was not to revive until the following century. Nevertheless, hawkers continued to have a rich variety of wares reflecting a widespread popular willingness to read and an ability to purchase to do so. In a similar fashion to the French *bibliothèque bleue*, there were adventure stories, many of them on long-established themes, as well as ballads, the moralising of exemplary works, and joke books.

The importance of humour is apt to be underrated in favour of an emphasis on sentiment, and this may well lead to an underrating of the appeal of many works. During the summer of 1784, Robert Arbuthnot reported:

> The only theatre open at present in London is Colman's Playhouse in the Haymarket. The pieces represented there are all little musical farces, most of them written by a Mr O'Keefe, which although devoid of common sense and probability have the property of exciting laughter in very great degree. Mr Colman certainly entertains the town with sufficient variety, for every fortnight almost a new farce is exhibited, which after running a few nights, is never afterwards heard of.[10]

Music played a major role in the theatre. Theatres had orchestras, and many plays were accompanied by music, not least due to the propensity of actors to burst out into verse. The publication of cheap new songs to familiar tunes such as *Chevy Chase* and *Lillibolero* suggests that these tunes had a wide currency. This musical capability lent itself to comic works. The 'after money' audience was a specific market for comic interludes which were given as after pieces. After the third act of the main piece, it was possible to purchase seats at half-price; but the appeal of farces or harlequin pantomimes or dramatic entertainments was great and they were put on frequently. John Rich's pantomimical *The Newcromancer: or Harlequin's Dr Faustus* ran for 291 performances in London from 1723 to 1745.[11] In forty-one seasons from 1720–21 to 1760–61, first at Lincoln's Inn Fields and then at Covent Garden, he staged pantomimes on nearly 2500 nights, while Drury Lane added another 1500. Pantomimes brought activity, speed and a show made up of costume, spectacle and scenery. They were easy to follow and so popular that managers were able to put up prices for performances. An anonymous letter in the *St James's Chronicle* of 15 May 1764 noted:

> The French are often pointed out to us as patterns of politeness, and I have in particular heard great encomiums made on the regularity, the decency, and the agreeableness of their comedies: whereas our theatres have, on the contrary, been called the storehouses of obscenity, indecency and ribaldry.

James Dance (1722–74), who took the surname Love, a comedian who was linked to Drury Lane from 1762, was responsible for a number of pantomimes, including *The Witches* (1762), *Rites of Hecate* (1764), and *The Hermit* (1766). The occult therefore could be comic. Playbills and newspaper advertisements for plays make it clear that, alongside the plays, came farces and interlude, that were generally more comic. To take *Swinney's Birmingham and Stafford Chronicle*, the issue of 4 August 1791 reported:

> The Hon. General Burgoyne's elegant comedy of *The Heiress*, with the laughable farce of the Ghost; and by desire, singing between the acts by Mr Sedgwick, with the Wapping Landlady ... will be performed tomorrow evening.

A week later, the advertisements for evenings at New Street Theatre in Birmingham offered on 12 August *Henry IV: Part One* followed by 'A pantomimical interlude, consisting of singing and dancing, called Harlequin at All; or The Whim of a Moment. The whole to conclude with The Humours of Bromsgrove Races to which will be added A Farce (performed here but once) written by Mrs [Elizabeth] Inchbald called Animal Magnetism'. At the Theatre Royal in Margate, the evening fare on 9 October 1798 concluded with the farce *Barnaby Brittle: or A Wife at her Wit's End*.

Such works were not only produced and printed in the second half of the century. Earlier, some were a response to political events such as the Jacobite rising of 1715–16. In 1717, two 'tragi-comical farces' by Philips commenting on it appeared: the third edition of *The Earl of Mar marr'd: With the Humours of Jockey the Highlander*, and its sequel *The Pretender's Flight: Or, A Mock Coronation. With the Humours of the factious Harry St. John*, the latter a reference to the exiled Tory politician, Viscount Bolingbroke. Others were non-political. In 1737, Drury Lane saw *The Eunuch: or the Darby Captain*, a musical farce adapted from Terence by Thomas Cooke, a prominent translator of Classical texts. Farce and pantomime both included stock characters and situations and also offered opportunities for responding not only to events but also to new cultural themes with, for example, landscape increasingly presented towards the close of the century in terms of Romantic values.[12]

The popularity of such works was high, although not to everyone's taste. In the *Champion* of 9 September 1740, Henry Fielding complained about 'miserable farces, below the dignity of the theatre', and congratulated the management of Drury Lane for raising its sights so that audiences did not have to put up with 'tumbling, farce and puppet-show'. Henry Ley wrote from Exeter in March 1793:

> All the town are going this evening to Mr Hughes' benefit as a reward for his liberality in giving two nights towards the fund for seamen. I could not, however, prevail upon myself to see in Exeter, such a play as 'Every man has his fault', with a harlequin entertainment, which I had so often rejected, in London – and indeed there is no place to be had.[13]

The ephemeral nature of farces has led to an underrating of their importance, and this is more generally true of humour, much of which was very specific. There was also a moral dimension to humour, as Mist noted in the dedication to the volume of his collected miscellany that appeared in 1727:

> the whole aim and design of the following papers has been to censure and correct those monstrous vices and corruptions, which have of late so openly showed themselves in all public affairs, as well as to ridicule the

little follies and impertinences of fops, coquets, prudes, pedants, and coxcombs of all sorts.

This aim joined satire on stage and in print with caricatures and the world of fairground shows.

In part, the relationship between sections of elite and popular culture derived from the greater interest in the latter displayed by artists and intellectuals. By the 1770s, as also elsewhere in Europe,[14] there was more interest in the supposed lifestyle of the peasantry, and they were now generally associated with exemplary behaviour. This interest matched growing fascination with landscape, although the latter was often empty of people, other than the narrator or viewer, especially if the emphasis was on the apparently sublime aspects of wild, particularly mountainous, landscape. The routine grind and miseries of rural life were generally ignored and, instead, an idealised view was presented, as with the stylised charm of Gainsborough's cottages. He covered much of the rural lifestyle, with paintings for example of *The Harvest Wagon* (*c.* 1767 and again in 1784–85) or *Peasant Ploughing with Two Horses*, and of *Peasants Going to Market* (*c.* 1769). There was an idyllic quality to some of them, as in *Rocky Wooded Landscape with Rustic Lovers, Herdsman and Cows* (*c.* 1771), and in his 1770s paintings of attractive children in rustic settings, for example *Miss Isabella Franks* (*c.* 1775), who is shown with a lamb.[15] In France, Jean-Baptiste Greuze (1725–1805) used peasant life for sentimental effect and didactic purpose.

Pastoralism was also seen not only in the parks of stately homes but also in songs, most famously the biblical 'He Shall Feed His Flock' from Handel's *Messiah*; and poetry such as James Thomson's *The Seasons* (1726–30), Christopher Smart's *Song for the Haymakers* (1748) and John Dyer's *The Fleece* (1757). Sentimental comic operas, especially Isaac Bickerstaff's *Love in a Village* (1762) and *The Maid of the Mill* (1765), and William Boyce's *The Shepherd's Lottery* (1751), also took pastoral themes. Less distinguished writers contributed to the genre, Robert Lloyd writing *Arcadia: or The Shepherd's Wedding. A Dramatic Pastoral* (1761). Poems in newspapers frequently dwelt on pastoral themes. *Swinney's Birmingham and Stafford Chronicle* of 18 April 1776 included an anonymous *Pastoral Elegy on the Death of Miss A-h-d* in which the bereft lover compares himself to Corydon, a staple of pastoral verse. It ends:

> Ye shepherds who hear me complain,
> And blame me in grief that I pine!

> Which of you can point out a swain
> Whose sorrows are equal to mine?

This style went back to at least the first decade of the century. The issue of 21 July 1791 included William Fernyhough's *On the Meeting of the Archers, Held Lately near Woolsley Bridge*, in which the cast included nymphs and an unoriginal comparison was drawn with Cupid's arrows. On 18 August 1791, illustrating the tendency of local or amateur work to model itself on literary successes, appeared *Elegiac Sonnet to the Willow: In the Character of Sterne's Maria. By Mrs Hughes*, a pastoral.

Indeed the engagement of poets with the genre had led to a 'pastoral war' in the 1710s, with Ambrose Philips' *Pastorals* (1709) criticiced by Alexander Pope and parodied in John Gay's *The Shepherd's Week* (1714). Unlike Philips, Gay was willing to engage with the difficulties of rural life, including hard toil: he offers the reader, and the painterly choice of image is instructive, 'a picture, or rather a lively landscape of thy own country, just as thou mightest see it, didst thou take a walk into the fields at the proper season'. If this served the purpose of parody, it also acted as a valuable corrective, underlining the importance of realism, in contrast to the elegiac, if not utopian, character of much pastoral writing. The idea of a native 'Doric' pastoral, contrasting with an artificial, high Classical genre, was advanced. The influence of the Classical tradition was also seen in John Philips' blank verse poem *Cider* (1708), dealing with the growing of cider-apples and the manufacture of cider, which was modeled on Virgil's *Georgics*. Another aspect of pastoralism was humour at the expense of comical rustics as in *The Merry Cobler* (1735) by Charles Coffey and *Harlequin's Invasion* by David Garrick.[16]

If there were few pictures of peasants there were also few of servants, other than as adjuncts to their masters and mistresses. Those pictures that remain, for example *Jane Ebbrell Aged 87* (1793) by John Walters of Denbigh, which survives in the place of her employment, the servants' hall at Erddig, serve as a reminder of how few exist. The painting was commissioned by the house-owner, Philip Yorke, who began a tradition of having the Erddig house and estate servants painted. As fictional figures, sometimes members of the gentry in disguise or changelings, servants played a greater role in novels, most prominently in *Pamela* and *Joseph Andrews*, while, in 1784, Exeter's theatre audience could see *The Noble Peasant: or Love and Glory*.

Nevertheless, signs of sensibility were generally restricted to those of higher rank. As a result, they alone were shown responding to crises and distress in an uplifting fashion, and one that displayed an awareness of deeper currents, such as the sublime. It was a measure of Thomas Holcroft's radicalism that the hero of his novel *Anna St Ives* (1792), Frank Henley, was a servant very different to the usual model for heroes in novels, Samuel Richardson's Sir Charles Grandison, from the 1753–54 novel of that title. Earlier, Thomas Day's *History of Sandford and Merton* (1783–89), an exemplary tale for children, presented the meritorious Harry Sandford, the son of a farmer, and Tommy Merton, the lazy son of an affluent gentleman; establishing a contrast also seen with Hogarth's apprentices (1747). Although Day's book was to be very successful (at least in terms of selling well), Day was scarcely representative in his background. A disciple of the radical thinker and writer Jean-Jacques Rousseau, he educated two foundlings in order to make one suitable to be his wife; the experiment was a dismal failure. Servants might be praised, for example for constancy, but they could also be sharply criticized. In Swift's 'A Description of the Morning' maidservants are morally delinquent, and he also wrote a how-not-to-behave guide for servants.

The folk tales of the bulk of the population were regarded as of less interest than those of ancient time, and much attention was devoted to the latter in what is termed the Pre-Romantic period: the 1760s–80s. To the antiquarian tradition of interest in ancient literature, such as the Anglo-Saxon studies of the clergyman Edward Lye (1694–1767), was added a fascination with ancient 'folk' literature which was presented as offering an imaginative perspective capable of reviving culture. Thomas Gray's poem *The Bard* (1757) played an important role in presenting an alternative to urban and rural restraint. Based on the subsequently discredited Welsh tradition mentioned in Thomas Carte's *History of England* (1750) that the conquering Edward I of England (1272–1307) ordered the execution of all Welsh bards, Gray had been inspired to complete the poem when he heard a Welsh harpist play at Cambridge. His image of the bard or poet was not one of urban poise, but, instead, reflected the importance of picturesque landscape for bardic and primitivist literature:

> On a rock, whose haughty brow
> Frowns o'er old
> Conway's foaming flood,

Robed in the sable garb or woe,
With haggard eyes, the Poete stood;
Loose his beard and hoary hair
Stream'd like a meteor
through the troubled air.

A crucial role in strengthening interest in 'folk' literature was played by a Scottish writer, James Macpherson (1736–96) who touched off an interest and debate throughout Britain. Publishing poems that he claimed to have translated from the Gaelic of a third-century Highland bard called Ossian, Macpherson won fame with his *Fragments of Ancient Poetry Collected in the Highlands of Scotland* (1760). This was followed by *Fingal* (1761), dedicated to George III's Scottish favourite, John, 3rd Earl of Bute, the preface of which proclaimed the superiority of Celtic to Greek heroic poetry, and by *Temora* (1763). These works, in part his own creation, in part based on genuine Gaelic poems and ballads, enjoyed a phenomenal success and made primitivism, especially Romantic symbolism, popular. Aside from the subject, there was a quest for spontaneity, at odds with the balanced character of most contemporary poetry, and this was linked to a departure from pictorial description in favour of what was to be an influential emphasis on what could be termed psychological scenery.[17] The visual arts also paid tribute to Ossian, a large head of whom was the first of John Bacon's sculptures to win notice.

Impressed by Macpherson, Thomas Percy (1729–1811), a grocer's son who sought to show his descent from the medieval Dukes of Northumberland, published *Reliques of Ancient English Poetry* (1765), an edition of old ballads which promoted a revival of interest in the subject: four editions of Percy's *Reliques* had appeared by 1794.[18] He had already published *Five Pieces of Runic Poetry Translated from the Icelandic Language* (1763). As a publisher of ballad collections, Percy was followed by David Herd and Joseph Ritson. Based in Stockton, Ritson (1752–1803) was an example of the vitality of provincial culture and of the extent to which vegetarianism did not necessarily lead to equanimity: he was a particularly virulent critic of Percy. An eager researcher of ballads, Ritson was an active publisher of his findings, his works including a *Select Collection of English Songs* (1783), which contained engravings by William Blake, and a preface on the development of national song. Other works by Ritson included *Gammer Gurton's Garland: or The Nursery Parnassus* (Stockton, 1783), an anthology of nursery rhymes, and *Robin Hood:*

A Collection of all the Ancient Poems, Songs, and Ballads Now Extant Relating to that Celebrated English Outlaw (1795), which was illustrated by Thomas Bewick. Ritson was particularly important for his work on local verse, which led to *Bishopric Garland: or Durham Minstrel* (Durham, 1784), *Yorkshire Garland* (York, 1788), *The North Country Chorister* (Durham, 1792), and *The Northumbrian Garland: or Newcastle Nightingale* (Newcastle, 1793).

'Medievalism' also led to the success of Thomas Chatterton (1752–1770), who invented and wrote the works of a fifteenth-century poet Thomas Rowley, and whose suicide helped span interest in moral judgement with the Romantic cult of doomed youth: he was to be praised by Coleridge, Keats, Shelley and Wordsworth. Enthusiasm for medieval antiquities was developed by William Stukeley (1687–1765), who also played a major role in the growing interest in pre-Roman antiquities: he believed Avebury to be a 'Temple of the British Druids' and laid out such a temple near his home in Grantham.[19] Stukeley's interest in antiquities was both academic in flavour and capable of serving the cause of cultural nationalism, as it asserted the distinctiveness and longevity of a national culture. Interest in the Druids persisted despite Stukeley's views being regarded as unreliably eccentric by his fellow antiquarians from mid-century.

The English were not alone in their interest in folk tales. Also impressed by Ossian, the German philosopher Johann Gottfried Herder (1744–1803), court preacher at Weimar from 1776 until his death, published several collections of German folksongs which he believed important as the root of poetry and a source of national consciousness.

If in England the peasantry appeared less interesting and uplifting as an artistic topic than ancient Celts and medieval Britons, it was also the case that very few peasants became artists enjoying elite patronage. George Crabbe observed in *The Village* (1783)

> Save honest Duck, what son of verse could share
> The poet's rapture and the peasant's care?

Stephen Duck (1705–56), the 'Thresher Poet' and author of *The Thresher's Labour* (1730), was an agricultural labourer who taught himself to read and write. Thanks to the support of the local clergy, he won fame and, in 1730, Queen Caroline's patronage, although he was not a great poet. The 1736 version of his poem, part of a collection of his poetry, was, compared to the 1730 version, more polite in the use of words and somewhat distanced from the experience of work. He was no longer a labourer and, instead, was influenced by Classical norms. In 1746, Duck moved yet further from his origins when he was ordained, and eventually this removal may have led to his early death.[20]

John Bancks or Banks (1709–51), the 'Weaver Poet', failed to emulate Duck's success in winning patronage, but Robert Dodsley (1703–64) made a successful transition from footman-poet to bookshop owner, playwright, and major publisher. In the former role he had come to prominence with *Servitude* (1729) and *A Muse in Livery* (1732). These did not challenge social assumptions: the first was on how footmen should behave. James Woodhouse (1735–1820), a shoemaker poet, owed his advance to the patronage of a nearby landlord, William Shenstone, and in 1764 (reissued 1766), 1788 and 1803 published collections of his poetry. Other works of this type included *Miscellanies in Verse and Prose by John Lucas, Cobler* (1776).

Female plebeian poets included Mary Barber, Mary Leapor, Ann Yearsley and Mary Collier (1688?–1762), the last a Hampshire washerwoman who became a housekeeper on a farm. Collier's *The Woman's Labour* (1739) covered the burdens of working women – childcare, housework and employment. It was in part a reply to Duck's critical depiction of women agrarian workers. Leapor (1722–46), the daughter of a gardener, went into service, eventually at Edgcote House, which she celebrated in her most important poem *Crumble Hall*. She died of measles before the publication by subscription of her poetry, which was much praised, including by David Garrick and Samuel Richardson, reflecting the popularity of poets deemed natural; although it was only recently that she was rescued from the neglect into which her reputation had subsequently fallen.[21] In her poem *Mira's Will*, Leapor gave mock-instructions to her executors, including

> Bestow my Patience to compose the lives
> Of slighted virgins and neglected wives.

Yearsley (1752–1806), a Bristol milkseller educated by Hannah More, published four volumes of poetry, as well as a novel and a play. Her *Poem on the Inhumanity of the Slave Trade* (1788) was an important contribution to abolitionist literature. Yearsley had read Milton's much reprinted *Paradise Lost* and Young's *Night-Thoughts*, an indication of the poetry popularly available.[22]

More significant were the numerous but anonymous individuals who shaped and reshaped folk ballads, passing on traditional tales orally and thus reshaping them at the same time that they created new ones. Many of these ballads were printed as broadsides and in chapbooks, an inexpensive literature aimed at the literate poor, which were also prone to draw on biblical texts. Ballads themselves frequently challenged themes in more established (or socially prominent) literature. Thus, the stress on female delicacy and on politeness in many works was at variance with the presentation of heroines in numerous ballads as female warriors.[23] This literature, in turn, influenced more established literary currents, as writers of literary ballads and ballad operas sought to employ its themes and language.

The success of John Gay's *The Beggar's Opera* (1728) was followed by a decade in which ballad operas enjoyed a vogue on the London stage. Charles Johnson (1679–1748), one of the most active dramatists of the period, some of whose plays drew heavily on earlier works, produced *The Village Opera* in 1729, while, the following year, John Hippesley adapted Thomas Daggett's *The Country Wake* into *Flora: or Hob in the Well*, a comic ballad opera recounting the travails of the somewhat simple Hob. Related, though not identical trends, led to the development of *opera buffa* in Italy, the *opera comique* in France, the *tonadilla* in Spain, the *Singspiel* in Austria, and, from the 1770s, Russian comic opera which employed settings in rural life.

The humble did not only take a role in literature. Thomas Britton, a London coal-seller, painted by Woolaston in his smock with his coal-measure in his hand, organised a musical club that held weekly concerts in his cramped house from 1678 until his death in 1714. These attracted both distinguished performers, professionals and amateurs, including Handel and Pepusch, and an audience including members of the social elite. Britton was also a bibliophile and this brought him into touch with those of the socially prominent who shared his interest, including the Earl of Oxford.

The cultural world described in other chapters was in part brought at the direct expense of the poor, and both urban and rural space was organised in order to reflect the interests of the elite. Stately homes and landscaped parks led in many cases to the movement of settlements, as when the Oxfordshire riverside village of Nuneham Courtenay and its church were destroyed to make way for Earl Harcourt's new Palladian villa and park of Nuneham Courtenay in 1759, although Harcourt did provide the displaced villagers with well-built, spacious houses a mile away. Indeed tenants were usually rehoused in improved cottages, as by Lord Dorchester at Milton Abbas. Nevertheless, the disruption was considerable. The village at Shugborough was bought up and demolished by Thomas Anson between 1731 and 1773 in order to create open parkland in front of the house. To improve the park at Attingham, Tern Mill was demolished in 1787–89, the village of Berwick Maviston was pulled down in 1802, and part of the town of Atcham in 1806. Villages were also swept aside for Bowood, Kedleston, Stowe and Wimpole. Oliver Goldsmith complained in the *Deserted Village* (1770) about the tyrant that had destroyed 'sweet Auburn' village:

> The man of wealth and pride
> Takes up a space that many poor supplied;
> Space for his lake, his park's extended bounds
> Space for his horses, equipage and hounds.

Although a benign account of the countryside drew on the conventional contrast of rural virtue with urban vice, there was also an awareness of rural bleakness and the harshness of nature, as in George Crabbe's poem *The Village* (1783). Based on the author's experience of Suffolk poverty, it was a stark rejoinder to the pastoral and the sentimental:

> Fled are those times, when, in harmonious strains,
> The rustic Poet prais'd his native Plains;
> No Shepherds now in smooth alternative verse,
> Their Country's beauty or their Nymphs' rehearse
>
> ...
>
> I grant indeed that Fields and Flocks have charms,
> For him that gazes or for him that farms;
> But when amid such pleasing scenes I trace
> The poor laborious natives on the place,
> And see the mid-day sun, with fervid ray,
> On their bare heads and dewy temples play;
>
> ...
>
> Then shall I dare these real ills to hide,
> In tinsel trappings of poetic pride?
>
> ...
>
> Theirs is yon House that holds the Parish Poor,
> Whose walls of mud scarce bear the broken door
>
> ...
>
> There Children dwell who know no Parents' care;
> Parents, who know no Children's love, dwell there;

The pictorial quality of Crabbe's account also offered a rejoinder to painters who did not show farm workers suffering from the sun, although some paintings of rural life were scarcely bucolic. The milk-maid in Hogarth's *Evening* (1736) is a faceless worker, going about her mundane task. The walls are of brick not mud in William Redmore Bigg's *A Cottage Interior* (1793), but the face of the woman was that of toil and anxiety, and her figure is scarcely buxomly or Boucheresque. Earlier, in George Farquhar's play *The Beaux' Strategem* (1707), Mrs Sullen had voiced gentler doubts about the portrayal of the countryside:

> Not that I disapprove rural pleasures, as the poets have painted them; in their landscape, every Phyllis has her Corydon, every murmuring Stream, and every flowery mead, gives fresh alarums to love. Besides, you'll find that their couples were never married.

The state of rural society, whether deteriorating or already grim, under pressure from agrarian change, raises the question of the extent to which popular culture as a whole was in a state of crisis due to the demise of traditional rural pastimes that expressed communal solidity under pressure from agrarian reorganisation, as well as from the early signs of Evangelicalism, industrialisation and urbanisation, a process that gathered pace in the early nineteenth century. Such an account draws on the idea of the dichotomy of elite and popular culture, with a growing difference between them as the elite abandoned a shared world view and similar pastimes.

This analysis, however, is overly stark and, to a degree, confuses undoubted changes in fashion with a more problematic, and profound schism. Research on much of the topic is limited, but, in at least some respects, there are signs not only of the vitality of popular culture but also of the continuation or indeed creation of new links spanning social divides. For example, the establishment of large numbers of military bands attached to militia and other volunteer military units brought together elite and populace, with a convergence of musical tastes, not least the dissemination of elite support for wind bands and of the oper-atic repertoire. The tradition of band playing amongst working men developed after the 1757 Militia Act, as militia bandsmen formed a pool of experienced players on which civilian bands could draw.[24] The Church also bridged divides. As a young servant, James Mastin, later a clergyman, was encouraged by his clerical master to develop his skills in writing ballads. Mastin learned psalmody and music and to play the flute and ring the church bells.[25]

If rural society was presented by Goldsmith and Crabbe as a once stable world under pressure and changing in part due to greed, urban life was seen as an inherently unstable pressure-cooker. Low life congregated on the pages of novels, notably Daniel Defoe's *Moll Flanders* (1722) and the works of Fielding, and on the canvases of Hogarth. Sex was clearly a major theme. 'An Essay on the Present State of Music Among the Common People, and the Influence of Bad Music on Their Morals', published in the *Monthly Miscellany* of February 1774, complained about the impact of a generally-underrated cultural form:

> What has made London a sink of filth and wickedness, one monstrous mass of corruption. Why, the ballads that are chanted in every street and lane of the City ... a ballad-singer, standing in the chief place of concourse, with a crowded audience round him, inflaming their appetites and passions, winning his way into their hearts, by means of music often too sweet, and raising at his will the various devils of unbridled lust, shameless lasciviousness, discontent, sedition and unrest.[26]

The verses in question were generally light in tone. For example, the poetry in the *Moral and Political Magazine of the London Corresponding Society* (1796) included 'The Frenchman's Blunder', a work on prostitution and politics, beginning:

> A Frenchman, lately come to town,
> Quite gallant, gay, and debonair,
> Rambling one ev'ning up and down,
> Pick'd up a nymph both frail and fair.[27]

Some novelists sought to catch the note and tempo of the vernacular, as when Fielding, in his *Life of Jonathan Wild* (1743), uses the villain to offer a different manner and tone to that of eulogistic history. *En route* to meeting his beloved Laetitia, Jonathan Wild

> accidentally met with a young lady of his acquaintance, Miss Molly Straddle ... Miss Molly, seeing Mr Wild, stopped him, and with a familiarity peculiar to a genteel town education, tapped, or rather slapped him on the back, and asked him to treat her with a pint of wine at a neighbouring tavern ... the young lady declared she would grant no favour till he had made her a present.

In the dialogue in the novels, the varied ambiguities of speech are repeatedly used by Fielding to sketch character as well as to comic effect.

A very different attempt to capture the vernacular was offered by Wordsworth and Coleridge in their *Lyrical Ballads* (1798). This sought to display a 'prosaic' poetry that would show how far the language used by the bulk of the population could serve the ends of poetry. Wordsworth, in fact, did not live up to this idea. Although sometimes simple, his language remained refined. Instead, the Scottish poet Robert Burns was the innovator in this quarter, melding folksong and 'higher' forms in a language of an acutely varying register. Wordsworth's idea of a 'prosaic' poetry was far less influential on contemporaries than it was to become subsequently. It reflected, however, the situation of cultural and political flux at the close of the century.

7

Books and Newspapers

We must read what the world reads at the moment. It has been maintained that this superfoetation, this teeming of the press in modern times, is prejudicial to good literature, because it obliges us to read so much of what is of inferiour value, in order to be in the fashion; so that better works are neglected for want of time, because a man will have more gratification of his vanity in conversation, from having read modern books, than from having read the best works of antiquity. But it must be considered, that we have now more knowledge generally diffused; all our ladies read now, which is a great extension. Modern writers are the moons of literature; they shine with reflected light, with light borrowed from the ancients.

Samuel Johnson opining over dinner at Allan Ramsay's, 29 April 1778, as reported by James Boswell.

The culture of print expanded in both scale and variety during the century. Most of the means by which new ideas and works were diffused, such as books, newspapers and engravings, were far from new, but they became more insistent in English culture and society. The lapse in 1695 of the Licensing Act, which required publications to have approval prior to their appearance, was followed by the spread of provincial printing, hitherto in England and Wales limited to Cambridge and Oxford. The first press in Exeter was founded in 1698 and the first long-lasting one in Cornwall in 1753, although in some towns the first printer did not appear until later, in Bedford not until Bartholomew Hyatt, first mentioned only in 1766.[1] As a result of the spread of printing, books began to be published in many towns by provincial booksellers, the first in Chichester, *An Easy Introduction to the English Grammar*, appearing in 1770. The Eighteenth-Century Short Title Catalogue has revealed considerable activity outside London, although the metropolis dominated the world of print.[2] Benjamin Collins of Salisbury printed more than thirty works. The Act had also limited the right to print in London to the master printers of the Stationers Company of London, while only four founders of type were permitted, and the number of apprentices, journeymen and presses per printer was regulated. All this was swept away.

The presses not only brought out more, but also different types of books and newspapers. The century saw the first daily, Sunday and provincial papers. Thanks to the expansion of both London and provincial circulations, total sales of newspapers rose. An idea of the local impact of the press can be gauged from the notice in *Swinney's Birmingham and Stafford Chronicle* of 11 April 1776: 'Through the neglect of the London carrier, we are under the necessity of printing upwards of two thousand of this day's publication on unstamped paper'. Excluding London, the number of English newspapers rose from about 24 in 1723, 32 in 1753 and 35 in 1760, to 50 in 1782, and continued thereafter to expand. On 1799, the first number of *Portsmouth Telegraph; or Mottley's Naval and Military Journal* appeared. The total annual sale of newspapers in England was about 2.5 million in 1713, and about 14 million in 1780. This expansion provided plentiful work, most of it poorly paid, and many literary figures wrote for newspapers and journals, including Addison, Fielding, Goldsmith, Johnson, Steele and Swift. They had to match their style and content to the journal for which they wrote, but their ability to do so reflected the partisanship that linked the overlapping worlds of literature and journalism.[3]

The development of the press encouraged the spread of a regular, wide-ranging and responsive world of printed news and opinion. Much of this was political. Delarivier Manley's novel *The Secret History of Queen Zarah and the Zarazians* (1705), an attack on the 1st Duke of Marlborough and, in particular, on his wife Sarah, claimed:

> The youth of that country, encouraged by their parents' examples, aspire to be Privy Counsellors before they get rid of the rod of their schoolmasters; and apprentice boys assume the air of statesmen before they have learned the mystery of trade. Mechanics of the meanest rank plead for a liberty to abuse their betters.

Readers of newspapers provided a ready subject for dramatists, whether Politic and Dabble in Fielding's *Rape upon Rape* (1730)[4] or Dangle in Sheridan's *The Critic* (1779). It was not only politics that was debated in the world of print. Critical artistic journalism also became important. The *Tatler*, a tri-weekly periodical that appeared in 1709–11, written by Steele and Addison, included discussion of poetry. It was succeeded by the *Spectator* (1711–12), also edited by Steele and Addison, an influential work that was reprinted in bound editions at least fifty times during the century, and that helped establish the essay as a form of authoritative commentary. Essay journals varied greatly in their popularity and impact, but Johnson's essays in the *Rambler* (1750–52) and the *Idler* (1758–60) helped to strengthen the prominence of the format. Reviews, such as the *Critical Review* (1756–63) and the *British Magazine*, guided book purchasers, and thus helped to define the market and to interpret and shape taste.

Reviewing also provided a way for writers to be introduced to the world of publishers. Michael de la Roche's *New Memoirs of Literature: Containing an Account of New Books ... at Home and Abroad* (1725–27) provided not only criticism of works but also full details of their particulars: title, place of publication, price, size and other details. Interest was not restricted to British works, the *Flying-Post* of 1723 offering extracts from the *Bibliothèque Germanique*, while the *Weekly Miscellany* printed regular accounts of new Continental books in the 1730s.

Critical reviews were not only published in the capital. One launched in Birmingham in 1775 cost 2½ d. an issue:

Theatrical exhibitions, as they afford the most rational entertainments, have also a forcible influence on the manners of a people. In all ages, and in all nations, encouragement of the drama has been proportionate to the progress of civilization. It is therefore a matter of no small moment, that the generality of mankind may not be misled in those places where vice and folly are to be exposed to just contempt, or that their taste should be vitiated by undue representations. For these reasons, a society of gentlemen have agreed to lay before the public, every Saturday, a paper entitled the *Theatrical Critique*; in which the most inviolable impartiality will be maintained with respect to the pieces represented, and the respective merits of each actor of both houses. Their applause will be conferred without reluctance, and their censure without timidity, on those only who deserve them. If then directing the judgment, to meliorate the morals, to affect the heart, and to refine the taste, are objects worthy the attention of the public, they flatter themselves with the approbation, to which, by their unwearied efforts, they will endeavour to demonstrate the justness of their claim. Those who are well versed in these matters, will be pleased to see their own ideas arranged with methodical propriety, while the unskillful will be enabled to adjust their notions of theatrical merit with precision, and be prevented from lavishing their unmeaning and random praises, or casting unjust and illiberal reflexions.[5]

The *Bath and Bristol Magazine,* which included poetry and literary reviews, followed in 1776.

Magazines had an impact across the cultural world. Books started to appear as parts in magazines, and the *Gentleman's Magazine* also printed songs. Daniel Defoe's *Moll Flanders* was serialised in the *London Post* in 1720–23;[6] Tobias Smollett published *The Life and Adventures of Sir Launcelot Greaves* in the *British Magazine* (1760–61) which he edited; and Oliver Goldsmith's *Memoirs of M. de Voltaire* appeared in the *Lady's Magazine* from February to November 1761.

Not only books were reviewed. Music journalism developed in response to the increase in public interest in music. It provided a forum for a stylistic debate that opposed new operatic forms to the dominant *opera seria,* a world of Classical mythology, serious heroism, and solemn music brought to life in London by Italian singers. The role of music as a moral force was also debated. For the theatre, *Cotes's Weekly Journal: or The English Stage-Player* appeared in 1734, providing both news and plays.

Cultural matters were not only debated in the specialist press, but were also considered in general London and provincial newspapers, and theatrical news became a regular feature of the ordinary press. The sheer amount of space devoted to theatre is very striking. Newspapers did not hesitate to tell their readers what they ought to think of particular plays and of the purpose of theatre. On 17 April 1787, the *Morning Chronicle* criticised the production of the tragedy *Julia:* 'On Saturday evening, it was half an hour after nine o'clock before the curtain dropped, after the Epilogue was delivered; nine o'clock ought to be the period of conclusion'. The following year, the advertisements for the daily London evening paper, the *Star* offered 'the occurrences of the present day ... drama and the opera and every fashionable place of public amusement'.

At times, the discussion was distinctly lacking in critical discrimination, possibly because many printers were also booksellers. On 23 February 1728, James Ralph's recent work was pushed hard by Andrew Brice in his paper *Brice's Weekly Journal:*

The celebrated poem entitled *Night,* whereof a small specimen was some time since given in this paper, is now published, and may be had of the

printer, hereof, price 18*d*. it being esteemed by the most competent judges
one of the finest performances of its kind ever published in the English
tongue, not Milton's himself excepted, most of whose beauties, elegances,
and sublimity, it comprehends, but none of his defects. In short, its truly
Homer in a nut-shell; and will charm any reader of polite good sense, and
who has any gust of poetry, to an hundred times, perusal.

Most books that were pushed were published in London, but there was
also a degree of provincial identity: a study of the Newcastle press has
argued that it created a 'distinctive and influential regional platform for
the exchange of ideas about cultural value', and that more was at stake
than emulating developments in London.[7] The press certainly provided
plenty of space for local poets. In 1727, 'Cassio' sent *Mist's Weekly Journal* a love poem in February as he expected springtime wars to crowd
the paper later.[8] Much of the poetry was weak: cloyingly sentimental or
dependent on puns or unfunny rhymes. John Delap, an unsuccessful
clerical playwright, whose tragedy *The Captives* failed in March 1786, was
mocked as follows:

> How hard is your hap,
> Poor Doctor Delap,
> To receive such a slap,
> When you wish'd for a clap,
> Indeed, my old Chap,
> Your Tragedy sap
> Is no better than pap;
> Then take off, Delap,
> Your Ossian scrap,
> And let Smith no more nap
> In fair Siddons's lap,
> Or you'll meet with, mayhap,
> Another damn'd rap,
> That will Split your square cap.[9]

The content and tone of books reflected more developed views on
taste. The rise of the novel can best be seen as an important instance
of the embourgeoisement of culture, although only if that is regarded
as a matter of patronage more than content. Earlier, there had been
an emphasis by authors on seeking the support of individual patrons,
presented as crucial protectors, and therefore as responsible for the
cultural health of the nation. In practice, patronage from such patrons
could indeed make it easier for authors to deal with publishers and

could provide some funds, but there was also a wider social position-ing, noted by Fielding in the preface to his *Historical Register for the Year 1736*, which was dedicated to the public, whereas, he noted for his publisher:

> What, says he, does more service to a book or raises curiosity in a reader equal with 'dedicated to his Grace the Duke of —', or 'the Right Hon-ourable the Earl of —' in an advertisement? I think the patron here may properly be said to give a name to the book.[10]

Novels, in contrast, created and responded to a large readership, and were not dependent on a distinguished list of subscribers, or on politi-cal patronage. Fielding's *Joseph Andrews* sold 6500 copies in 1742. In contrast, the more rarified appeal of epics, and therefore their lower potential sales, were not compatible with the commercial literary cli-mate. The need to secure the patronage of the public to ensure the success of novels created an additional reason to emphasise reviews. An advertisement in *Swinney's Birmingham and Stafford Chronicle* of 19 May 1791 for *The History of Sir Geoffrey Restless and his Brother Charles* noted that it was by the author of *The Trifler* and that 'The *Critical Review* for July 1777, in speaking of the *Trifler* has the following words ...' The role and variety of reviews led Sheridan to note in his play *The Critic*: 'puffing is of various sorts; the principal are, the puff direct, the puff preliminary, the puff collateral, the puff collusive, and the puff oblique, or puff by implication'.

Sales were not the sole means by which novels secured the market. In addition, the growth of circulation, proprietary and subscription libraries, as well as the serial publication of books, permitted those who could not afford to purchase them to read them. A new public library opened in Bristol in 1740, and the first English circulating library in 1757, and there were about one thousand such libraries by the end of the cen-tury. The first of the many proprietary libraries, whose members owned shares, was the Liverpool Library, formed in 1758: membership was already 140 in 1758, 300 by 1770, and over 400 by 1799. Between 1758 and 1800, the library acquired an average of almost 200 books annually.[11] Proprietary libraries followed in Warrington (1760), Manchester (1765), Leeds (1768), Sheffield (1771), Hull (1775) and Birmingham (1779). In Norwich, the Public Library, in fact a private subscription library, was established in 1784. Towns offered their potential readers institutional choices: in Kendal, where a book club was formed in 1761, a newsroom followed in 1779, a subscription library in 1794, and an 'Economical Library' for the less affluent in 1797.

Libraries provided opportunity not only to read but also to meet and socialise, including for cards, dances and concerts. Book clubs, such as that at Spalding, also had social purposes.[12] In 1760, the first circulating library in Brighton was established, the founder Edmund Baker, a Tunbridge Wells bookseller and bookbinder, adding a rotunda in 1762 as a bandstand. This was an instructive instance of the range of activities of the individual entrepreneurs of culture, and thus of the need to be cautious in separating out the individual arts for analysis.[13] In Margate, William Garner, the owner of the Marine Library, was also a leading actor at the Theatre Royal in the 1790s.

In most towns, competition rapidly followed the establishment of the first library. In his *Diary Kept on an Excursion to Little Hampton, near Arundel, and Brighthelmston [Brighton], in Sussex, in 1778: and Also to the Latter Place in 1779* (1780), Peregrine Phillips commented on the constant struggle between the libraries, and upon their popularity and fashionability: 'The company encreases fast, and is very genteel'.[14] Judged by library catalogues, history, biography and travels were particularly popular. Aside from libraries, the number of bookshops increased. In the second half of the century, Derby usually had four booksellers. London, however, dominated the world of publishing and bookselling. It is not simply a contrivance of the plot that has Fielding in *Joseph Andrews* send Parson Adams to London in order to get his nine volumes of sermons published.

The spread of libraries, bookshops and printers helped encourage not only the dissemination of national works but also local ones. In 1783, Bennett Jaques, a Chichester printer, printed William Hayley's *Ode to Mr Wright of Derby*, following in 1784 with Charlotte Smith's *Elegiac Sonnets*. Chichester-born Hayley, a landowner who lived in Sussex, was an active poet and playwright, who ranged from an *Elegy on the Ancient Greek Model* (1779) to *The Two Connoisseurs: A Comedy* (1785) and *The Happy Prescription: or The Lady Relieved from her Lovers* (1785). His publications indicated the non-exclusive nature of the relationship between London and the provinces: most appeared in London, not least his most popular poem *The Triumphs of Temper* (1781), but some in Chichester. Hayley in turn gave Charlotte Smith her crucial start into print: the *Elegiac Sonnets* were dedicated to him and printed at Chichester.

Far from conforming to a common tone, form or intention, novels varied greatly in content and approach, a trend encouraged by the size and diversity of the reading public. The rise of the novel was for a long time discussed in terms of the works of Daniel Defoe, Samuel Richardson and Henry Fielding, but this neglected what was a far greater range of early novels, many written by women, and, in doing so, misleadingly simplified the origins of the genre. Although English writers played the key role in its eighteenth-century development, there were important seventeenth-century precursors, including Cervantes's *Don Quixote*, and indeed a range of literary types that the novel looked to, including picaresque tales, travel books and romances. The latter were particularly important in England in the early eighteenth century, such that a novel then was a short story of romantic love, for example Eliza Haywood's successful *Love in Excess* (1719–20).

The common feature of the early novels of these decades was their claim to realism. This can be seen in Defoe's *Robinson Crusoe* (1719), *Colonel Jack* (1721), *Moll Flanders* (1722), *A Journal of the Plague Year* (1722) and *Roxana* (1724). Their subjects were very different and they looked back to varied influences – *Robinson Crusoe* to travel literature and spiritual autobiography, *Colonel Jack*, *Moll Flanders* and *Roxana* to picaresque tales – but the common theme in these alleged autobiographies was authenticity, and they had affinities with criminal biographies, a very popular genre. The romantic tales, such as those of Haywood, also claimed to be accounts of real life and manners, while the most distinctive novelistic account, Swift's *Gulliver's Travels* (1726), proclaimed itself a true account.

Gulliver's Travels' combination of traveller's tale, picaresque novella and satire proved inimitable, and there was little development in prose fiction until Samuel Richardson's first novel, *Pamela* (1740), a very popular book on the prudence of virtue and the virtue of prudence, with the title continuing *or Virtue Rewarded*. The appeal of the novel reflected in part its ability to span sexual frisson with clear morality, to move from page-turning perils for Pamela to a happy ending, and to employ the form of letters in order to provide the sympathetic insight of the heroine. Pamela, a young maidservant, resists the lascivious advances of Mr B, in part thwarting attempted rapes by fainting at opportune moments. In the end, a realisation of Pamela's virtues and an appreciation of her virtue leads him to propose marriage, thus fulfilling the fantasy of social aspiration: Pamela marries her employer. The importance of writings to the structure and form of the novel was seen not only with the letters but also because the theft of Pamela's journal leads Mr B to this appreciation. *Pamela*'s content and success invited skits and parody, especially Fielding's satirical *An Apology for the Life of Mrs Shamela Andrews* (1741) and his *Joseph Andrews* (1742), as well as James Dance's comedy *Pamela* (1742). John Cleland employed the epistolary style of *Pamela* in his pornographic novel *Memoirs of a Woman of Pleasure* (1749), otherwise known as *Fanny Hill.* Thus, the novels of the 1740s displayed considerable diversity in content.

A common theme, however, was psychological accuracy. Richardson's narratives sought to reveal the detailed workings of the human heart. They were composed of letters, which allowed him to vary the tone by using different styles for his writers; and helped give *Pamela* an impetus and an urgency matching the plot of virtue vying with seduction, while Fielding insisted that his novels were 'true histories' in that they revealed the truth of behaviour, an approach especially suited to the ironic voice he adopted as narrator, comparable also to that he had also taken in his plays, such as *Tom Thumb* (1730). Thus, in the last chapter of *Joseph Andrews* 'this true history is brought to a happy conclusion'. History indeed frequently appeared in the title of novels, as in James Ridley's *The History of James Lovegrove, Esquire* (1761).

While novels sought to be true histories, conversely, historical writing was supposed to capture character, the anonymous *Reflections on Ancient and Modern History* (Oxford, 1746) praising Classical writers because of 'that nice discernment of the several lines and features of human nature, which are so strongly expressed in all the characters, throughout their histories'.[15] The Classical account of history was challenged, however, by Sarah Fielding in *The Lives of Cleopatra and Octavia* (1757), with her female protagonists returning to tell their tales and to claim the spotlight from a traditionally male-dominated narrative.

History did not only offer character out of interest. There was also the presentation of history as a morally exemplary tale, which brought history, novels and the theatre together. Far from being differentiated, the relationship of history or politics and morality was strongly focused because of the obvious political importance of a small number of individuals and because of the notion of kingship and governance as moral activities. The anonymous writer of the *Reflections on Ancient and Modern History* complained in 1746 that 'with modern writers everything is either vice or virtue'.[16] As the relationship appeared timeless, it seemed pertinent to apply admonitory tales in a modern context, as with the comparisons of Sir Robert Walpole indiscriminately with Charles I's favourite Buckingham, Henry VIII's Wolsey and Tiberius's Sejanus, and the equivalent use of historical examples on stage. Belief that history possessed a cyclical quality contributed to this, as time was not held to compromise the moral power of Classical exemplars.

Furthermore, the stress on personal drives, rather than on social, economic or institutional or geo-political forces, ensured that in history, as in literature, the emphasis was on personality and narrative. Elizabeth Montagu claimed in 1762, 'Few people know anything of the English history but what they learn from Shakespeare; for our story is rather a tissue of personal adventures and catastrophes than a series of political events'.[17] In both history and novels, there was an emphasis on individual free-will, not determinism, in short a world that was best understood in moral terms and where there was no sense of changing moral standards. Indeed the novel offered for ordinary people the guidance outlined in the London newspaper the *Test* on 12 February 1757:

> The mechanism of government is too intricate and subtle, in all its various motions, for a common eye to perceive the nice dependencies and the secret springs, that give play to the complex machinery; and, in consequence, the generality of people while the great political movements are passing before them, are full of undiscerning astonishment, and only gaze on in expectation of the event. Afterwards indeed when the historian gives his narrative of facts, when he rejudges the actions of the great, and, from the ends which they had in view, and the means by which they pursued those ends, ascertains the colour of their characters, then the minds of men are opened, and they perceive honour and conquest, or disappointment and disgrace naturally following one another, like necessary effects from their apparent respective causes.

The different styles of Richardson and Fielding helped energise novel-writing as they encouraged debate as to best practice, while both had their imitators. With its emphasis on the female plight and perspective, Richardson looked forward to the sentimental novel, as did his stress on an appropriate gentlemanly behaviour. This was an important aspect of the role of the novel as instructional fiction.

The novel as the true depiction of life was taken a stage further in Laurence Sterne's very popular *The Life and Opinions of Tristram Shandy, Gentleman* (1760–67). As the first-person narrator, he presented the confusion of perception in a fashion that extended to the appearance of the book. Volume nine, chapter 25 of this is as follows:

> When we have got to the end of this chapter (but not before) we must all turn back to the two blank chapters, on the account of which my honour has lain bleeding this half hour – I stop it, by pulling off one of my yellow slippers and throwing it with all my violence to the opposite side of my room, with a declaration at the heel of it –
>
> – That whatever resemblance it may bear to half the chapters which are written in the world, or for aught I know may be now writing in it – that it was as casual as the foam of Zeuxis his horse: besides, I look upon a chapter which has, *only nothing in it*, with respect; and considering what worse things there are in the world – That it is no way a proper substitute for satire –
>
> – Why then was it left so? And here without staying for my reply, shall I be called as many blockheads, numskulls, doddypoles, dunderheads, ninnyhammers, goosecaps, jolt-heads, nincompoops, sh-t-a-beds – and other unsavoury appellations, as ever the cake-bakers of Lerné, cast in the teeth of King Gargantua's shepherds – And I'll let them do it, as Bridget said, as much as they please; for how was it possible they should foresee the necessity I was under of writing the 25th chapter of my book, before the 18th, etc?
>
> – So I don't take it amiss – All I wish is, that it may be a lesson to the world '*to let people tell their stories their own way*'.

The freedom of writing in this novel was arresting, but so also was another source of uncertainty: the abandonment of the omniscient narrator with panoptic vision, able apparently to manipulate events and characters as he or she chose. Instead, in *Tristram Shandy*, Sterne presents the story as if the novelist has only an uncertain grip on events, characters and, indeed, perception. Clearly-delineated episodes are tossed hither and thither in a sea of whimsical chaos. His arresting approach was much imitated, at least up to the 1790s.

Tristram Shandy contained sentimental scenes, but the sentimental novel was a more fully-fledged type that was particularly influential in the 1760s and 1770s, and popular across Europe, with love-intrigues playing a role in novels such as Frances Brooke's *The History of Emily Montague* (1769). Her use of the term 'history', which to contemporaries meant narrative, seen also in her *The History of Julia Mandeville* (1763), remained typical in the presentation of the genre. Such novels were particularly designed for women, as was noted in an advertisement in the

25 April 1776 issue of *Swinney's Birmingham and Stafford Chronicle* for 'Isabella: or The Rewards of Good-Nature. A Sentimental Novel.* Intended chiefly to convey united amusements and instruction to the fair sex'.

Sentimentality and history joined novels to another important, but underrated, art form of the period, gossip. Indeed, especially with the epistolary novels, there was a note of appropriate, if not exemplary, gossip in their themes and tone. History, novels and gossip all offered accounts of individuals and thus focused on how best to understand and represent individuality, not least with reference to social norms.[18]

Sentimental novels required a commitment from narrator and reader that was very different in tone and consequences to the ironic authorial distancing of Fielding, or the undercutting shifting of perspective of Smollett. As yet further evidence of how the possibilities of the novel developed qualities and forms of imagination, the sentimental novel was also taken in a distinctive direction in the Gothic novel, which put sentimental characters and themes under particular strain, and largely omitted the explicit love intrigues of sentimental fiction, sublimating them into more extreme desires and threats. The Gothic novel, of which the most influential exemplar was Horace Walpole's *The Castle of Otranto* (1764), departed from the existing conventions of the novel, not least by breaking with the emphasis on realism. Indeed, Walpole deliberately emphasised the need to employ 'fancy', and, as the plot lines amply demonstrated, this was repeatedly done in Gothic novels. Walpole had visited Naples in 1740 as part of his Grand Tour, but did not travel on to Otranto. In 1786, when Lady Craven gave Walpole a drawing of the castle, the delighted Walpole responded, 'I did not even know that there was a castle of Otranto'; the book's descriptions of the castle and its environs indeed are extremely sparse. This was far from Johnson's sense of novels as displaying 'life in its true state'. Boswell recorded that Walpole was not one of Johnson's 'true admirers', while Johnson 'allowed that he got together a great many curious little things, and told them in an elegant manner'.

A painterly equivalent to the Gothic novel was provided by Joshua Reynolds's *Ugolino and his Children in the Dungeon* (1773), a dramatic history painting based on an episode in Dante's *Inferno*, in which the imprisoned count has to decide to starve to death or to eat his similarly imprisoned sons and grandsons when they die. When exhibited at the Royal Academy, this caused a stir comparable to that of Walpole's novel. The Gothic novel was often about foreignness, and the psychological and real threats it posed, and this was an aspect of a more general presentation of the outside world. Difficult individuals in novels were often foreign, as with the wilful Sicilian protagonists of John Moore's first novel *Zeluco: Various Views of Human Nature, Taken from Life and Manners, Foreign and Domestic* (1786).

Dr Johnson claimed that novels showed 'life in its true state'. In part, this reflected the extent to which the Romantic focus on the exalting character of the imagination, and on its ability to endow some literature (art, music etc.) with great quality, had not been anticipated in any measure in the first half of the century. Instead, the ideas and assumptions associated with Romanticism were all largely innovations of the period of eighteenth-century expression termed the sublime, of which the Gothic novel was a key product. The Romantic focus on the imagination was to overturn the role of earlier rules in establishing merit, and to separate literature from other writings, This creates problems for modern readings of the century as a whole, some of which overly reflect the focus and priorities of Romanticism.

By the end of the century, about 150 novels, ninety of them new, were being published annually, and, indeed, in his piece on 'Modern Novels' in the *Annual Register* of 1797 George Colman the Younger referred to the 'small fry of scribblers' wriggling 'through the mud in shoals'. Many of the novels themselves were multi–volume: Jenny Warton's *Peggy and Patty: or The Sisters of Ashdale* offered four volumes of sentimentality. The extent of the market was indicated by the frequency with which the financially embarrassed Charlotte Smith published novels. Having translated Prévost's *Manon Lescaut* (1785), she brought out from 1788 a series of sentimental novels reflecting love of nature. The success of her first, the four-volume *Emmeline: or The Orphan of the Castle* (1788) led her to write the five-volume *Ethelinde: or The Recluse of the Lake* (1790), the four-volume *Celestina* (1792), the three-volume *Desmond* (1793), the four-volume *Old Manor House* (1793), and the four-volume *The Banished Man* (1794). Her other novels included *The Young Philosopher* (1798) and *The Solitary Wanderer* (1799): the former included among its notes of pathos, a scene of losing a daughter in London and another of madness, the latter a frequent theme of such novels.

That the writings of many (but by no means all) were published was part of a major expansion in publishing, in which individual works vied for attention. In *Gulliver's Travels* (1726), Swift noted 'that writers of travels, like dictionary-makers are sunk into oblivion by the weight and bulk of those who come last'. As there were few technical innovations, profitability depended on increased sales, and publishers such as William Strahan in London, producing sizeable editions, had to be sensitive to the market. The Edinburgh-born Strahan (1715–85) was publisher to many of the greats of the age, including Blackstone, Blair, Gibbon, Hume, Johnson, Robertson and Smith. He made a lot of money and became an MP. Like Robert Dodsley (1703–64), who published Akenside, Goldsmith, Gray, Johnson, Pope and Shenstone among others, Strahan indicated how publishers played a dynamic role helping shape individuals works and major projects. Indeed Dodsley played a key role in Johnson's *Dictionary* as well as producing literary anthologies.[19] To boost sales, publishers found it sensible to produce accessible editions of texts. James Bruce's five-volume travelogue was published in an abridged version from 1790.

The profits to be gained from the growing market encouraged a slow process of differentiation within the trade in which the role of publisher was in part separated from that of bookseller. It also led some publishers, encouraged by the weakness of the Copyright Act for the Encouragement of Learning of 1710, to produce pirate editions, part of the Grub Street free-for-all satirised by Fielding in his play *The Author's Farce and the Pleasures of the Town* (1730). Thomas Johnson did so for some of Pope's works, including his translation of *Iliad*. Later, Pope had to cope with piracy by James Watson.

Booksellers and libraries also encouraged and benefited from the growth in readership, and there was often an overlap, with individuals serving as all or two of publishers, booksellers and librarians. Thomas Lockett, a Dorset printer and bookseller, listed items for sale in his printing shop in 1788 including

> Books that will improve the Mind
> Novels for the Young and Old,
> Pretty stories, roundly told.
> ...
> but also medicines, paints and newspapers.[20]

The publication of plays provided another area of opportunity that extended the market and also provided profit for playwrights. James Moore was given £100 for the right to publish his comedy *The Rival Modes* (1727), which went through three editions that year.

The growth of the reading public did not only bring profit to publishers and booksellers. It also affected literature. In the field of history, authors such as Edward Gibbon, David Hume and William Robertson, and hack writers such as Richard Rolt, were able to write for a large and immediate readership, producing a clearly commercial product, in contrast to the Classical model of history for the benefit of friends and a posthumous public. Gibbon and Robertson both made substantial sums, and attempts were made to raise the dignity of writers. This was exemplified by Johnson, who lived by his pen, including for writing periodicals, but was determined to break with the pejorative connotations of writing for Grub Street. Johnson's rejection in 1755 of the Earl of Chesterfield's attempt to patronise his *Dictionary* was an affirmation of the value of authorship, as well as a testimony to the diligent effort involved in writing: 'Seven years . . . during which time I have been pushing on my work through difficulties of which it is useless to complain'. In the preface he noted that the *Dictionary* was written 'without any patronage of the great'. The work itself established the author as the man who fixed the language, not least by excluding fashionable words.

Authorship was further enhanced by Johnson's careful criticism of fifty-two writers in the *Lives of the Poets* (1779–1781), which helped establish the national literary heritage.[21] The value of authorship, however, was unstable and moulded by the developing pressures of the commercial world, a process captured by the issues of copyright and the relationship between authors and publishers, and sometimes focused by questions of book piracy (unauthorised publication), plagiarism and forgery.[22] These reflected the drive to probe and profit from market opportunities. In number 101 of the *Tatler*, Richard Steele complained about booksellers selling cheap reprints: 'These miscreants are a set of wretches we authors call pirates, who print any book, poem, or sermon, as soon as it appears in the world, in a smaller volume: and sell it, as all other thieves do stolen goods, at a cheaper rate'. Understandable from the perspective of an author, this view said little on behalf of the drive to expand the market. Relations between authors and booksellers were frequently poor. In 1762, Samuel Foote parodied the Irish bookseller George Faulkner as Peter Paragraph in his successful play *The Orators*.

The development of the market encouraged the appearance of numerous historical works. For example John Bancks or Banks (1709–51) wrote lives of Christ, Cromwell, Peter the Great, Marlborough, Prince Eugene and William III, a history of the Habsburgs, as well as poetry, and played a major role in two leading opposition London newspapers. Local history was also a field that expanded, in part drawing on the widespread interest in antiquarianism. Antiquarians such as Thomas Tanner, Edmund Gibson and William Stukely all wrote the chronology and narrative of the places they studied: making sense of the past really meant putting events in their order. William Hutton, who opened the first circulating library in Birmingham, published a well-received *History of Birmingham* (1781), as well as *The Battle of Bosworth* (1788), *A Dissertation on Juries* (1789), a *History of the Hundred Courts* (1790), and *A History of Derby* (1791).[23]

Much English history lacked intellectual subtlety and philosophical profundity. It could, however, be suggested that the vigour of the writing and the clarity of the prejudices expressed meant that these works were more attuned to popular attitudes than those of some of the more famous historians of the period. More typical than the self-consciously enlightened writers who were subsequently to gain attention was the anticlericalism and xenophobia of Richard Rolt (1725?–70). Dependent on his works for a living, Rolt adopted a polemical style and a didactic method, as in *The Lives of the Principal Reformers, Both Englishmen and Foreigners, Comprehending the General History of the Reformation: From its Beginning in 1360, by Dr John Wickliffe, to its Establishment in 1600 under Queen Elizabeth. With an Introduction; Wherein the Reformation is Amply Vindicated and its Necessity Fully Shown From the Degeneracy of the Clergy, and the Tyranny of the Popes* (1759). In this, and in other books, Rolt presented religious freedom and liberty as inseparable. A feeling of struggle, of embattled values, characterises his work: Protestantism had to be fought for.

Earlier works by Rolt had been marked by a similar feeling of struggle, directed against France, which was presented as the 'natural enemy' of Britain. In response, Rolt called for a revival of ancient virtues, arguing that national strength depended upon public culture – the liberty and religion of the people, rather than on the size of the armed forces or other criteria. Liberty and religion were in turn reliant upon the moral calibre of the people and this was threatened by subversion encouraged by ministerial corruption. Rolt indeed claimed that France had once enjoyed a constitution and 'happiness' similar to Britain's.[24] This had been lost, a point which underlined the fragility of the British constitution and the need for continued vigilance. Just as the Saxons had been 'effeminated' by Catholicism,[25] so could the British be by a variety of factors, and, in the *Memoirs of the Life of ... John Lindesay, Earl of Crawford* (1753), Rolt bewailed that the nobility, in contrast to his subject and hero, had lost their martial skills; Crawford indeed was a Scot. In common with many writers, especially those of an opposition or critical disposition, Rolt regarded the Glorious Revolution of 1688 as no more than a stage along the road. In this perspective, the Revolutionary Settlement could not prevent threats, and the price of political and religious liberty was eternal vigilance.

Oppressed by a corrupt present, and seeking to show that it represented an unnecessary aberration, Rolt – like other writers – looked back to a glorious past, especially to the reign of Queen Elizabeth I. In 1756, when he jointly edited *The Universal Visiter and Memoralist*, he published a poem in it beginning 'Illustrious Raleigh! Britain's noblest friend'. Elizabeth was greatly praised in Rolt's work for her defence of Protestantism, her vigorous foreign policy, and the challenge to Spain's position in the Americas. Elizabeth was an acceptable counterpoint to the Whig hero, William III, and those in the 1730s who opposed the erection of a statue to him in Bristol wanted one for Elizabeth. She was also an 'alternative' to Queen Anne and her foreign policy a contrast to those of Marlborough and Walpole. Elizabeth was English, a key moulder of the Church of England, had apparently ensured that foreign policy had served national goals, and was sufficiently historical to prove both uncontroversial and malleable, without being so ancient as to offer only tenuous parallels to the present, as was the case with pre-Reformation monarchs such as Edward III. At a time of national humiliation in the early stages of the Seven Years' War, the *Monitor*, a leading London newspaper, in its issue of 26 November 1757, asked, 'Who can forget the days when Elizabeth out of her cabinet gave laws to all Europe: set the captives free and of a distressed state made them High and Mighty?'

The feeling that the national position, its constitution, liberty, international security and religion were all under threat accounts for Rolt's views on the didactic purposes of history: he argued that it revealed the threats challenging the nation, and the fate that would befall the island if vigilance was lost. Rolt ended his life of Archbishop Cranmer, burnt under Queen Mary, by stating that her reign 'ought to be transmitted down to posterity, in characters of blood, as her persecution was the most terrible that raged since the time of Diocletian'.[26] Rolt was quite clear that history should be didactic: 'It was not the true intent of history so much to load the memory of the reader with a copious collection of public records, as it is to elevate his thoughts and enrich his understanding'.[27]

Rolt was not alone in his concerns. The Nonconformist London minister Samuel Chandler wrote a preface to a translation of Limborch's *History of the Inquisition*:

> There being, as I apprehend, no way so proper to expose the doctrine and practice of persecution, as by a fair representation of the unspeakable mischiefs that have been occasioned by it; nor any other method so likely to render it the universal abhorrence of mankind, as to let them see, by past examples what miseries they must expect, if God should ever, for our sins, subject us again to the yoke of ecclesiastical power; which, wherever 'tis not kept under strict restraint, will usurp upon the authority and dignity of princes, and trample under foot all the civil and religious liberties of mankind.[28]

Chandler's preface led to controversy. An Anglican cleric, William Berriman, published a criticism in 1733 which led to three replies by Chandler in 1733–34, collected as a *History of Persecution* (1736). For Chandler, the battle against Catholicism was central to national identity, culture, and interest. Ten editions of his *Great Britain's Memorial against the Pretender and Popery* (1745) appeared during the '45. This clear sense of history made present by the Catholic threat – of historical writings firmly located in contemporary ideological suppositions by their anti-Catholicism – did not cease with the collapse of Jacobitism. In 1769, Edward Lewis, an Oxfordshire rector, published *The Patriot King: Displayed in the Life of Henry VIII, King of England, from the Time of his Quarrel with the Pope till his Death*, a violently anti-Catholic work.

History, like other countries, offered a vista of possible developments for England, and, if that was a frightening perspective, this was claimed to be part of its educational value. This value, frequently in practice partisan, was often presented directly in the titles of works, as in the 1713 pamphlet on the overweening ambition of great men, *The Life of Edward Seymour, Duke of Somerset, Lord General, and Lord Protector ... With Some Parallel Instances to the Case of John Duke of M-h [Marlborough], Late Great Favourite [and] the Sudden Fall of ... John Dudley, Duke of Northumberland*.

Newspapers stressed the value of history, the *True Briton* of 9 September 1723 arguing that 'No study is so useful to mankind as history, where, as in a glass, men may see the virtues and vices of great persons in former ages, and be taught to pursue the one, and avoid the other'.

For opposition newspapers, history provided a safe perspective from which to attack ministers, as well as offering the suggestion that the cause of opposition was both timeless and necessary, and that evil governments would eventually collapse. On 11 May 1728, the *Craftsman* claimed:

> History gives us frequent examples where the best princes have by such ministers lost the affections of the best people; who are naturally disposed to overlook the personal failings or accidental miscarriages of their sovereign, and are never so much irritated as when he endeavours to support a tyrannical over-grown favourite against their general demand for justice.

Historical works frequently appeared in newspapers, and their partisan intention or applicability encouraged criticism. Gilbert Burnet's Whig *History of My Own Time* was attacked in 1723–24 by *Mist's Weekly Journal* and also criticised in *Historical and Critical Remarks on Bishop Burnet's History of His Own Time* (1725) by the Jacobite Bevil Higgons. This was countered in the Whig *London Journal* on 30 January and 6 February 1725, leading to a second edition in 1727 that rebutted the paper's defence of Burnet. Higgons also published *A Short View of English History* (1723), which refuted Burnet's claims of the Pretender's illegitimacy, and was the author of *The Generous Conqueror* (1702), a play defending the Jacobite claim. In turn, in 1730, the *London Journal* complained that in the opposition *Craftsman* 'The History of England is racked and tortured', a criticism of Viscount Bolingbroke's essays in the paper, while in 1734 the *Daily Courant* carried a life of Rienzi as a warning against popular disorder and pseudo-patriotism, and another pro-government paper, *Read's Weekly Journal,* published parts of Burnet's *History.*[29]

An emphasis on the uplifting quality of true art also led to a stress on the value of history. The *Way to the Temple of True Honour and Fame by The Paths of Heroic Virtue Exemplified in the Most Entertaining Lives of the Most Eminent Persons of Both Sexes on the Plan Laid Down by Sir William Temple, in his Essay of Heroic Virtue* (Devizes, 1773) by William Cooke, an Oxford Fellow and a chaplain to the widowed Marchioness of Tweeddale, juxtaposed true art with fiction. The verse on the title page declared:

> Abhor'd the Tale, which vain amusement brings,
> Tempts the frail mind, and tickles till it stings,
> But blessed those lines, that in each faithful page

> Impart the fruits of far experienced age,
> Founded on truth, the youthful heart which mend,
> And precious use with various pleasure blend.

Dedications individually and in sum are an important branch of literature, as well as of critical attitudes, and this one was no exception. Criticising 'writings calculated to enflame the passions, and debauch the youth of both sexes', Cooke claimed that 'Real history, which imparts the knowledge of past events, affords the best instructions for the regulation and good conduct of human life'.

Novels and history were far from alone in the world of books. Works were also produced to supply new and developing specialisations. For the popular world of horticulture, Peter Miller's *The Gardener's Dictionary* (1724), Robert Furber's *Short Introduction to Gardening* (1733), James Lee's *Introduction to Botany* (1760), William Hanbury's *A Complete Body of Planting and Gardening*, John Kennedy's *Treatise upon Planting* (1776) and Loddiges's *The Botanical Cabinet* (1777) were followed in 1786 by the *Botanical Magazine*.[30] The new plants described were an aspect of an interaction with the wider world, as was the burgeoning field of travel literature, which included works such as George Anson's *Voyage Round the World* (1748). At the same time, there was an attempt to systematise and order experience. In the case of gardening this led to George Mason's *Design in Gardening* (1768), William Mason's *The English Garden* (1772) and Horace Walpole's *History of the Modern Taste in Gardening* (1780).

Authors sought to make their writings as comprehensible as possible to the anonymous, expanding literate population, and modern concepts of authorship developed. Books, magazines, newspapers and dictionaries assisted the spread of new ideas, transmitting the grand themes of artistic and intellectual life. Treatises on taste (aesthetics) were designed to guide appreciation and patronage.[31] Gerard Langbaine's *Account of the English Dramatik Poets* (1691) offered a tabular ranking that sought to establish a national dramatic heritage free of borrowings from French romances. The designs for James Gibbs's St Martin-in-the-Fields in his *Book of Architecture* (1728) influenced designs elsewhere. In a powerful assertion of the value of the Moderns and of their role as more than simply transmitters of Classical knowledge, this was the first English book devoted to the designs of a contemporary architect. The second edition of Batty Langley's *Ancient Architecture Restored* was entitled

Gothic Architecture, Improved by Rules and Proportions (1747); he had already published *New Principles of Gardening* (1728), and Hogarth's *The Analysis of Beauty* followed in 1753. The study of English art was established with the publication by Horace Walpole of *Anecdotes of Painting in England* (1762–80), which were based on the notebooks of George Vertue (1683–1756), Draughtsman and Sub-Director of the Society of Antiquaries and a noted engraver. James Granger's *Biographical History of England ... Adapted to a Methodical Catalogue of Engraved British Heads: Intended as an Essay towards Reducing our Biography to System, and a Help to the Knowledge of Portraits* (1769) was intended to assist print collectors, and indeed led to a rapid rise in the price of engraved portraits.

Ephraim Chambers' *Cyclopaedia: or An Universal Dictionary of Arts and Sciences* (1728) attempted a classification of all knowledge, and was successful, with new editions printed in 1738, 1739, 1741 and 1746. This was followed by the *Encyclopaedia Britannica* in 1768–71. Published by a consortium of Edinburgh printers, but dependent on the British market, this was a reply to the French *Encyclopédie* and a reflection of the market opportunities provided by public interest in the expanding world of knowledge.

Encyclopaedias were not the sole compendia to appear. A number of dictionaries appeared including Nathan Bailey's *Dictionarium Britannicum* (1730), but, once published, the field was dominated by Samuel Johnson's massive *Dictionary of the English Language* (1755), which sought to clarify meanings and included an English grammar. The plan of 1747 declared 'The chief intent ... to preserve the purity and ascertain the meaning of our English idiom'. Johnson's citations reflected his sense of the role of a national canon of literature: half of all the quotations in the *Dictionary* came from only seven sources – Shakespeare, Dryden, Milton, Addison, Pope and the Authorised Version of the Bible, all works produced over the previous 170 years, many over the previous eighty, and thus an affirmation of the value of recent literature. Similarly, Hogarth, in his self-portrait of 1745 presented himself alongside volumes of Milton, Shakespeare and Swift.

Although the codification of language does not suit the tastes of some modern ahistorical commentators, who see it as a form of stultification and have therefore regarded Johnson's *Dictionary* as regressive, to contemporaries, Johnson's achievement was an epic one, which it certainly was on the personal level. In his *Dictionary* he had single-handedly ordered the language, creating a work that rivalled the lexicons of French and Italian academies. In his poem *On Johnson's 'Dictionary'*, David Garrick wote:

> And Johnson, well arm'd like a hero of yore,
> Has beat forty French, and will beat forty more!

Johnson himself wrote in the *Dictionary*, 'We have long preserved our constitution, let us make some struggles for our language'. The moral nationalism of the tone was appropriate for a country moving towards full-scale war with France:

> The words which our authors have introduced by their knowledge of foreign languages, or ignorance of their own, by vanity or wantonness, by compliance with fashion or lust of innovation, I have registered as they occurred, though commonly only to censure them, and warn others against the folly of naturalizing useless foreigners to the injury of the natives.

Seeking to clarify meanings, Johnson was also aware of the changing nature of the language. Indeed, this sense of impermanence was a characteristic feature of Tory writers, pessimistic about the chances of a well-ordered society, and it was especially notable among Anglicans conscious of the challenges to the position of the church. Changes in the text reflected Johnson's attempt to fix the shifting language, but this was a struggle in which he increasingly doubted his ability. Johnson moved from the confidence of the *Plan of the Dictionary* to the subsequent resignation of the preface, written after the work on the first edition had ended.[32]

The publication of collections and guides was frequent and varied. For example, in 1772 John Aikin published *Essays on Song-Writing: with A Collection of Such English Songs as are Most Eminent for Poetical Merit*, while John Walter published an English-Welsh dictionary in parts in 1770–94. Compendia included collections of literary works, and these were actively pushed in the press. Alongside collections came histories that sought to fix what was important and that provided a sense of continuity, as in Benjamin Victor's *History of the Theatres of London and Dublin from 1730* (1761–71), and Clara Reeve's *The Progress of Romance through Times, Centuries and Manners* (1785). What was instructive was the sense of a canon being established by anthologies and taken forward by new works. The *Daily Universal Register* of 1 January 1785 advertised

Four volumes of Farces, with elegant frontispieces, are now first published as a supplement to *Bell's British Theatre*, comprising fifty-seven of the best and most modern farces and entertainments now performing on the British stage ... may be had also the most valuable collection of English Plays that has ever been printed, viz. Bell's British Theatre, In twenty-one volumes, consisting of one hundred and five of the most esteemed English plays and operas, elegantly printed, complete, and correct, as the authors left them; besides being adapted to the use of the theatres, by the mode of printing, which distinguishes the variations observed on the stage, each play is enriched with a dramatic print, representing the most favoured performers in some spirited scene; they are all depicted from life, and compose a very capital collection of animated prints.

Publications and visual images therefore complemented each other.

The culture of print accustomed part of the population to experience information and news through publications, lessening the role and sway of oral culture. Two thousand copies of the folio edition of Johnson's *Dictionary* were printed and the price was £4 10s. It was soon followed by a second edition published in 165 weekly sections at 6d. each. Earlier, the sale of Young's *Night-Thoughts* had become large scale after 1750 when Robert Dodsley and Andrew Millar published their one-volume edition, and by 1765 there had been seventeen editions of the collected *Night-Thoughts*. Even in published work there was a sense of the 'bespoke' in the format of books. Many were printed in blue-paper wrappers so that purchasers could choose a binding to go with them. Many works were published in large and standard paper editions so that a book-collector or follower of a particular author could obtain a particular edition.

Editions also sought to expand markets. Indeed an 1777 edition of Young's *Night-Thoughts* included a glossary to define difficult words. The drive to appeal to the market played a role in the many editions of Shakespeare, not least Thomas Bowdler's *The Family Shakespeare* (1818) with its determined assault on apparent improprieties. Abridgements were another instance of the search for market share by the very sophisticated publishing and bookselling trade. The desire and ability to respond to market opportunities was a commercial aspect of the wider organisation of the growth in writing and printing in order to accord with cultural, social and political needs and priorities. This helped shape the rise of disciplinarity, professionalism, and the notion and practice of literature that led to literary hierarchies still influential today.[33]

8

Styles

... certain men called *Virtuosi*, whom, by the near relation their title bore to virtue, I took at first to be a set of rigid moralists: but, upon enquiry, I discovered that they were a company of fiddlers, eunuchs, painters, builders, gardeners, and, above, all, gentlemen that had traveled into Italy ... assume a sort of legislative authority over the body of their countrymen: they bid one man pull down his house, and build another, which he can neither pay for, nor inhabit; they take a dislike to the furniture of a second, and command him to change it for a different one more expensive and less commodious; they order a third to go and languish at an opera, when he had rather be halloing in a bear garden ... all the laws of it are changed once in every seven years; and that which before was right itself, becomes at once a high crime and a misdemeanour.

George Lyttelton, *Letters from a Persian in England* (1735).[1]

Eighteenth-century satirists, such as Alexander Pope and Jonathan Swift, would have been much amused by the vocabulary, tone and content of modern academic debates about cultural trends and causes. Such amusement is not without reason, but, at the same time, it is necessary to appreciate that great works do not exist in a vacuum. The most familiar approach to the culture of the period is to focus on developments in style and artistic movements, which for this century takes us eventually from the Baroque to Romanticism. There are, however, many problems in describing changes in style, particularly since developments can be perceived fully only through an appreciation of specific texts, objects and performances. The appropriateness of the accepted stylistic vocabulary is also open to question: a description, vocabulary or chronology of change that might suit portraiture is not necessarily appropriate for opera, or poetry, or architecture. Although stylistic labels do serve purposes, they are unable to capture the full picture. For example, movements such as the English Baroque, associated in particular with Sir Christopher Wren and Sir John Vanbrugh, and with a Grand Style or Manner across the arts, are open to very different definitions. Even in the important but restricted case of architecture, there was a difference in Baroque terms between the tradition of Wren and William Talman and that of Vanbrugh and Nicholas Hawksmoor. The East Front of Dyrham Park, designed by Talman, was very different to Easton Neston, a contemporary seat where Hawksmoor boldly used giant Classical orders. The arbitrary character of some definitions extends from styles to periodisation. The conventional periodisation for Baroque and Classical came from the History of 'Art', but the terms as applied to the visual arts are not synchronous with those as used for music. There are also issues of national definition: the French and the British mean something different by Classicism.

While common themes can be discerned in some fields of cultural activity, it is generally more appropriate to write in terms of stylistic tendencies, rather than to suggest that distinct uniformities can be discerned. Alongside this point should come a caution in assuming that different styles and influences clashed and competed. Public criticisms of existing styles were indeed part of the establishment of an identity for newer styles, but it is also appropriate to note the coexistence and often overlap of apparently competing styles and influences, and, indeed, considerable mutual influence. Thus, alongside criticism of Baroque architecture on behalf of the Palladian style, came a melding of elements of both styles, as in the work of James Gibbs.

These different styles can in part be related to the disparate goals sought by both patrons and artists, but great care is necessary on this head. If some art was seen as a public medium that could improve society, rather than as a private luxury, the latter was also important and goals could coexist. Similarly, a stylistic device could be used to different ends. Thus, the letter was used as the form for Samuel Richardson's serious and influential novel *Pamela* (1740), as well as in Christopher Anstey's comic depiction of the Blunderhead family in his *New Bath Guide* (1766), both successful works.

The ready availability of periodicals, the presence of a range of artistic bodies and learned societies, and the forcing hand of entrepreneurial activity, helped create a cultural climate that was receptive to new ideas and works, and willing to consider new stylistic devices, and even styles. This was seen across the arts. Music provides a good instance. For example, in Norwich, where there was a very active musical life, both public and performers were ready to respond to quite rapid change, and, at the end of the century, concert-goers were able to hear the latest British and German works.[2] The foundation and growth of provincial festivals was a feature of the century.

The willingness to accept frequent revisions of taste was also recorded in individual buildings. Powderham Castle, the seat of the Earls of Devon, gained grand bookcases by John Channon with a continental-style decoration (1740) and a grand staircase supported by exuberant Baroque decoration (1754–56), but also a large Neo-Gothic apsidal-ended music room added by James Wyatt in 1794–96. The desire to be fashionable was also mocked by satirists. In her novel *Camilla* (1796), Fanny Burney presented Mr Dubster showing guests around his grounds, which included the development of an island in a pool in front of his house:

> Mr Dubster then displayed the ingenious intermixture of circles and dia-
> monds projected for the embellishment of his grotto; the first of which
> were to be formed with cockle-shells, which he meant to colour with blue
> paint; and the second he proposed shaping with bits of shining black coal.

As England was part of a European culture, all the major stylistic and thematic changes occurred on a continent-wide scale, although there were significant national variations and differences in chronology, while individual writers and artists could also make an important contribu-tion. Thus, as an aspect of artisan culture, the poet and artist William Blake (1757–1827) developed a distinctive way to engrave both text and illustrations on the same plate.

At the beginning of the eighteenth century, the most important Euro-pean architectural style was Baroque. Although to varying degrees emanating from Rome and associated with Catholicism, Baroque was also a style, or even ethos, seen in England in particular with the archi-tecture of Wren and Vanbrugh, the music of Purcell, the drama of Dryden, and the formulaic structure of performances of Italian *opera seria*. Thanks to the extensive use of paint, moulding and sculpture, Baroque architecture made great play of painterly and sculptural quali-ties that from decorated ceilings and walls contributed to a grandeur that overpowered the spectator, taking him or her into a world that was above and beyond them. This could be further accentuated by devices such as *trompe l'oeil* and mirrors. This emphasis on spectacle and scale

– the great domes at St Paul's Cathedral and Greenwich Hospital being the first large domes and lanterns in England – was particularly suited to the grandeur of position, especially of monarchy, aristocracy and established church. As such, it offered less to the middling orders and to their needs to participate in cultural life other than as audience. Visitors to Castle Howard were warned of their status by approaching through a substantial arch crowned with a pyramid above heavy machicolations. Nobility was a key theme. Joseph Addison in his *Dialogues upon Medals* claimed:

> There is no inscription fitter for a medal, in my opinion, than a quotation that besides its aptness has something in it lofty and sublime: for such a one strikes in with the natural greatness of the soul, and produces a high idea of the person or action it celebrates.

All the viewer was designed to do in response to Kneller's *The Triumph of Marlborough* (c. 1706), a sketch for a Rubenesque work of martial glory joining Earth to Heavens in a fantasy that would have seemed incongruous later in the century, was spectate.

A highpoint of the English Baroque was the Painted Hall at Greenwich, part of Christopher Wren's Royal Hospital for Seamen, which indicated the staged quality of its architecture and decorative theme. In 1708, James Thornhill was commissioned to paint the Great Hall. His rich painting of the ceiling (1708–12), an explicitly grand state painting, was a triumphant work proclaiming national power. The painting represents William III and Mary bringing Peace and Liberty to Britain and Europe. Oxford was also a centre of the Baroque, buildings including the Sheldonian Theatre, the Radcliffe Camera and the interiors of Queen's and Trinity College chapels. Thornhill was also responsible for the 'Apothesis of Archbishop Chichele', a fresco at the east end of the chapel of All Souls College, Oxford, which, with its sky-lit character, painted architectural details, massed angels and ascending layout would not have been out of place in Rome.[3]

A less grandiose Baroque can be seen at Beningbrough Hall, built under the supervision of William Thornton, who had worked under Vanbrugh at Castle Howard. Beningbrough has a two-storey hall of architectural quality and fine plasterwork, both aspects associated with the Baroque. For those who worshipped, the assertive bulk of Nicholas Hawksmoor, as in his St George-in-the-East, London (1714–29), encapsulated Baroque values of scale. Interior decorating was greatly influenced by Italian artists who came over to work at houses such as Burghley. Italian *stuccatori* applying stucco were particularly influential and helped both spread and satisfy fashion within provincial networks. For example, from the Hall and High Saloon at Castle Howard, they went on to tackle the interior of merchants' houses in Leeds, and the scenic aspect of the opera house at the Queen's/King's Theatre in London.

At the same time, the phrase English Baroque can encompass very different tones and has to consider contemporary criticisms of these works, not least a Palladianism that rejected what was seen as the impure Classicism of the Baroque in favour of a return to true Classical forms. This had a politico-cultural dimension, as the Baroque could be presented in terms of a papalism, Italianism and even Frenchification of these forms, with Palladianism a return to them comparable to that of the Primitive Church and of virtuous, public, non-authoritarian, politics.

Whatever the goals of their creators, forms and styles had certain connotations. This was seen with the contemporary Grand Style in literature. Whereas Shakespeare had used prose alongside iambic pentameters, there had been a major shift in the seventeenth century, associated in particular with Milton and Dryden, to an emphasis on epic poetry with a consistent pentameter rhythm, and the use of polysyllables, rather than monosyllables. Couplets were preferred to blank verse. When Pope died he was planning an epic entitled *Brutus*. This reflected not simply a strong Latinity in literary culture, seen not only with Pope but also with writers very much perceived as English, such as Samuel (Dr) Johnson, but also a striving for significance in themes, similes and characterisation, not least an association of exalted characters with Classical gods and heroes. Uplifting language appeared appropriate for uplifted characters, and the Grand Style did not lend itself to comedy, which was handled differently, not least with a strong reliance on wordplay. The declamatory acting style that went with such uplift was associated in particular with James Quin (1693–1766), who was noted for playing the roles of Bajazet, Brutus and Cato. The equivalent on canvas was a preference for the noble, and for nobles, for heroic behaviour and elevated stances. This was an art that was statuesque, not intimate, and its corollary was the emphasis on passion and grand gestures in the Italian operas popular in London.

The variety of cosmopolitan influences was seen with the Rococo style that followed the Baroque. At the same time, there was a critical response to the Rococo located in a different social and moral context: the Rococo aesthetic, with its emphasis on pleasure,[4] was different to the ethos and ambience of sentimentality which was also most popular in mid-century.

Rococo is a term commonly associated for England with painting and interior decoration, rather than architecture. The Rococo style in Britain rarely got beyond individual objects. Very labour-intensive, and therefore expensive, whole decorative schemes in Rococo style are rare and limited to the homes of the very rich. Charles-Nicolas Cochin, who first used the term Rococo in a critique of 1755, referred to it as a style of furnishing and interior decoration, the latter characterised by mirrors and wall panels in carved wood, asymmetry, flowing curves, and shell and leaf patterns. Thus, the Master's Chair of the Fruiterer's Company produced in 1748 was light, swirling, sinuous and decorated, with the cabriole legs rising from lion-paw feet and headed by men-of-the-woods masks. The term Rococo may have been derived from *rocaille*, the rock-like watery and shelly substance used for artificial caves, and *coquille* (shell). Applied to other art forms, the Rococo placed an emphasis on ornamentation even if an underlying order lay behind it. Rococo embellished the rich ornamentation of Baroque, but without its apparent solidity or at least grandeur, it was freer in shape and suggestion, and lacked the rigidity of the ordered rules of Classical architectural detail.[5]

The Baroque was also replaced by an emphasis on a more refined and less demonstrative feeling that from the 1740s has been described in terms of a sensibility that was as much moral as aesthetic. The rise of sentimentality represented a different impulse to the Rococo. According to the adage 'scratch a cynic and you find a romantic', sentimentality possibly was the counterpart of political and social cynicism. Its manifestations were varied, including an ostentatious moderating of the amorality and bawdy of much late-seventeenth-century comedy. It had already been lessened by the religious criticism of commentators such as Jeremy Collier, the Societies for the Reformation of Manners being joined in a more positive fashion by essayists in periodicals urging restraint and an awareness of social value, an argument pushed in particular by the *Spectator*. Many plays now encouraged a bourgeois consciousness equally opposed to indulgence, whether decadent aristocratic mores or popular ignorance and vice. Colley Cibber, Poet Laureate from 1730 until 1757, made his name with *Love's Last Shift*

(1696), a sentimental comedy of marital reconciliation (husband brought back from rakish lifestyle by his disguised wife), and this was followed by a series of such comedies, including Cibber's *The Careless Husband* (1704) and *The Provoked Husband* (1728). In Richard Steele's *The Conscious Lovers* (1722), virtue and sensitivity are rewarded. Earlier playwrights were tidied up for modern tastes, as with Cibber's version of Shakespeare's *Richard III* (1700).

Similarly, a number of painters moved from a grandiloquent style in portraiture toward a focus more on private character. This was seen in particular with the work of Joseph Highmore (1692–1780), one of the leading portraitists from the reign of George II, for example in his portrait of William Fellowes of Shotesham Park commissioned in 1748 as a present for his friend Robert Marsham. Rather than making an heroic statement, portraitists increasingly sought to offer individual personality, consciously seeing themselves as akin to biographers.[6] Biography, indeed, developed in this period with, for example, Oliver Goldsmith's lives of Bolingbroke, Richard Nash and Thomas Tarnell, and Johnson's *Poets*. This was linked to a rise of 'biographical' culture.

The cult of 'sensibility', of sentiment and fine emotion, at once individual and formulaic, had a considerable influence on the theatre and the newly-emerging novels of the period, helping, as a result of the interacting development of fashion and psychological receptivity, to shift the focus from tragedy and epic to more domestic genres and themes, particularly the sentimental play and the novel.[7] By calling forward a response, the depiction of distress gave the audience an opportunity to show their goodness and morality. A poised compassion towards virtue in distress made it possible to display a refined feeling that was artistically meritorious. While this appears a modern trait, the idea of seeking 'entertainment' in for example the lottery at the ragged schools also had a distinctly old-fashioned flavour. By the 1780s, sensibility was increasingly to be seen as affectation, although a comic ambivalence can already be seen with Yorick, the protagonist in Laurence Sterne's *Sentimental Journey through France and Italy* (1768). Despite the portrayal of bogus sensibility or, indeed, criticism of sensibility itself, it went on being important in both published work and private reflection.

Sensibility and sentimentalism were associated, with the latter reflecting in particular a greater emphasis on the display of feelings in the shape of emotionalism.[8] The morality of Samuel Richardson's popular novels, *Pamela* (1740) and *Clarissa* (1747–48), were seen as displaying admirable sentiment in terms of moral lessons and emotional honesty, and many other sentimental novels followed including Henry Brooke's *The Fool of Quality* (1766–72). Sentimental comedies, such as Hugh Kelly's *False Delicacy* (1768), also benefited from the vogue for the display of feelings, although this was a matter of benevolent gentility, not raw emotion. Three years later, when Aphra Behn's *Oroonoko: or The Royal Slave* (1688) was performed in Exeter, the proprietor in the playbill noted that the original script had been altered, so that what he saw as the pernicious immorality of the comic scenes could be replaced by more acceptable sentiments of fidelity, generosity and affection.[9] In the 1740s, although the leading actor and theatrical entrepreneur David Garrick acted in Benjamin Hoadly the younger's successful comedy *The Suspicious Husband* (1747), the taste of which was to be regarded as questionable, he also sought to raise the moral tone of the theatre, as others, such as John Dennis, Aaron Hill and James Thomson, had earlier sought to do. In Germany 'reform' theatre sought to offer improving plays. It was intended to improve spoken language and banish coarse humour.

In England, the sentimental comedy that resulted generally lacked bite, and English theatre did not greatly flourish in the second half of the century, but its morality reflected audience wishes; although these are not easy to recover, and surviving comments indicate a variety of responses. Samuel Johnson, not the famous one but the young son of William Johnson of Torrington, wrote from London to his sister Elizabeth in 1774:

> I have been at one play since I writ you my journal. *The Beggar's Opera* with *The Druids*: my inducement for going was to hear Signor Rossignol's most amusing imitations of singing birds, which he does to that perfection that it is impossible to distinguish them from the finest notes of the nightingale, canary bird, goldfinch, linnet, etc; for all appearance of the human voice is entirely lost; the sound is produced with a very great effort and exertion of the lungs, and he is obliged to stop for breath and drink a glass of water in the middle of his performance.

The young Samuel was not much of a theatregoer, but his letters home indicated that going there was expected. The following January, he

> went to the play with cousin John, which is the only time since I have been here, which is owing to two reasons, want of time, and an indifference for new plays, which have swarmed this winter. *Matilda* is the play which I

saw; but I would rather read two plays to you, than see such a one again, though they say this is the queen of the hive. I thought it a drone.

Going to see prominent actors was clearly a goal in visiting the theatre. The next day, Johnson's uncle intended 'to see Garrick in the *Wonder*, and their Majesties who were at the play'. The royal presence stamped plays as respectable, while the actors were also celebrated for elite audiences in a number of ways, not simply portraits and the whole genre of theatrical paintings but also porcelain. At Belton House the porcelain collection includes a pair of white Bow figures of Henry Woodward as the Fine Gentleman and Kitty Clive as the Fine Lady in Garrick's face *Lethe*, first performed at Drury Lane in 1740. In February 1775 Johnson

> went to see Garrick act Leon in *Rule a Wife and have a Wife*, we got very good seats, and I was for the only time since I have been here very much entertained with the play, and indeed as much at King and Mrs Abingdon as at Garrick, for I hardly think that Garrick exceeded either of them; the farce was a pantomime.

Two days later, because his aunt had taken twelve places, his cousin and he saw *The Rivals*, 'though very much against our inclination', and four days after that went to *Braganza*:

> this play had been so exceedingly cried up that the boxes were all taken for fifteen nights before the play came out; this was the first night … I suppose Garrick appeared to support the great encomium which he had bestowed … it met with great applause, but people's expectations were by no means satisfied; there is no one epithet will express my opinion of it better than insipid.[10]

The focus was on established forms, a civilised tone, comedies of manners, and the testing, but in the end affirmation, of emotional and family stability. If lovers were apart due to mischance or parental disapproval, these were overcome. In *The Clandestine Marriage* (1766) by George Colman the Elder and David Garrick, the secret marriage of Fanny, the daughter of a wealthy merchant, and Lovewell, his clerk, is forgiven at the magnanimous request of Lord Ogleby; Fanny herself confesses to self-reproach and says she 'must be miserable for ever' if she does not receive her father's forgiveness. At the close of the popular *The West Indian* (1771), by Richard Cumberland (satirised as Sir Fretful Plagiary in Sheridan's *The Critic*), there was a typically contrived denouement, at once dramatic and sentimental. Belcour discovers that he is the son of Stockwell, who declares:

> How happily has this evening concluded, and yet how threatening was its approach! ... Belcour, I have watched you with a patient, but inquiring eye, and I have discovered through the veil of some irregularities, a heart beaming with benevolence, an animated nature, fallible indeed, but not incorrigible; and your election of this excellent young lady makes me glory in acknowledging you to be my son.

In Thomas Holcroft's very successful comedy *The Road to Ruin* (1792), the discovery of a new will and the surprising saving of the failing family bank bring the scenario to rights. In fiction, Oliver Goldsmith's sole novel, *The Vicar of Wakefield* (1766), was also reliant on an improbable happy ending which required the actions of a benign knight, the revelation that neither a fake marriage nor a death from grief had occurred (the marriage was in fact a real one), and the change of heart of a swindler. Alongside villains, such as in Fanny Burney's novel *Cecilia* (1782) the Honourable Compton Delville, one of the villainous guardians of the protagonist, came those capable of showing sensibility. If Squire Thornhill in *The Vicar of Wakefield* proves a malevolent force, his uncle, Sir William, acts as restorer. In Thomas Morton's successful musical melodrama *The Children in the Wood* (1793), the murderous villain out to have the children killed is the wicked Sir Rowland:

> soon their silence shall be eternal. My brother being concluded dead, that lustrous orb being set in night, shall these pygmy satellites eclipse me? No. That fellow I am sure of. From his eye remorse is banished, and unmasked murder lowers upon his brow.

Social harmony, however, is restored, Lord Alford and Lady Helen regaining their children, while Walter proves an honest yokel.

Hogarth criticised aristocratic mores, but most painters depicted aristocrats in an exemplary light. Instead of seeing the commercialisation of leisure as a triumph of bourgeois culture, the role of the middling orders was largely one of patronising both new and traditional artistic forms, rather than developing or demanding distinct styles. Alongside plots that matched a desire for sensibility came acting associated with Garrick that was seen as more measured and less demonstrative than the earlier declamatory style. The comparable music was the light, easy (but carefully contrived) elegance of Johann Christian Bach's sonatas and concertos of the 1760s and 1770s, and the music written for Vauxhall

Garden by James Horn, who was composer and organist at Vauxhall Gardens from 1774 to 1820. In poetry, there was a shift in emphasis from satire to sensibility.

The art to which the pressure for a moral culture gave rise is generally described as Neo-Classical, although that was not a term used in the period, the 'true style' being the favoured description.[11] The idea that culture should be exemplary had never been lost, while, once a public debate about the purpose of art and the artist developed, it was likely that it would have taken the attitude, critical of the Rococo and of cultural borrowings, that was adopted in mid-century. Criticisms focused not so much on the quality of the work as on its purpose, or apparent lack of it, for artist and patron, matching the criticism of Boucher and praise of Greuze in France by Diderot.[12]

Although there was an increasing sense of the happiness of the individual (and of society) as an important goal of human society, critics found art for what they saw as mere pleasure inadequate. Instead, they sought a didactic art capable of arousing sentiment and morality, rather than of confirming comfort. In his 'Discourses' as President of the Royal Academy, Joshua Reynolds propounded a purposeful view of art, rather as the German painter Anton Raphael Mengs had done in his *Gedanken* (1762). In 1770, Reynolds claimed that a true painter 'instead of endeavouring to amuse mankind with the minute neatness of his imitation ... must endeavour to improve them by the grandeur of his ideas'. He offered an exemplary portrayal, but this did not have to mean grandiloquence. In his portrait of the surgeon William Hunter, who in 1768 became the first Professor of Anatomy to the Royal Academy, Reynolds depicted a man of simple dress, the focus, being on his face, hands and work, rather than on the trappings of power.

Improvement was not simply a matter of rules. Indeed, in 1769, in his second Discourse, Reynolds suggested that once thoroughly grounded in the discipline, the painter might 'try the power of his imagination ... The mind that has been thus disciplined, may be indulged in the warmest enthusiasm, and venture to play on the borders of the wildest extravagance'. Nevertheless, truth had to be the basis. In 1774, Reynolds criticised Philip James de Loutherbourg for not basing his paintings on observation: 'There are many good landscapes of Loutherbourg, but they are very much *manierata*. They seem to be the works of a man who has taken his ideas at second hand, from other pictures instead of nature'.[13]

The exclusive court and aristocratic circles that patronised the Rococo and favoured cosmopolitan styles were not especially interested in public debate. Nevertheless, they also were affected by the Neo-Classical current by the 1760s. This had a number of manifestations including, most simply, the depiction of characters, in fiction, on stage or on canvas, in Classical poses. Recently returned from Italy, George Romney, in 1776, painted Elizabeth, Viscountess Bulkeley as Hebe, the wife of Hercules and daughter of Jupiter, who appears behind her in the portrait in the guise of an eagle. Her plain dress with its draperies is reminiscent of those in Classical reliefs. Classical plans and motifs dominated buildings, not only secular works but also, increasingly, ecclesiastical ones. Begun in 1760, although not completed and consecrated until 1812, Gibside Chapel, the work of the architect James Paine, was based on the buildings of Roman antiquity and churches of Palladio which Paine had seen on a visit to Italy. A Classical building on the plan of a Greek cross, with a double portico closing the vista along the avenue, its six Ionic columns line the entrance façade. Above the portico is a pediment in front of a parapet carrying urns. The work on the estate was funded by the coal wealth of George Bowes, MP for Durham County who died in 1760 leaving a fortune estimated at £600,000. Neo-Classical architecture was characterised by an absence of Baroque ornamentation and Rococo exuberance. Instead, the emphasis was on a geometry of clarity, with clean straight lines and plain surface. Simplicity was a key Neo-Classical value, being associated with integrity, both individual and collective.[14]

Neo-Classical themes were also seen in interior decoration, especially in the work of Robert and James Adam in the 1770s, as well as in the pottery designs used by Josiah Wedgwood. The influential light elegant style in interior decorating introduced by Robert Adam, when he returned from Italy in 1757, included ornamental motifs from Classical antiquity, especially after the discoveries at Pompeii. At Kedleston, where he was active in the 1760s, Robert Adam designed twelve painted benches for the Marble Hall, the design inspired by a sarcophagus in the Pantheon. The design by William Ivory for the plasterwork on the ceiling in the Peter the Great Room in Blickling Hall derived from ceilings discovered in Pompeii and Herculaneum. Rediscovered in 1748, Pompeii made a major impact from when it was professionally excavated beginning in the 1770s.

Sculptures appeared particularly apt for Neo-Classical buildings. The first gold medal for sculpture awarded by the Royal Academy was given to John Bacon in 1769 for a bas-relief representing Aeneas escaping from Troy. Thomas Banks, who was in Rome from 1772 until 1779, initially thanks to support from the Royal Academy, produced relief sculptures, including *The Death of Germanicus* for Thomas Coke of Holkham and *Caractacus* for George Grenville, the commissions reflecting familiarity with Roman history. Classical models and remains had an air of reborn integrity, and Neo-Classicism possessed a quality of statuesque drama seen not only in architecture and sculpture but also in painting, particularly with the popular Classical manner of Reynolds. This also affected other painters. Joseph Wright of Derby abandoned his 'Flemish' style in favour of Reynolds's manner, as the Italian school of painting was considered superior to the Dutch school.

The use of the term Neo-Classicism by implication locates Classical influences in the second half of the century. This was certainly true of Greek models, but, in practice, these influences could be found throughout the period, albeit with varying impulses. Augustan is a term applied to the writers of the first half of the century, especially Pope and Swift; and Goldsmith wrote *An Account of the Augustan Age in England* (1759). The writers of this period were much impressed by Virgil, Horace and Ovid, Latin poets of the reign of Augustus, especially by Virgil's *Eclogues* and *Georgics*, both of which greatly influenced Pope. The heroic pentameter couplets that dominated poetry were particularly valuable for creating balancing links within and between lines, providing a structure that offered much to satire, but that was also to lend itself to the poetry of sensibility.

Goldsmith's *Account* implied that by 1759 there had been a falling off in quality. There had certainly been a shift in mood. The preference for satire over sensibility seen earlier had been reversed, although neither approach was absent in either period. The more reflective and intimate and less 'public' poetry of the period of sensibility, famously represented in Thomas Gray's *Elegy Written in a Country Churchyard* (1751), was not without important Classical roots, as the notion of withdrawal from the corruption of the city was a powerful one among the influential Roman models of the period. Nor were poets alone in looking back to Classical roots and models. Homer's lost *Margites* served Henry Fielding as an alleged model for his novels, which he claimed were 'comic epics in prose'.

The emphasis on elegant clarity in sentiment and expression seen in the English Augustan writers has equivalents in Neo-Classical activity in other art forms later in the century, but there were also differences. In both periods, however, there was an assumption that the educated public would understand Classical references and be interested in Classical themes. Thus, playwrights produced works such as Colley Cibber's *Perolla and Izadora* (1706), set during the Second Punic War, as well as Charles Beckingham's *Scipio Africanus* (1718) and Philip Frowde's *The Fall of Saguntum* (1727), on topics that would attract no attention today. Addison's *Cato* (1713) was a greatly influential play recalling a heroic Roman at a time when the Whigs were confronting what the future would be after Queen Anne died. Richard Glover (1712–1785) made his name as a writer for the Patriots against Walpole, with his lengthy and much reprinted epic poem *Leonidas* (1737), and later wrote a series of tragedies on Classical themes – *Boadicea* (1753), *Medea* (1761) and *Jason* (1799), as well as another lengthy epic poem, *The Athenaid* (1787). Much of this Classical history was fundamental to the Italian opera produced in London.

The range of Classical influence is indicated by the use of Roman dress in portraiture and funeral statuary, for example Henry Cheere's full-length funerary statue of Robert Davies in Roman dress in Mold church. John Miller (ed. 1798) and his wife Anne (1741–81), who had visited Italy in 1770–71, established a literary society at their seat of Bath Easton. This centred on an attempt to honour the Classical world by recreating elements of it. Guests were asked to write poems which they put in an antique urn the Millers had bought in Frascati, and wreaths of myrtle were used to crown the best three competitors.

For the aristocracy in particular, the oligarchic system of republican Rome appeared an apt model, but it was not only the aristocracy that was attracted to the comparison. The potency of the Classical inheritance helps explain concern about corruptions of it, and therefore the philological emphasis on producing (and reading) accurate texts, a more particular anxiety in the first half of the century. This offered one way in which the Moderns could add to the contribution of the Ancients, and ensured that controversy could develop over works judged problematic, such as Pope's edition of Shakespeare (1725) and Conyers Middleton's *Life of Cicero* (1741): the former was criticised in Theobald's *Shakespeare Restored* (1726), while the authenticity of documents cited by Middleton was questioned in James Tunstall in works published in 1741 and 1744.

The Classical influence did not prevent a debate over the respective merits of Ancients and Moderns, which led to such works as Swift's *The Battle of the Books* (1704) and *A Tale of a Tub* (1704), mock-heroic satires that supported the Ancients, and to Pope's attack on the Moderns in *The Dunciad* (1728). This debate testified to the role of the Classics as a standard for judgement.[15] The opening chapter of *Joseph Andrews* offered a determined preference for the Modern when Fielding referred to 'those ancient writers which of late days are little read, being written in obsolete, and, as they are generally thought, unintelligible languages, such as Plutarch, Nepos, and others which I heard of in my youth'. Instead, he expresses a preference for the vernacular: 'our own language affords many [actions] of excellent use and instruction, finely calculated to sow the seeds of virtue in youth, and very easy to be comprehended by persons of moderate capacity'.

The debate between Ancients and Moderns became less potent, certainly in the literary world in the second half of the century, as the rise of the novel put the emphasis very much on Modern forms, while Classical themes were more generally reshaped. Nevertheless, there were still echoes of the debate. In 1766, Louis Dutens, a Huguenot immigrant patronised by the Duke of Northumberland, published a work translated three years later as *An Inquiry into the Origin of the Discoveries attributed to the Moderns: Wherein it is Demonstrated, that our Most Celebrated Philosophers have, for the Most Part, Taken What they Advance from ... the Antients; and that Many Important Truths in Religion were Known to the Pagan Sages.* The Ancients and Moderns debate became central to music in the 1770s and 1780s, with the foundation of the Concerts of Ancient Music, while the role of the Classical world in shaping aesthetic judgements continued to be reiterated. In 1786, the fifth edition of Nicholas Tindal's *A Guide to Classical Learning: or Polymetis Abridged* (1st edition 1764) was advertised as 'absolutely necessary, not only for the right understanding of the Classics, but also for forming in young minds a true taste for the beauties of poetry, sculpture and painting'.[16] Advertising, however, tended to benefit the Moderns because the idea of novelty was seen as an important seller.

The cultural tensions of mid century continued in the second half of the century. No one category is adequate to cover the variety of artistic developments from then until the close of the century. Neo-Classicism and pre-Romanticism vied for attention, but so also did the Neo-Gothic and *Chinoserie*.[17] Romanticism, itself a retrospective concept, has been variously defined, with an increased emphasis since the early 1980s on social and political elements, not least a greater awareness of the political and social interests of nearly all the major writers.[18] An older view of what would be seen as the Romanticism of the 1790s also still has value. In this, Romanticism is associated with the individual emotions of the artist, often at variance with social and cultural conventions, and inspired by the intoxicating power and wildness of elemental natural forces. There were certainly harbingers of this emphasis, and in them a changing appreciation of nature was important. James Thomson in his preface to *Winter* (1726) presented nature in reflective terms rather than with the emotional intensity seen toward the close of the century:

> I know no subject more elevating, more amusing; more ready to awake the poetical enthusiasm, the philosophical reflection, and the moral sentiment, than the *Works of Nature*. Where can we meet with such variety, such beauty, such magnificence? All that enlarges, and transports, the soul? What more inspiring than a calm, wide, survey of them? In every dress *Nature* is greatly charming.

In the second half of the century, in contrast, there was an interest in landscape painting with a new appreciation of the 'sublime' qualities of savage landscape, which contrasted with earlier formal gardens. Nature was increasingly seen as an elemental creative force, not as a pleasing and inconsequential landscape, and the human soul as a seat of passion, rather than harmony. The changing nature of the emphasis on sensibility, and its growing linkage with the notion of spiritual awareness, were very important in forming proto-Romantic taste. What can be seen as an early anticipation was provided by the poet Mark Akenside in his *The Pleasures of Imagination* (1744), a didactic poem that stressed the value of a well-formed imagination. The equivalent in portraiture was the attempt to give subjects natural and open expressions, as in Reynolds's *Mrs Levina Luther* (1763–66).

Towards the close of the century, a fashion for picturesque landscape was widely diffused and it served to direct popular tastes towards what would later be seen as Romantic values. Linked to this came an interest that was pronounced from mid century, sometimes pseudo-melancholic, and at once reflecting sensibility and looking towards proto-Romanticism in ruins which were increasingly presented as an innate part of the landscape.[19] William Mason closed his paean to 'Landscape' in *The English Garden* (1772):

> most happy, if thy vale below
> Wash, with the crystal coolness of its rills,
> Some mouldring abbey's ivy-vested wall.

Similarly, from Thomas Warton's 'The Solemn Noon of Night' in *The Pleasures of Melancholy* (1747) came the appeal of 'yon ruin'd Abbey's moss-grown piles'. 'Berry Pomeroy Castle' by the Exeter-based landscape painter Francis Towne (1739–1816) showed trees growing up among the ruins. Thomas Whately captured what was seen as the suggestible nature of the human imagination, and therefore its openness to the arts:

> At the sight of a ruin, reflections on the change, the decay, and the desolation before us, naturally occur; and they introduce a long succession of others, all tinctured with that melancholy which these have inspired.[20]

An interest in ruins was related to the focus on mortality by those later termed the 'graveyard poets'. Locating their meditations in nocturnal churchyards, writers such as Robert Blair and Edward Young sought sublime effects that meshed religious thoughts and fine sensibility, moving beyond melancholia to find a more active reflection. Although not addicted to churchyards, the same was true of William Bowles's popular *Fourteen Sonnets Written Chiefly on Picturesque Spots during a Journey* (1789). Bowles, like Gray and Young, was a cleric, but the theme of the meditation on death could not always be readily comprehended within Christian belief, although there was little downright rejection of it. Aside from poetry on mortality, there was also prose fiction, although that was less common. 'J.S.' in *Swinney's Birmingham and Stafford Chronicle* of 11 January 1776 published an allusive dream essay on time, pleasure and death, with time's inexorable triumph the major theme.

Melancholy was not the theme in Edmund Burke's aesthetic *Philosophical Enquiry into the Origin of our Ideas of the Sublime and the Beautiful* (1759), which put an emphasis on the extent to which the sublime could transform the reader and spectator, and emphasised that terror was important in creating the sense of the sublime. Sublime was a word used of Handel's music at the time, but it was defined by Burke as whatever led to ideas of danger, pain or terror: he suggested obscurity, vastness, privation and infinity. Burke argued that, if the source of these ideas was imaginary, they could cause delight. Emotions and potent sensory experiences, rather than nobility, reason and dignity, were crucial for Burke.[21] Burke's argument was important in the Gothic impulse, for example in the novels of Ann Radcliffe, and, particularly in their popularity, and also in early Romanticism. In Radcliffe's *The*

Italian (1797), the captured Ellena offered an appropriate response to the darkening forcefulness of the landscape that she was thrust into with all the attention of an enraptured spectator of an awesome painting, and, indeed, there are references to illustrations:

> It was when the heat and the light were declining that the carriage entered a rocky defile, which shewed, as through a telescope reversed, distant plains, and mountains opening beyond, lighted up with all the purple splendor of the setting sun. Along this deep and shadowy perspective a river, which was seen descending among the cliffs of a mountain, rolled with impetuous force, fretting and foaming amidst the dark rocks in its descent, and then flowing in a limpid lapse to the brink of other precipices, whence again it fell with thundering strength to the abyss, throwing its misty clouds of spray high in the air, and seeming to claim the sole empire of this solitary wild. Its bed took up the whole breadth of the chasm, which some strong convulsion of the earth seemed to have formed, not leaving space even for a road along its margin. The road, therefore, was carried high among the cliffs, that impended over the river, and seemed as if suspended in air; while the gloom and vastness of the precipes, which towered above and sunk below it, together with the amazing force and uproar of the falling waters, combined to render the pass more terrific than the pencil could describe, or language can express. Ellena ascended it, not with indifference but with calmness; she experienced somewhat of a dreadful pleasure in looking down upon the irresistible flood; but this emotion was heightened into awe, when she perceived that the road led to a slight bridge, which, thrown across the chasm at an immense height, united two opposite cliffs, between which the whole cataract of the river descended. The bridge, which was defended only by a slender railing, appeared as if hung amidst the clouds. Ellena, while she was crossing it, almost forgot her misfortunes.

The sublime had earlier been thought of without reference to terror, but in Burke's sense it did not have to wait for Gothic novels. Indeed, it could be seen across a host of activities, for example the acting of David Garrick, both his re-creation of Shakespeare's Macbeth from 1744 and his depiction of Hamlet faced with the ghost of his father.[22] This matched support for the presentation of moments of strong emotion by painters, a presentation that could link sensibility to Romanticism.

The idea of the soul as a seat of passion, and passion often as the cause of anguish, was most luridly expressed by the Swiss painter Johann Heinrich Füssli (he anglicised his name as Henry Fuseli) (1741–1825), who spent most of the period from 1764 in England, becom-

ing a member of the Royal Academy in 1790. He offered visions of hor-
rific fantasy, comparable to some of the contemporary Gothic novels.
Influenced by reading Rousseau, Fuseli was a precursor of Romanticism.
He argued that the individual and society, art and morality, were in
conflict, and that the arts were a divine gift which elevated man by their
force, impact and terror. Praised by George III and William Blake, his
most famous painting was *Nightmare* (1781; exhibited 1782), a Gothic
fantasy that offered powerful vision of the mysterious and the subcon-
scious. Producing work designed to arouse the imagination, not least for
the Shakespeare Gallery and to illustrate Milton's *Paradise Lost*, Fuseli
painted visions that exposed the limited sway of social order and psychological balance and harmony, and depths in human experience
which reason could not explain. His paintings looked toward the
unfixed, metaphorical quality that was to be so important to so much
Romantic work,[23] and that was also pronounced in Gothic literature,
such as Ann Radcliffe's novels, although at the end of her novels she
provides a rational explanation to what had seemed supernatural.

While the theme helped explain the link, Reynolds's massive *Macbeth
and the Witches*, painted in the late 1780s, echoed aspects of Fuseli's
work. The grip of *Macbeth* on the imagination reflected interest in the
supernatural and in fantastical stories, but was also in accord with the
instinctive response by audiences then increasingly fashionable in contrast to the earlier intellectual response. This was an aspect of a shift
from text to a theatrical experience in which emotional atmosphere created by other means, such as the scene-painting, was more important
than hitherto.

Drama that tested contemporary boundaries was provided in a different way by William Beckford's *Vathek: An Arabian Tale* (1786), a novel
about the quest for deadly knowledge and legendary power in which the
explicit defiance of established morality was in part expressed by a sexual adventurousness seen as part of its subject's desire to fulfil his
sensuality. This looked to the exoticism of some Gothic fiction, and to
troubled villains, such as Ambrosio, the protagonist of Matthew Lewis's
lurid novel *The Monk* (1796). Ambrosio is presented as a victim of his
own irrational impulses, specifically lustful self-destructive drives, which
are at the end of the novel unconvincingly attributed to diabolical
forces. He was more frightening than the creations of Horace Walpole
and Ann Radcliffe. Like the paintings of Füssli, the plots of Gothic literature tested conventional notions of probability, not least the

established patterns of expressing and moulding experience with reference to the interior and natural world. Gothic fiction reworked many of the images of landscape poetry: monastic stonework and trees became ruined abbeys and sinister woods that both served as malign settings for the plot and also represented the psychological strains of the psyche. This was very different to the metropolitan settings that had dominated the culture of print at the start of the century.

The emphasis on the wilful protagonist was very much located in Romantic fascination with the ego. To be heroic, however, the Romantic hero required a brooding quality, a dignified melancholy and mysterious introspection, that separated him from the more easily driven and readily explained villains of Gothic novels, although Schedoni, the complex, troubled, austere monkish villain of Ann Radcliffe's *The Italian* (1797) showed signs of being such a hero.

Dramatic accounts of character were offered by painters, as with Reynolds' 1784 portrait of *Mrs Siddons as the Tragic Muse* (1784). Siddons (Sarah Kemble, 1755–1831), the leading tragic actress of the age, was successful in showing that the Gothic could be theatrical and, in this, that the potent psychology of the paranormal that Gothic had come to express, could be channelled to dramatic effect.[24] Reynolds's rich, dark painting with its figures of Pity and Terror looked forward to Romanticism. The painting was a great success, praised by James Barry as 'The finest picture of the kind, perhaps in the world, indeed it is something more than a portrait'. The last point reflects the shift in Reynolds's later portraits away from conversation pieces and towards a style that is more otherworldly, with more clouds and smoke.[25]

Pictorial representation in turn influenced the theatre: Sarah Siddons was wheeled along the stage at Drury Lane as the tragic muse in a 1785 production of Garrick's *Jubilee*. Similarly, the theatre frequently provided occasion for painters. Hogarth was commissioned to depict a scene from John Gay's *The Beggar's Opera*, and produced a frontispiece for the published version of Henry Fielding's play *Tom Thumb the Great*. Siddons herself was held up for praise by Frances Crewe because she relied on 'feelings' not 'attitudes'. Vital simplicity was applauded:

> *Action* is the Language of Nature ... Mrs Siddons would make us weep, or rage, in short just as she chose to affect us ... There must, I know, be *Machinery* in everything, but ought we see it? ... What Sir Joshua Reynolds somewhere says of drapery, is exactly what I think of imitation, "It should be woollen, or silk, or linen, it should be *drapery*, it should be nothing

more". An actress should not be Italian, or French, or English, she should be a woman and nothing more.[26]

Debates about style were linked to a flourishing literature of criticism as well as to a more widespread process of criticism in which attempts were made to improve the quality of individual works. The character of critical works – in book, pamphlet and periodical form – reflected the contentious nature of the public sphere and a sense of reader interest. Joseph Addison's popular play *Cato* (1713) led to the publication of a number of commentaries that discussed whether the rules of drama had been observed in the play. Most were praiseworthy, although in John Dennis' *Remarks upon Cato* (1713) there was criticism of a lack of appropriate morality. Institutional formats aided debate: the commencement in 1769 of annual exhibitions by the recently-established Royal Academy of Arts encouraged art criticism. Across the century, much of the criticism was didactic in tone, reflecting, in part, a belief that the arts were of more general social and cultural importance, but it was frequently also felt necessary to add a humorous tone in order to attract readers, as in *The Dramatic Censor, or Critical Companion. Being an instructive and entertaining preceptor for the playhouse* (1776). Some writers made their name as critics, John Dennis producing *The Advancement and Reformation of Modern Poetry* (1701) and *The Grounds of Criticism in Poetry* (1704). More prominent writers and artists also tried their hand at criticism, Alexander Pope producing an *Essay on Criticism* (1711) in heroic couplets. Critics also became figures of fun in satires, Dennis appearing as Sir Tremendous in the farce *Three Hours After Marriage* (1717) and, alongside Lewis Theobald, in Thomas Parnell's book *Homer's Battle of the Frogs and Mice, with the Remarks of Zoilus, to which is prefixed the Life of the said Zoilus* (1717).

Revisions to, and criticism about, particular works, both interacted with more general issues about style and also reflected the specific needs of individual genres. This can be seen in a letter from William Pitt the Elder, not a figure generally associated with the arts. In September 1751, he wrote to James Oswald, a fellow MP, about a manuscript play the latter had sent him to read. Pitt had read it with George Lyttelton

> with much pleasure. We both found great spirit and imagery in it, as well as much deep and strong sense; there is likewise character. We think the business had better open between Agis and the mother, and leave out an unnecessary preceding scene. The great situation of the judgement is well

kept up, in part: towards the end of it, something more of dignity and greatness might be thrown in to hold it up to the last. With all this merit no one can answer for the success of the play.[27]

Pitt's sentiments reflect not only his interest in culture, but also a Classical stress on dignity and greatness.

The emphases and trends that contributed to the stylistic blend have left very different traces. In particular, because they lent themselves to critical debate, there is an emphasis on serious discussion rather than on comedy, let alone on what might be seen as low comedy: buffoonery or farce, but this emphasis bears no necessary reference to popularity. Thomas Morton's comedies, especially *The Way to Get Married* (1796), *A Cure for the Heart-Ache* (1797) and *Speed the Plough* (1800), were staged at Covent Garden, were popular and were frequently revived, but he rates few mentions today. Whereas this might be an appropriate literary response to the stock characters and scenarios of the plays, it is but part of the general critical problem of addressing the variety of the period.

9

London and the Provinces

It does not follow, that works of merit can *only* originate in the metropolis of England; and that, unless a new book is distinguished by a *London* title page ... it is beneath the notice of the curious.

John Tisdal, *Flora's Banquet* (1782).

John Tisdal, a Belfast printer, was defiant when he published *Flora's Banquet*, a collection of Irish poems he had edited, but the promised second volume did not appear. Although the century saw a major increase in public cultural activity outside London, in England it was very much dominated by the metropolis. Within England, although three-tenths of the population in 1800 lived in towns of between 2,500 and 100,000 inhabitants, there was no equivalent, outside London, to the strong and distinctive Scottish public culture, with its self-conscious creation of the Edinburgh New Town as a northern metropolis, the integration of folk airs in musical culture, the spread of 'Ossian', and the strong publishing base by late century.

London dominated the public gaze. In mid century, Antonio Canaletto, with his splendid canvases, used talents developed to depict Venice in order to show the glories of modern London, as Marco Ricci had done earlier in the century. A modern pride in London was expressed in Canaletto's views, with recent or new buildings such as St Paul's Cathedral, Greenwich Observatory, Somerset House, Westminster Bridge, and the rebuilt towers of Westminster Abbey playing a prominent role (although he also painted Warwick Castle).[1] A less grand view, but one that more accurately captured the city's expansion, was offered by other painters, for example Richard Wilson in his *Westminster Bridge under Construction* (1744), with the blue openness of the River Thames and the sky being spanned by the new bridge.

London was central to English life and culture. In 1700, London had

more than half a million people, nearly 10 per cent of the English population, and also more than all the other English towns (settlements
with more than about 2000 people) together. Only five of the latter had
more than 10,000 inhabitants: Norwich, Bristol, Newcastle, Exeter and
York, although some smaller towns, most obviously Oxford and Cambridge, had more 'cultural' influence than their larger provincial
counterparts. Although London's share of the national population did
not rise during the century, by 1800, thanks to the growth in the latter,
its population had doubled to make it the most populous city in Europe,
or the Americas (and the third most populous in the world),[2] and it was
over ten times larger than the second city in England.[3]

The energy of London was captured across the arts and provided the
context for much of national culture. Under the shadow of St Paul's
were published accounts of the diversions of the capital, such as James
Ralph's *The Touchstone: or ... Essays on the Reigning Diversions of the
Town* (1728), and Henry Fielding's *A Trip through the Town* (1735); and
a particular genre of unbuttoned travelogues, for example *A Trip
through London: Containing Observations on Men and Things, viz ... A
remarkable rencounter between a bawd and a sodomite ... of a person of
quality's cloaths sold off his back in the Mall by auction, by his Valet de
chambre ... of the Exeter-' Change beauties ... practices of petty-foggers
exposed* (1728), and the anonymous *London Unmasked: or The New Town
Spy. Exhibiting a striking picture of the world as it goes. In a ramble
through the regions of novelty, whim, fashion and taste, as found in the
cities of London and Westminster, their purlieus and vicinities ... particularly fortune-hunters, matrimonial brokers, modern Messelinas, dissipated
fops, demireps, sycophants, loungers or time-killers, military fribbles,
French, Italian and other foreign leaches, duellists, rapacious quackers,
griping usurers, black legs, body snatchers etc ... By the Man in the Moon*
(1784).

Ned Ward (1667–1731), a tavern keeper who was the master of such
works, offered a distinctive account of eighteenth-century life. In his
Labour in Vain: or What Signifies Little or Nothing (1700), he presented
a series of lost causes, including an old man's marrying a young woman,
and expecting life-time benefit from a covetous man. Such timeless
themes spanned social groups, although Ward also added more specific
instances, such as being a Jacobite. An old man marrying a young
woman was indeed central to the plot of *Three Hours After Marriage*
(1717), a farce largely by John Gay, who in 1716 also wrote *Trivia: or The*

Art of Walking the Streets of London. Alongside Ward's works should be put the frequent joke books of the period, such as those of Joe Miller or, less successfully, Robert Baker, which have been unduly neglected as a guide to attitudes and values. Many of the jokes, for example about tailors' yards, were sexual.

Jokes were also staged, as with George Alexander Stevens's 'Lecture on Heads'. Stevens (1710–1784), a London tradesman who became an actor, was also the author of novels and plays, and wrote a large number of popular songs. Keenly aware of the need for topicality, Stevens cashed in on events, writing, in response to victories in the Seven Years' War (1756–63), *The French Flogged: or English Tars in America*, a play staged in 1761, and, after George III's popular visit to the fleet at Portsmouth in 1773, followed with *The Trip to Portsmouth*. His activities included editing *The Beauties of All the Magazines Selected* (1762–64), as well as writing *The Adventures of a Speculist: or A Journey through London* which appeared posthumously in 1788, but he was best known for the 'Lecture' which used busts and wig blocks to satirise prominent individuals and recognisable types. Representations of the prominent were a source of considerable interest. They included engravings, figures, including those advertised in the *Newcastle Courant* of 13 April (os) 1734 'in a new composition, which far exceeds wax', and Stevens's 'Lecture'. First presented in 1764, this humorous monologue review became a great success, bringing Stevens, who took the 'Lecture' to North America, considerable wealth. Numerous published editions appeared, and the 'Lecture' played a prominent role on stage and in print throughout the rest of the century.[4] The accessible populist character of Stevens's songs were captured in his 'The Hogan of Houghton', a popular drinking song still being reprinted in newspapers in the 1790s, that claimed that Homer would have done well to drink the strong beer it celebrated.

The backdrop to this activity was the vitality of the capital. London's dominant position owed much to its place in trade and industry, but also reflected the city's role as the centre of government, the law and consumption, and its position in the world of print, which became even more important as a shaper of news, opinion and fashion. Even Welsh publishing was dominated by London presses. London newspapers circulated throughout England, and were also crucial sources for the provincial press. The turnpike and postal systems also radiated from London.[5] London led the way in national societies such as the SPCK and London parishes were more important in the Church.

London was also significant in influencing notions of urban life and in providing both setting and topics for cultural activity. As a subject, it was the most striking in the country until the cult for landscape late in the century. Its role was seen in the titles of works, for example poetry, such as John Gay's *Trivia: or The Art of Walking the Streets of London* (1716) and Samuel Johnson's *London* (1738), and also in response to the metropolis. London was presented as a site of liberty, trade and progress, a Whiggish rendition, but also in terms of moral, political and economic disorder and dissolution. Urban living therefore served to delineate, if not define, issues. Whigs tend to take the former view and Tories the latter. In the Tory Alexander Pope's *The Rape of the Lock* (two versions, 1712, 1714), the witty satire about a lack of values is set in London society. It was not necessary, however, to be a Tory in order to criticise London. Joseph Yorke, a member of the 'Old Corps' Whig establishment, wrote in 1763:

> Don't you think that the overgrown size of our metropolis is one great cause of the frivolousness, idleness and debauchery of the times. I have often wondered that the legislature has not long since laboured to put bounds to its increase, for it is really too big for the good observance of the law or the gospel.[6]

The city grew significantly, especially at the beginning of the century, when the West End estates of landlords such as Sir Richard Grosvenor and Lord Burlington were developed as prime residential property. Celia Fiennes recorded 'There was formerly in the city several houses of the noblemens with large gardens and out houses, but of late are pulled down and built into streets and squares and called by the names of the noblemen, and this is the practise by almost all'. As the nobility moved west from the Covent Garden area, Mayfair and St. James's became the select side of town and the streets there still bear the names of the politicians of the period, for example Harley Street.[7] Building and gentrification helped make the area safer. Leading aristocrats built or rebuilt grand London houses, such as Burlington, Carlton, Chandos, Chesterfield, Derby, Devonshire and Spencer Houses. Robert Taylor built a house in Piccadilly for the Duke of Grafton, while Robert Adam played a major role in the refurbishment of Northumberland House.[8]

The financial and economic importance of London also led to some significant artistic work in the old-established part of the city. Sir James Thornhill in 1725–27 provided painted decorations for the ceiling of the

New Council Chamber in the Guildhall, offering Baroque themes and images, with the oval medallion in the centre providing a personification of the City of London as a young woman attended by Pallas Athena (symbolising wisdom), Peace, Plenty, and two cherubs. George Dance the Elder (1700–68), Surveyor to the Corporation of London, designed the Mansion House begun in 1739, and the Excise Office in Broad Street, and his son, George the Younger, who succeeded him as Surveyor, was responsible for the rebuilding of Newgate Prison. Robert Taylor (1714–1788) did sculptural work on the façades of the Bank of England and the Mansion House, before becoming an architect. As architect to the Bank of England, he made extensive additions in Neo-Classical style, including wings on either side of the original façade. His London work included the Stone Buildings in Lincoln's Inn. As an instance of the prominence that could come from architecture, Taylor became Sheriff of London, was knighted and left a large fortune.

Within the existing built up area, the physical creation of London was an evolutionary, not a revolutionary, process, with development out of existing housing types and traditional layouts. The ability to change and upgrade the structure of new houses, plus the high level of maintenance they required, particularly in the painting of woodwork, made them perfectly suited to a consumer society geared towards the continued renewal and replacement of products. This was a process of change, however, that reflected and sustained social distinctions, as was seen in open spaces within London. Squares tended to be public, rather than private, arenas until the 1720s. Then the emphasis came to be on exclusivity with the open spaces enclosed, and this helped further a process of social exclusion.[9]

London developed as a centre of consumption and leisure, although the living conditions of much of the population was far from easy.[10] The amount of fixed, specialised investment in leisure rose greatly with theatres, pleasure gardens, picture galleries, auction houses, and the ubiquitous coffee houses. In 1753, the British Museum was established by Act of Parliament as the first national museum of its kind in the world. The museum acted as though it was an encyclopaedia, with sequences of rooms, their layout, and the juxtaposition of objects within them, providing a means of understanding relationships within the world of objects and specimens.[11] 12,000 people visited it in 1784, although the rules banned children and sought to prevent 'persons of mean and low degree' from gaining access.

The presence of publishers in the capital was also important, helping support the profitability of literary, musical and visual works. Across the arts, London provided venues, performers, audiences, and entrepreneurs seeking to produce multiple links between them. Changes in any of the factors of production could alter the cultural world. For example, the enlargement of Covent Garden in 1792 and of Drury Lane in 1794 led to theatres that were less intimate and instead more conducive to the drama of spectacle, and this was conducive to the taste for Gothic drama in the 1790s,[12] as well as to the increase in payments to playwrights, and the profits of theatre owners and lessees.

Pleasure gardens, especially Ranelagh and Vauxhall, were not only places to see and be seen, eat and meet, set and spot fashions, find spouses or whores, but also major sites of entertainment, especially of music. In the season, Vauxhall, which was developed from 1728 by Jonathan Tyers, had two programmes of music each evening, featuring music by leading composers. Johann Christian Bach wrote songs for Vauxhall in the 1760s and 1770s. On the model of these pleasure gardens came others, such as Marylebone.[13] A varied mix of emulation and diversity in pleasure gardens reflected entrepreneurship, such as that of Daniel Gough, a tavern keeper, at Marylebone, and also an attempt to match services to the varied pockets of consumers. In addition to pleasure gardens, sixty-four of which are known for London, there were parks, such as St James's. The last changed in about 1770 when 'Capability' Brown replaced the rectilinear 'Canal' and walks with the natural look, the former becoming what is now called the Serpentine, and also with the development of Buckingham House as part of the vista.

The pull of London attracted talent not only from abroad but also from the provinces. Born in Whickham, County Durham, the son of a music-master, William Shield (1748–1829) played at concerts in Newcastle before being appointed leader of the theatre orchestra at Scarborough and conductor of the concerts there, a pairing that illustrated the mutual dependence of much of provincial cultural life. In 1770, he moved to become leader of the Durham theatre orchestra and conductor of the Newcastle concerts. Although young, Shield was already a key figure in the musical life of the region, but next season he moved to become a violin player in London. He began an active life in metropolitan musical life, including being composer at Covent Garden, which in turn was to lead to becoming master of musicians in ordinary to the king in 1817 and to burial at Westminster Abbey in 1829.

Economically, it was the City that dominated London, but the polite society that lived to the west was the prime topic of artistic endeavour, whether portraits or satire.[14] Henry Fielding saw London in terms of a corrupt Court and aristocracy at its West End, with their commerce in vice, and the more acceptable commercial metropolis. London was a setting for villainy for many artists and writers, for example of the snares that bedevil William Booth in Fielding's novel *Amelia* (1751). William Wordsworth's Preface to his *Lyrical Ballads* (1798) asserted the pernicious consequences of the move to the cities, but, in practice, this social phenomenon helped to produce an appetite for recreational literature.

'All the world's a desert beyond Hyde Park', complained the ridiculous Sir Fopling Flutter in Sir George Etherege's comedy *The Man of Mode* (1676), while in 1749 Thomas Bowlby, a travelling army official, offered a reminder that not all towns shared in the urban renaissance when he described Durham 'the Town I have now the misfortune to live in is another Avignon [a papal possession], a beautiful situation and the nursery of indolence and priest-craft'.[15]

In fact, London's development greatly influenced that of other cities,[16] not least because of the importance of image. The designs of London's new houses were given wider impact through publications such as Richard Neve's *The City and Country Purchaser and Builder's Dictionary*, which first appeared in 1703, with a second edition in 1726. There was also great interest in what to put in the houses, and this resonated with issues of taste, emulation, and the use of publications to spread designs, as in a London book of 1760 *Household Furniture in Genteel Taste for the Year 1760 by a Society of Upholsterers, Cabinet-Makers, etc. Containing upwards of 180 Designs on 60 Copper Plates. Consisting of china, breakfast, side-boards, dressing, toilet, card, writing, clan, library, slab, and night tables, chairs, couches, french-stools, cabinets, commodes, china shelves and cases, trays, chests, stands for candles, tea kettles, pedestals, stair-case lights, bureaus, beds, ornamental bed-posts, corniches, brackets, fire-screens, desk, book and clock-cases, frames for glasses, sconce and chimney-pieces, girandoles, lanthorns, Chandalears, etc, etc, with scales*. This included designs by Robert Manwaring, William Ince, John Mayhew, Thomas Chippendale and Thomas Johnson. The literary equivalent included works such as Charles Vyse's *New London Spelling Book* (1776). Influence, however, only operated up to a point. For example, provincial silversmiths, such as those in Exeter, were influenced by London designs but also produced work with unique features.

The London pleasure gardens were showpieces for all kinds of art and music, and they, and the walks and assembly rooms of London, were emulated in other cities and towns. London's squares were imitated in cities such as Bristol. The social basis of London's development – a major expansion in the middling orders and a growing practice by the rural elite of spending part of the year there, was matched in regional capitals, such as Norwich and Nottingham, country centres, such as Warwick, and developing entertainment centres, particularly spa towns, such as Tunbridge Wells and Bath, while the range of goods and services provided in small towns increased.[17] Thirty-four new spas were founded in England between 1700 and 1750, and even more in the second half of the century.[18] Although many aspects of London's culture were copied in provincial towns, there were also important differences. One of the most important was the price of culture. The cost of paintings was very different, with portraits costing more in London and Bath than elsewhere.[19]

The period is often associated with urban elegance, as in the squares of the West End of London. Brick buildings with large windows were built in a regular 'Classical' style, along and around new streets, squares, crescents and circles. Brick replaced timber-frame in houses for the well-to-do, for example in Norwich from the late seventeenth century. Queen's Square begun in 1699 set the fashion for brick-built houses in Bristol, and was responsible for the growth of brickworks there. In Bristol, the very spacious Prince's Street (1725) was followed by King's Square and Brunswick Square laid out between 1755 and 1769.

In nearby Bath, where the first Pump Room was built in 1706, followed in 1708 by Harrison's Assembly Rooms, the suburbs laid out to the north of the old core were influential on the establishment of urban forms. Circles, even if not the invention of John Wood Senior, were first used on any scale by him in Bath. Wood began the King's Circus in 1754, the design and decoration reflecting his masonic and druidical beliefs, and his son began the Royal Crescent in 1767. Palladianism greatly influenced the extension of Bath, not only with the Circus (1754–64) and the Royal Crescent (1767–74), but also with John Wood the Elder's Queen Square (1728–34) and Assembly Rooms (1730), his son's Assembly Rooms (1769–71), and the Palladian Bridge created in the nearby gardens of Prior Park. Alongside its development as a fashionable resort, such construction helped make Bath an attractive topic and space for the descriptive poetry, prose and painting of the period, as in

Mary Chandler's poem *A Description of Bath* (1733). The development of Bath as a city of orderly leisure owed much to Richard 'Beau' Nash, who in 1705 was appointed first Master of Ceremonies. His 'Rules' for the behaviour of visitors to Bath were first published in 1742, part of the process by which the codification of social propriety was expressed (and debated) in print.[20] In Exeter, Bedford Circus built from 1773, probably by Matthew Nosworthy, was followed in 1792 by Barnfield Crescent. In Plymouth, Durnford Street and Emma Place were laid out in 1773 as a fashionable residential area.

Alongside light, roomy and attractive private houses for the affluent,[21] of which there are massed examples in the Georgian terraces of Bath, the Clifton section of Bristol and other cities, numerous public and philanthropic buildings were also built, and they featured in the novels and paintings of the period, as well as providing work for architects. Theatres, assembly rooms, subscription libraries and other leisure facilities were opened in many towns, alongside public outdoor space: parks, walks and racecourses. In 1732 York, socially the capital of the north of England, gained a magnificent Assembly Rooms that showed that the Palladian style could be used for a public building: Lord Burlington drew on Palladio for the design. The young Samuel Johnson, not the great Dr Johnson, described a far less grand subscription assembly at Islington near London that he visited and danced at in 1775:

> This assembly is quite a sociable meeting where the greatest part of the company is known to each other, and very like ours, a dancing room and a cold room, tea about 10, and breaking up about 12, two or three fiddles, a tabor and pipe, and I believe a hautboy, and a horn, admittances 5 shilling, twelve or fourteen couples, but generally I believe nearer to twenty; minuets and country dances, two or three handsome ladies, and one very handsome, one very good natured man (Captain Shirley) to unite the company together, and this I think a recipe for an agreeable assembly. All kinds of liquors such as punch are included.[22]

Gentility and equality were fused. The assurance of the former made it possible in theory for the company to set aside status and act as equals, sidelining the concerns about social fluidity that played such a corrosive role in mixing. At the same time, these concerns were reiterated not only in society but also in fiction, particularly with satirical discussion about social mixing and, more threateningly, with the criticism of self-serving hypocrisy. Indeed, social mixing played a large role in real and fictional dramas about seduction and misalliances. The challenges to honour that

led to duels represented another threat, and this was recorded fiction-
ally, in Sheridan's *The Rivals* and also in Smollett's novels *Roderick
Random*, *Humphry Clinker* and *Peregrine Pickle*. However threatening,
social mixing had its limits, and the organisation of space, both within
towns, and in individual sites such as buildings excluded the bulk of the
population in the cause of an uneasy mix of hierarchy, status and
profit.[23]

The social world that fostered the demand for new buildings and
spaces was matched by the wealth of a growing economy and by entrepreneurial activity to provide many opportunities for artistic skill.
Although not all towns moved at the same pace towards what has been
seen as an urban renaissance, in many towns provincial architects, such
as Joseph Pickford in Derby, Richard Gillow and Thomas Harrison in
Lancaster, John Johnson in Chelmsford and William Belwood in York,
were responsible for fine buildings.[24] As a result, the urban fabric
changed considerably. Stockton, an important port for North Sea trade,
acquired a new parish church (1712), customs house (1730), town hall
(1735) and theatre (1766). Exeter gained the Devon and Exeter Hospital
(1743) and the Law Courts (1773–75).

New buildings often marked a major change in local consciousness,
not least as a replacement of past settings of authority, as with the new
Guildhall in Worcester designed by Thomas White and constructed
between 1721 and 1727. In mid century, Nottingham replaced its
medieval timber-framed Guildhall with a brick one with a colonnaded
front. Bristol's Council House had been rebuilt in 1704, while, in 1784,
James Essex, the leading Cambridge architect, designed and built a new
Guildhall.

More generally, the image of towns altered. Timber and thatch were
seen as dated, unattractive, non-utilitarian and, increasingly, non-
urban, as were long-established street patterns. A devastating fire in
Warwick in 1694 led to the establishment of the Warwick Fire Com-
missioners who by 1704 had distributed charity money not only to
encourage builders but also to compensate for land taken to widen
streets.[25] Later in the century, the Priory Estate, centred on Old Square,
played a major role in the gentrification of Birmingham: occupants were
not allowed to keep pigs, dump sewage, or open butcher's or black-
smith's shops. This was an instance of the social polarisation that
stemmed from urban improvement. Alongside issues of access to cultural facilities came those of social acceptability. Such activity reflected

a concern with the urban environment, a confidence that it could be improved, and a determination to act. Towns appeared to be one of the principal products of human activity, the section of the environment most amenable to action, and where society was open to regulation. This reflected interacting functional, moral and aesthetic criteria and requirements that were aspects of the cultural activism of the period.

Although some churches were rebuilt, new stone and brick buildings increasingly offered new definitions of town function, with an emphasis in particular on leisure and retail, and, more generally, on private space open to those who could pay (shops, subscription rooms), rather than spaces and places open to all (market places, churches). Old gates and walls were demolished. In Newcastle, literally a fortress against Jacobitism in 1715 and 1745, the gates and walls were demolished between 1763 and 1812, and the town instead gained a theatre in 1788. Such remarks underrate the degree of disruption and contention caused by changes in both urban land use and the values of the townscape. There were also differences in the building process, for example between patrons and architects, while there was tension between the skills of the craftsmen and the professionalising power of the architect.

Furthermore, aesthetically and practically, the transfer of Classical ideas to houses, churches and public buildings was not easy, as the prototypes were mostly ancient temples and baths, and it proved necessary to design a new architectural grammar for design and ornamentation. This encouraged recourse to books of designs. Architectural and related publications brought together a demand for such works with the entrepreneurial activism of the world of print. Practical knowledge was combined with Classical models. In 1735, 'in a neat pocket volume', appeared James Smith's *The Carpenter's Companion*, which offered not only guidance but also 'the five Orders of the Architecture, in a more easy and concise method, than any yet published'. Classical models encouraged the use of columns at the entrance to all sorts of buildings, for example Salutation Inn at Topsham, which also received a Venetian window and a broken pediment, possibly in a rebuilding.

The opportunities for architects from the new forums for sociability were considerable. The influential Assembly Rooms at York were largely built in 1731–32. Assemblies were first held in Newcastle in 1716, and new assembly rooms opened there in 1736 and 1776, expanding the cultural life of the city,[26] while Norwich, Bristol and Sheffield gained assembly rooms in 1754, 1755 and 1762 respectively. The buildings themselves were seen more brightly as the night was more thoroughly lit with the introduction of street lighting. The main streets of Lancaster were lit from 1738. Nevertheless, until gas lighting, and later electricity, transformed the situation, the change between day and night was far more abrupt than is the case today. As Hogarth's *Night* indicated, night-time offered different sensations, experiences and dangers, and the role of moonlight was much more important than today.

Assembly rooms were part of the urban fabric of sociability through which ideas were disseminated and new ones introduced, a process aided by the establishment of clubs and societies. The Manchester Literary and Philosophical Society was founded in 1779. Together, towns were the principal context of cultural patronage by the middling orders. Exposure to novelty was not a process restricted to the major towns. The first theatre in Lincolnshire was built in Stamford soon after 1718. Others followed in Lincoln (*c.* 1731), Spalding (*c.* 1760), Gainsborough (1775), Boston (1777) and Grantham (1777). The circuits of the theatre company based in Richmond, Yorkshire spanned Yorkshire and Cumbria, including Beverley, Harrogate, Kendal, Northallerton, Ulverston and Whitby.[27] Companies brought London plays to audiences across the country, although that was not the sole way in which the actors had a local impact, as the provincial stage was not simply a passive recipient of London productions.

Instead, the need for plentiful plays helped provide opportunities for provincial playwrights. Robert Hitchcock, a Yorkshire actor, was also the author of a comedy *The Macaroni*, which was staged in Yorkshire in 1773 and printed in York next year, following up with another comedy *The Coquette: or The Mistakes of the Heart*, acted in Yorkshire and printed in Bath in 1777. The strength of local interest in the stage is suggested by the 544 subscribers listed in *The Miscellaneous Poems of J. Cawdell, Comedian: Consisting of a Variety of Serious and Comic Prologues, Epilogues, Pastorals, Songs, Descriptions, and Epigrams. Together with Several Sentimental Pieces*, published in Sunderland in 1785 by James Graham, a local bookseller. James Cawdell, depicted in the frontispiece on stage in Sunderland, was the manager and leading comic actor of the theatre there, and also a playwright, his works including *Melpomene's Overthrow* (1778), a comic masque, as well as *Battered Batavians* (1798), a response to the British defeat of the Dutch fleet the previous year at Camperdown. Provincial interest was also demonstrated by shows such as that put on by Mrs Wells in Dadley's Assembly Room in Birmingham on 6 August 1791 in which her imitations included Mrs Siddons and a scene from *Jane Shore*,[28] the latter indicating the length of impact of a play first staged in 1714.

Provincial society also became the setting for plays, and not simply in a fictional fashion as with *She Stoops To Conquer*. Shrewsbury was the backdrop for Farquhar's *The Recruiting Officer* and Lichfield for his *The Beaux' Strategem*. He had visited both as a recruiting officer in 1705–6, and the use of these locations was a deliberate break with the convention that London was the setting for comedy.

Towns also provided both subject and source of patronage for professional painters. The market place of Norwich, a city that acquired assembly rooms (1754), a theatre (1756), and a public subscription library (1784), was painted by Robert Dighton in 1799. It was not only major centres, such as Bath and Norwich, that could boast professional painters. Christopher Steele (1733–67) of Egremont, the teacher of George Romney, was partly responsible for the high quality of Cumbrian portrait painting.[29] Poetry also flourished in many towns. In 1792 Richard Polwhele, a Devon curate, edited *Poems chiefly by Gentlemen of Devonshire and Cornwall*, based on a literary society that met every three weeks in an Exeter tavern, reciting their writings before dining.

Towns were not separate from rural society. Indeed, there were important commercial and social links, and these were strengthened by improvements in communications, not least the postal services used for the letters that provided the structure for a large number of novels, most famously Samuel Richardson's *Pamela* (1740) and *Clarissa* (1747), Tobias Smollett's *Humphry Clinker* (1771), and Fanny Burney's *Evelina* (1778). Post Office revenues rose from £116,000 in 1698 to £210,000 in 1755. This reflected the foundation of new routes, such as Exeter-Bristol-Chester in 1700, and others that became more frequent, as the London to Bristol and Birmingham services did in the 1740s. Cross-posts were created by Ralph Allen. The sense of change was presented by a report in *Jackson's Oxford Journal* on 19 June 1773:

> The difference in the number of stage coaches, etc. travelling on the Western road, within these few years, is not a little remarkable. About ten years ago there only passed through Salisbury in the course of a week, to and from London and Exeter, six stage coaches, which carried six passengers each, making in the whole (if full) 36 passengers. At present there constantly pass, between the above places, in the same space of time, 24 stage

coaches, carrying six passengers each and 28 stage chaises, carrying three each, making in the whole, if full, 228 passengers.

A degree of urban-rural rapprochement and cohesion at elite level was an important factor encouraging stability and also contributing to a degree of cultural merging. Joseph Pickford (1734–82), the London-born architect who designed the Derby Assembly Rooms, also designed the Riding School at Calke Abbey, as well as Josiah Wedgwood's house and factories at Etruria.[30] It is important not to exaggerate: differences remained between urban and rural values. Enlightened clubs were primarily urban, for example in cathedral cities, and anything but representative of society as a whole. Nevertheless, there was a degree of interchange between towns and countryside based on a degree of shared values that was arguably greater than that of the two previous centuries. Although largely based in towns, enlightened clubs, such as the Spalding Gentlemen's Society founded in 1709, the Peterborough Gentlemen's Society founded in 1730, the Brazen Nose Society founded at Stamford in 1736, and the Northampton Philosophical Society founded in 1743, included many landed gentry among their members, mixing easily with local clerics and professional men.

If Jane Austen's settings were largely provincial, the concern with the uneasy equilibrium in courtship of romantic affection and the exigencies of the marital economy were not limited to town or country. Furthermore, a lack of urban homogeneity that reflected differences within towns aided integration with the views of the rest of society. This lack of homogeneity was noted by contemporaries, and contributed to the designation of only some towns as fashionable. Similarily, buffoonery was seen as more popular with the theatre audiences of Devonport and Plymouth than their more genteel Exeter counterparts.

More generally, alongside inclusive influences in the growth of provincial culture, there were many tensions. For example, some learned societies, including Birmingham's Lunar Society and the Manchester Literary and Philosophical Society, were associated with a Whig and Dissenting tradition, as was the Northamptonshire Philosophical Society,[31] while others lacked that slant. Indeed, alongside the inclusive notion, should come an awareness that much of provincial culture, especially the press, can be located at least in part in terms of divides, both the Whig-Tory division that lasted until the 1750s and 1760s, and ones that emerged subsequently, culminating in the 1790s with the appearance of revolution and repression.[32] Partisanship, not leisure, became at least a driving force for provincial culture. Alongside partisanship came a tension about the consequences of wealth that carried forward the critique of the monied interest voiced earlier in the century.[33]

The provinces were not simply sites for cultural activity but also increasingly topics of comment, with the landscape understood as a stimulus or subject for political comment.[34] An interest in the picturesque aspects of rural Britain was also an important aspect of the Pre-Romantic impulse. Visits to literary shrines, country houses, picturesque ruins and the natural landscape all became fashionable. This became even more the case when the French Revolution and the subsequent war, which Britain joined in 1793, brought the Grand Tour to a close, although already, prior to then, among British tourists to the Continent there had been a greater interest in picturesque landscape, and therefore mountains. George Keate's poem *The Alps* was published in 1763.

Travel within Britain was aided by the development of turnpike roads, especially from mid century. The first turnpike trust for Devon was established in 1753 and in Cornwall the year after.[35] Guidebooks, travel accounts and illustrations brought the Lake and Peak Districts, the Wye Valley, and other sites to a fashionable attention, not that they had been completely ignored before: Charles Cotton, for example, published *The Wonders of the Peake* (1681), a descriptive poem reprinted as late as 1725. In the dedication to his *Ode to the Sun* (1776), William Cumberland claimed:

> We penetrate the Glaciers, traverse the Rhone and the Rhine, whilst our own domestic lakes of Ulswater, Keswick, and Wyndermere exhibit scenes in so sublime a stile, with such beautiful colouring of rock, wood and water, backed with so tremendous a disposition of mountains, that if they do not fairly take the lead of all the views in Europe, yet they are indisputable such as no English traveler should leave behind.

This *Ode* and other early accounts of the Lakes, including John Dalton's *Descriptive Poem* of 1755 appeared in 1780 in the second edition of Thomas West's *A Guide to the Lakes: Dedicated to the Lovers of Landscape Studies, and to All who Have Visited, or Intended to Visit, the Lakes in Cumberland, Westmorland and Lancashire*. West (1720–1779), a Jesuit stationed in Cumbria, is a reminder of the great variety of types who contributed to cultural life. His book was the first major guide to picturesque mountain scenery. The popularity of West's work ensured seven editions by 1799 and eleven by 1821. The collectable and display quality of these editions was enhanced first with maps and, subsequently, with aquatints. From the fifth edition (1793), the sixteen aquatint *Views of the Lakes* by Samuel Alken, after drawings by J. Smith and J. Emes, were advertised as of an appropriate size to bind with the *Guide*. The more elegant nature of the production – the fifth edition having wider spaced type and broader margins – was an additional instance of the higher production values made possible and desirable by the profitability of this market.

Interest in the Lakes was further enhanced by William Gilpin's *Observations Relative Chiefly to Picturesque Beauty, made in the Year 1772, on Several Parts of England: Particularly the Mountains, and Lakes of Cumberland and Westmoreland* (1786). Gilpin's work lacked the precision seen in travel accounts earlier in the century, but proved particularly successful in striking an impressionistic note in which there was an emphasis on the personal response, a style matched with impressionistic aquatints. Popularity led to a second edition in 1788, with both text and plates revised in order to make the work more in accord with a market that wanted a sensibility focused on the sublime quality of landscape. This approach had already been seen in Gilpin's *Observations on the River Wye and Several Parts of South Wales, etc. Relative Chiefly to Picturesque Beauty: Made in the Year 1770* (1782) which proclaimed the goal of examining the region described 'by the ruins of picturesque beauty ... adapting the description of natural scenery to the principles of artificial landscape'. As a result the illustrations were of picturesque ideas, not topographical drawings.

The market in turn encouraged writers and artists to travel, write and paint. Landscape painting unrelated to the parkland of country houses developed, early examples including Thomas Gainsborough's *Extensive River Landscape* (c. 1748–50) and George Lambert's *Moorland Landscape with Rainstorm* (1751). Whereas George Lambert's *The Great Falls of the Tees* (1746) had depicted rustics, when he returned to the subject in 1761 they were replaced by tourists dwarfed by the monumental rocks and clouds. John Inigo Richards (1731–1810) was the earliest prominent painter to visit the Dartmoor region. Studying in London, but based for much of his life in Exeter, Francis Towne (1739–1816) was an instance of the interaction of metropolitan and provincial artistic circles. In Devon, he both taught drawing at country houses and also painted and sketched local landscapes. By exhibiting such works in London, his *View on the Exe* at the Royal Academy in 1779, he encouraged metropolitan interest in Devon landscapes. Travellers found not only subjects but also inspiration. Thomas Girtin (1775–1802), a watercolour painter who was a master of depicting light and shade, was much influenced by a visit to the north of England in 1796.[36]

Travel accounts, whether printed or not, were regarded as incomplete without illustrations. William Maton's *Tour in the Western Counties* (London, 1797) was illustrated with views sketched by the Reverend F. Rackett that were engraved by Aiken. Among those in the manuscript version but not reproduced in the book were picturesque sketches of Ivy Bridge and Pendennis Castle.[37] John Swete, an affluent cleric whose illustrated journals were not published until recently, entitled them 'Picturesque Sketches of Devon', employed the term picturesque 125 times in his first four surviving journals, wrote of the sublime, the romantic and the beautiful, and referred to Gilpin. Swete's values were seen in his description of a view near Torquay which he described in 1793, 'a greater variety of pleasing and romantic scenery will rarely be met with – rocks, woods, houses, a villa and the sea, are seen intermingled in the happiest manner, altogether forming a landscape of uncommon beauty'.[38] Many travellers took with them journals, sketchbooks and portable drawing aids, such as the Claude glass, a convex mirror that reflected the landscape tinted in miniature. Drawing manuals sought to aid the travellers.

William Combe poked fun with his *Dr Syntax in Search of the Picturesque* (1812), illustrated by Thomas Rowlandson, but the perception of the country was changing. The aesthetic redefinition of English landscape was linked to Edmund Burke's *Philosophical Enquiry into the Origin of Our Ideas of the Sublime and the Beautiful* (1759). The literature on rural aesthetics helped shape travelogues and it became prominent toward the close of the century, with Richard Payne Knight's *The Landscape: A Didactic Poem* (1794) and Uvedale Price's *An Essay on the Picturesque* (1794). Picturesque tourism also affected and shaped the response to abroad. Whereas the painter James Barry went to Italy in 1766–71 to look at ancient sculpture in order to equip himself to be a history painter, John Robert Cozens went there in 1776–79 and again in 1782–83 to look for dramatic scenery.

The quest for picturesque mountain scenery was amply realised in the pages of Gothic fiction. Crossing the Alps into Italy in Ann Radcliffe's *The Mysteries of Udolpho* (1794), Emily

> often as she travelled among the clouds, watched in silent awe their bil-
> lowy surges rolling below; sometimes, wholly closing upon the scene, they
> appeared like a world of chaos, and, at others, spreading thinly, they
> opened and admitted partial catches of the landscape – the torrent, whose
> astounding roar had never failed, tumbling down the rocky chasm, huge
> cliffs white with snow, or the dark summits of the pine forests, that
> stretched mid-way down the mountains.

Interest in the grandeur of untouched landscape was linked to a less sympathetic account of the appeal of urban life. The latter had always, in the Classical manner, been seen as lacking integrity,[39] but the world of urban order and gentility was an attempt to share in civilised values, values seen as conspicuously lacking in rural fastnesses. The Romantic movement transposed this, with the city as the culmination of a false consciousness, indeed corruption and decadence, that was opposed not to rural order but to an untrammelled naturalness seen in sublime land-scape. In *Lyrical Ballads* (1798) and 'Tintern Abbey' (1798) Wordsworth was the poet of this attitude, and he believed that it was directly relevant for the writer who could only be true to himself if he lived in such areas. This represented an integrity different to that of writers and artists a century earlier.

Home and Abroad

So much [our Bard] a Briton that he scorns to roam
To Foreign Climes to fetch his Hero home

Prologue of *King Charles the First* (1737).

In 1720, a significant moment in cultural independence occurred when James Thornhill became the first English-born artist to be knighted. Prior to that, the great names in English portraiture had been foreign-born, Van Dyck, Lely and John de Medina becoming knights and Godfrey Kneller, in 1715, a baronet. Indeed the German-born Kneller had dominated painting in England in the 1690s, 1700s and 1710s, becoming Principal Painter to the King in 1691 and Governor of the Academy of Painting established in 1711. Kneller did not die until 1723, but Thornhill's rise challenged his pre-eminence, although in decorative painting, not portraits. Thornhill, who became Serjeant-Painter to the King and the King's History Painter in 1720, worked at Chatsworth, Greenwich, Hampton Court, and St. Paul's Cathedral, making a fortune that enabled him to repurchase and rebuild his ancestral seat at Thornhill. His son-in-law, William Hogarth, another product of the London artistic world, advocated a specifically English style, although he ploughed a lonely furrow.

Any emphasis on an English style clashed with cosmopolitan tendencies that were particularly pronounced in the royal family and among the aristocracy. Cosmopolitanism was aided by travel, patronage, the rule of cultural intermediaries and the process of emulation. Travel helped to spread knowledge of present, as well as past, artistic developments among patrons.[1] Giovanni Antonio Pellegrini's fresco work for the Earl of Manchester at Kimbolton testified to the importance of diplomats in bringing back knowledge of foreign styles and artists, as well as providing an instance of an artist moving easily between countries and cultures; Pellegrini went on to work at Castle Howard. As the Grand Tour became fashionable, increasing numbers travelled for pleasure and, at a formative period in their life, were exposed to foreign culture. Artists, such as the painters James Barry, Alexander Cozens and his son John Robert Cozens, Nathaniel Dance, Gavin Hamilton, William Hoare, William Kent, William Marlow, John Parker, Willey Reveley, Joshua Reynolds, George Romney, Jonathan Skelton, Francis Towne, Richard Wilson and Joseph Wright of Derby, the sculptors Joseph Nollekens and Joseph Wilton, and the architects Matthew Brettingham and William Kent, also travelled in order to acquire training, employment and inspiration. This encouraged not only interest in foreign works and cultural ideas, but also a sense of relativism, seen, for example, in Joshua Reynolds's essay on beauty in the 10 November 1759 issue of the the *Idler*:

> It is custom alone determines our preference of the colour of the Europeans to the Aethiopians, and they, for the same reason, prefer their own colour to ours. I suppose no body will doubt, if one of their painters was to paint the goddess of beauty, but that he would represent her black, with thick lips, flat nose, and woolly hair, and, it seems to me, he would act very unnaturally if he did not; for by what criterion will any one dispute the propriety of his idea? We, indeed, say, that the form and colour of the European is preferable to that of the Aethiopian; but I know of no other reason we have for it, but that we are more accustomed to it.

Patronage was inspired by, and sustained, an elite cosmopolitan culture, while the role of intermediaries necessary to such a culture was facilitated by the appreciable number of foreigners in London. In the first half of the century, the number of Huguenot (French Protestant) refugees was particularly important, as they had close links with both France and the United Provinces.

Emulation and fashion were significant in encouraging cultural borrowing. At the level of elite culture, especially in the early decades of the century, there was a strong sense of inferiority to the cultural life and products of France and Italy. This led to an attempt to implant foreign fashions and also to the patronage of foreign artists. Richard, 3rd Earl of Burlington (1694–1754), who paid two visits to Italy, played a major role in the reception of Italian culture. An admirer of the work of Palladio, Burlington was an active builder, as well as a patron of Italian musicians, including Pietro and Prospero Castrucci and Filippo Amadei, whom he brought back from Italy in 1715, and painters.[2] The impact of Italy on architecture was such that James Cawthorn, headmaster of Tonbridge, wrote in his *Of Taste* (1756):

> Is there a portal, colonnade, or dome,
> The pride of Naples, or the boast of Rome,
> We raise it here, in storms of wind and hail,
> On the bleak bosom of a sunless vale;
> Careless alike of climate, soil and place ...
> Hence all our stucco'd walls, mosaic floors,
> Palladian windows, and Venetian doors.

Italian opera was also prominent, particularly in the 1710s and 1720s, and this was a matter not only of music and libretti but also of performers. Castrati began to perform in London in the 1690s, and there were various incremental developments towards full all-sung Italian opera in 1706–10. Towards the time of Handel's arrival, the genre became more stable in London, and the castrato Nicolini, praised for both voice and deportment by the *Spectator*, was one of the first serious Italians to make his mark in London. In 1711 appeared Handel's *Rinaldo*, the first new Italian opera written specifically for an English audience.[3] The leading Italian singers of the age spent much time in London, including the celebrated castrato Carlo Broschi, whose stage name was Farinelli. Francesco Bernardi (Senesino), another castrato, performed in many operas in London between 1720 and 1735, while Faustina Bordoni, a noted Venetian soprano, spent 1725–28 in London.

France was a major leader in fashion, including women's behaviour and clothes. This encouraged the demand for French clothes, hairdressers, cooks, food and wine in elite circles in London. French card games and pornography crossed the Channel, followed, in the 1780s, by ballooning.[4] The morning levée and the umbrella were introduced into Britain from France. Alongside the strength of Italian cultural influences, a large number of French artists visited England. Alexandre Desportes painted many hunting scenes on his visit in 1712–13, while Maurice Quentin La Tour, a portrait painter admired by Hogarth, had a successful visit to London in 1723. Another portraitist, Jean Van Loo, arrived in 1737 and spent a lucrative five years taking commissions from resentful English rivals. Adrien de Clermont spent from the mid 1710s to the mid 1750s in England, carrying out decorative painting at Kew, Strawberry Hill and Wilton. The draughtsman Hubert Gravelot arrived in London in 1733, training a whole generation of artists, including

Thomas Gainsborough, at the St Martin's Lane Academy, and stayed until the Jacobite rising in 1745 led him and his compatriot, the artist Philip Mercier, to leave for France. Charles Clerisseau was invited to London in 1771, and exhibited with much success at the Royal Academy. Few went to France to train, although Christopher Steele, a Cumbrian portrait-painter, spent a year in Paris around 1750 where he was trained by Charles Van Loo. He then returned to northern England, where his polished manners led to his being called 'Count' Steele. He was important for his role in developing the style of George Romney, who was apprenticed to him in 1755–57. The richness of the colour of Romney's early style and his skilful handling of drapery have been traced to this background. Alongside the French, there were important influences from the Low Countries, with the Van Aken brothers, Peter Tillemans, Peter Casteels, Joseph Nollekens and William Verelst all playing major roles in the first half of the century.

French influences were not limited to painting. Adaptations of French plays were common in the early decades of the century, Sir John Vanbrugh basing *The False Friend* (1702), *The Confederacy* (1705) and *The Mistake* (1705) on French writers. Ambrose Philips turned to a French version of the Classical inheritance with *The Distrest Mother* (1712), a version of Racine's *Andromaque* that lacks the flow of actable drama. James Miller's plays drew heavily on Molière, while Aaron Hill died in 1750, the night before his translation of Voltaire's *Merope* was to be performed. French novels were also translated. For example, Marie-Catherine Aulnoy's *The Prince of Carency: A Novel* was published in 1719, a second edition following in 1723, while Robert Chasles's scandalous amorous fiction appeared as *The Illustrious French Lovers: Being the Histories of the Amours of Several French Persons of Quality* (1727), a second edition following in 1739. French aesthetic treatises were also translated, Jean Baptiste Dubos's *Critical Reflections on Poetry, Painting and Music* being published in 1748.

Later in the century, works translated included Rousseau's *Emile*, translated by Thomas Nugent in 1763, while Frederick Reynolds's first play *Werter* (1785) was based on Goethe's novel and was often staged. The psychological intensity of German plays proved particularly popular in the closing years of the century, those of August von Kotzebue being successfully adapted, especially by Elizabeth Inchbald in *Lovers' Vows* (1798), Benjamin Thompson in *The Stranger* (1798) and Sheridan in *Pizarro* (1799). Another work that was frequently translated during the century was Miguel de Cervantes's *Don Quixote*, the picaresque style of which proved one of the models for English fiction, notably for Fielding's *Tom Jones*.

Ten tailors, three gilders, three embroiderers and one dancing master were among those on a list of thirty-six French Catholics living in Westminster in 1722.[5] They could all, with reason, have been seen as taking jobs and commissions from English artisans, and in Hogarth's *The Rake's Progress* profit from Rakewell's lack of discrimination.[6] French superiority in the luxury trades and services was widely acknowledged, but also feared and derided. In response, drawing schools were established, while the Anti-Gallican Association was founded in 1745, the year of a French-supported Jacobite invasion, 'to oppose the insidious arts of the French Nation' and 'to promote British manufactures – discourage the introduction of French modes and oppose the importation of French commodities'. The French invention of papier mâché for decorative work – a threat to the livelihood of carvers – was condemned.

Cultural influences were not all one-way. Translations spread interest in English literature. Modern authors, such as Henry Fielding, Samuel Richardson and Laurence Sterne, and earlier writers, in particular Shakespeare, had a considerable impact in the Low Countries and Germany, while, once translated into French, Pope (who drew heavily on Classical models) was very popular in France. A German translation of the *Spectator* was published in Hamburg. Shakespeare swept Germany in the early 1770s, leading C. P. E. Bach in 1773 to write a symphony that was influenced by the playwright. In Russia in 1741–1800, 245 books were published that can be traced back to original English-language works by British writers, many via a French translation. The Russian dramatist Alexander Sumarkov first produced his adaptation of *Hamlet* in 1750, although the anguished doubt of the original was replaced by clear moral purpose.[7]

At the elite level, cultural borrowing from the Continent continued, but there was also a shift in attitude towards England's cultural relations with the rest of Europe. Thanks to a burgeoning economy, an apparently successful political system, and a great and powerful world empire, there was less of a general sense of inferiority than there had been in the seventeenth century and more of a sense of an elect nation. In 'Italy and Britain' from his *Letter from Italy* (1701), Joseph Addison found Britain superior despite the climate: ''Tis Liberty that crowns Britannia's Isle'. By the eighteenth century, in spite of the popularity of Batoni, Mengs,

Piranesi and other Rome-based artists, it appeared that the country of Newton and Sloane, Reynolds and Watt, had little to learn from the Continent. If it did, a process of Anglicanisation occurred, as with the Palladian style of architecture which was presented through works such as Colen Campbell's *Vitruvius Britannicus* (1725): produced by a Scot for a largely English readership. Newton, knighted in 1705, was seen as a demonstration of national achievement.

Whig confidence about the nature and role of the constitution, and the view of England as a country of liberty and progress, broadened into a moulding of English culture that was seen both in attitudes towards cosmopolitanism and in response to the English heritage. Modern Italy was increasingly seen as a decayed civilisation, and commentators claimed Rome's mantle for Britain, by which most English commentators meant in effect England. As a result, the most important cultural borrowing – from the Classical world – was not seen as threatening. In *The Progress of Poesy* (1757), Thomas Gray followed poetry's development from Classical Greece and Rome to modern England. Indeed admiration for Rome helped unite the elite.[8] Alexander Pope, who was greatly influenced by Roman literary models, produced in his poem *Windsor Forest* (1713) a celebration of rising national power under Queen Anne; but, as a Tory rather than a Whig, he lambasted, in *The Dunciad* (1728), a lack of cultural quality under her Hanoverian successors, presenting them in his *Epistle to Burlington* (1731) and *Epistle to Augustus* as unworthy.

At the same time, cosmopolitan aspirations and tensions were affected by a public ideology that was defined in terms of opposition to abroad. Certainly until the end of the 1750s, it was from continental Europe, Scotland and Ireland that the threats feared and decried in England emanated. Fear centred on Catholicism and autocracy, which appeared, to most commentators, to be two sides of the same coin, mutually sustaining in their antipathy to Protestantism and liberty.[9] This tradition of hostility looked back to the English Reformation, the subsequent English succession crises which lasted until 1603, English intervention in Catholic-Protestant struggles elsewhere, the British civil wars of 1639–51, and the relationships between religion, politics, and the succession in the reigns of Charles II and James II and in the Revolution of 1688. Important cultural manifestations included the partial jettisoning of the Italian Catholic Palladio in favour of the English Protestant Inigo Jones in Palladianism's panteon of heroes, as well as the interest in Gothicism, more specifically the idea that the English were the descendants of the Saxons who had enjoyed a liberty that was lost with the Norman Conquest. The cult of King Alfred, a defender of the nation who could be presented as a bold Patriot, was an aspect of this. In architectural terms it led, for example in the gardens of Stowe, to Gothic alongside Classical references.[10]

At the popular level, there was a robust xenophobic reaction to foreign culture seen in particular in a hostility to the employment of continental artists, especially French actors.[11] Mademoiselle Roland, a French dancer, was pelted with stones and fruit when she appeared at Drury Lane in January 1739. The theme of the danger and cost of cultural borrowing was repeated endlessly in the press. The *Worcester Post-Man* of 9 December 1720 carried a London report announcing that 'The new French theatre in the Hay-Market is just finished; and the actors are soon expected from Paris to open there; at the same time that one of our own, for want of due encouragement, is ready to be pulled down'.

The consequences of cultural borrowing from France were frequently presented on the stage, in particular in attacks on Frenchified returned tourists, as in James Smythe's *Rival Modes* (1727), Arthur Murphy's *Englishman from Paris* (1756), and Samuel Foote's *A Trip to Calais* (1776). Smyth's play introduced the Earl of Late-Airs and his son Lord Toupet who merged cultural and social tensions: he was not only unwilling to wear anything English but also 'always avoided *aucune chose de Bourgeois*'. Foote introduced the Francophile Luke Lappelle who complained 'there is a roughness, a *bourgoisy* about our barbarians, that is not at all to my taste'. Cultural pretentiousness and praise of foreignness for its own sake were mocked in the *Connoisseur*, a London weekly of 1754–56, as well as by Hogarth and others. A harsher note was introduced in Francis Lynch's play *The Independent Patriot* (1737), which not only satirised the cultural gullibility of many tourists but also struck a chord of sexual jealousy, Spruce declaring:

> As for ladies women, milliners, mantua-makers, embroiders, and lower citizens daughters, they fall before a foreign minister like grass before a scythe – there's Count Pulvilio, with the complexion of a mulatto, and the face of a baboon, has soused two thirds of all the nymphs of my acquaintance ... He spoiled a certain tradesman's daughter, I thought to spend my days with.[12]

The reference to the Count's appearance reflected the harsh depiction of most foreigners, especially in caricature.[13] The device of presenting foreigners as animals was also employed in literature, as in John Arbuthnot's *History of John Bull* (1712).

Whereas public criticism of government was generally rebutted, albeit not always to the same extent or with identical vigour, the patriotic critique was commonly not countered, and there was little attempt to offer a printed defence of aristocratic mores and fashions. In the cultural sphere, as in the political, threats were identified as originating from abroad, but being dangerously abetted by domestic supporters motivated by a variety of causes, including folly and self-indulgence.

Partly as a result, the use of the vernacular was an issue in manner, style, and cultural politics. The critique of Italian opera was a major theme in the debate, with John Gay's *The Beggar's Opera* (1728) and Handel's oratorios recording the greater use and prestige of the native tongue. There had been earlier anticipations. John Hughes's vernacular opera *Calypso and Telemachus* (1712) was put on at the Queen's Theatre in the Haymarket despite the hostility of part of the Italian company. The following year, Pope's prologue to Addison's *Cato* called for a learning from the Classical of the value of native culture:

> With honest scorn the first famed Cato viewed
> Rome learning arts from Greece, whom she subdued;
> Our scene precariously subsists too long
> On French translation and Italian song.
> Dare to have sense yourselves; assert the stage,
> Be justly warmed with your own native rage.
> Such plays alone should please a British ear,

Gay reached for change with more than his use of the vernacular. Although in some respects it was just another play-with-songs (only with more songs than usual), *The Beggar's Opera* was also a stylistic revolution, especially with the replacement of sung recitative with the faster flowing spoken word. The use of old English airs in the work helped suggest that its novelty was as one with an important cultural continuity. Italian opera, in contrast, was held by hostile critics to be degenerate and morally dubious, the ambivalent sexuality of the singers – castrati and women dressed as men – supposedly symbolising its corrupt and alien nature.

Greater interest in England's cultural past, especially in the second half of the century, was part of the process by which a more self-confident nation focused on native values and models, although the *St James's Chronicle*, in its issue of 10 May 1766, referred to 'this Paris-loving-age'. Already, in his *Essay on the Theory of Painting* (1715), Jonathan Richardson had argued that the English could equal Italian 'old masters'. An English literary canon was defined in the middle decades of the century and, in this process, critical discussion interacted with the demands of the book trade and the shaping of the market. Shakespeare, the subject of John Dennis's *Three Letters on the Genius and Writings of Shakespeare* (1711), had been criticised by Charles Gildon in *The Laws of Poetry* (1721) for failing to abide by such laws. He was now praised as the National Poet, presented as better than French rivals, with his monument in Westminster Abbey from the late 1730s, and was the most frequently cited authority in Johnson's *Dictionary*. Indeed, in his preface to his edition of Shakespeare's plays, Johnson provided a criticism of Addison's *Cato* that made clear how tastes had changed:

> *Cato* affords a splendid exhibition of artificial and fictitious manners, and delivers just and noble sentiments, in diction easy, elevated and harmonious, but its hopes and fears communicate no vibration to the heart.

The defence of Shakespeare was conducted in a spirit of national rivalry. 'An old-fashioned Englishman', in a letter printed in the *St James's Chronicle* of 13 May 1769 claimed:

> We are a people that should be often roused to a sense of our blessings, and to the means of securing them. French clothes, French cookery, French literature, French plays, French shoes, and French hats, have so possessed us from top to toe, that if we do not guard against these encroaching refinements, we shall have even our immortal Shakespeare plucked from his eminence by French critics, and degraded to the character of buffoon and drunken savage, which the spirit of envy and ignorance has been pleased to call him by the pen of Monsieur de Voltaire ... while we can think and feel like Britons, we shall ever glory in the immortal productions of the greatest poet which any age or country has produced.

In *The Vicar of Wakefield* (1766), Goldsmith referred to 'other fashionable topics, such as pictures, taste, Shakespeare, and the musical glasses'. Garrick was responsible for Shakespeare's plays being staged more frequently, and actively promoted the Shakespeare Jubilee in 1769, the year of the publication of Elizabeth Montagu's *An Essay on the Writings and Genius of Shakespeare.* The Jubilee was wrecked by poor weather but Garrick then staged a play about the Jubilee at Drury Lane.[14] Shakespeare attracted other actors and entrepreneurs, and also editors. A more naturalistic approach to acting led Charles Macklin to make his name playing Shylock as a tragic character and to play Macbeth in Scots clothing in 1772. No fewer than six major editions of Shakespeare's complete works appeared that century: by Rowe (1709), Pope (1725), Theobald (1733), Warburton (1747), Johnson (1765) and Malone (1790), and other Shakespearean editors and commentators included Edward Capell (1768), and Isaac Reed and John Monk, both of whom published works in 1785.[15] Acting and editing were not always separate activities: James Dance (1722–74), who assumed the surname Love, was a comic actor of note, who was particularly successful as Falstaff, but he also sought to improve Shakespeare, publishing an altered *Timon of Athens* in 1768. Editions and commentary led to much debate, as with Thomas Edwards' attack, in *The Canons of Criticism* (7th edition, 1765), on Warburton's edition. Shakespeare interested other writers, for example Ann Radcliffe, who quoted him at the start of some of her chapters, while George Colman the Younger used him as a model for his plays *The Battle of Hexham* (1789) and *The Surrender of Calais* (1791), and also borrowed ideas for particular scenes.

Interest in Stratford-upon-Avon as a cultural shrine developed, and even a Shakespeare forgery industry flourished. Shakespeare and his plays attracted attention across the arts,[16] notably from painters. William Hogarth's *Falstaff Examining his Recruits* (1730) the first known painting of a Shakespeare scene, may also have been the depiction of a performance. Subsequently, many painters responded to Shakespeare, Angelica Kaufman producing an *Allegory of the Birth of Shakespeare.* Francis Hayman, George Romney and Thomas Jones all painted Prospero and Miranda spying the shipwrecked Ferdinand from *The Tempest.* Romney was particularly interested in Shakespeare, *King Lear in the Tempest Tearing off his Robes* being one of his first major paintings. Actors were depicted in Shakespearean roles, John Henderson as Macbeth by Romney, whose portrait captured the intensity that tragic actors increasingly sought. *Swinney's Birmingham and Stafford Chronicle* of 2 May 1776 carried an advertisement offering illustrations of thirty-six leading actors in Shakespearian roles.

There was also interest in some of Shakespeare's contemporaries. John Upton, who had already published *Critical Observations on*

Shakespeare (1746), brought out *Remarks on Three Plays of Benjamin Jonson* in 1749 and an edition of Spenser's *Faerie Queene* in 1758, while Peter Whalley produced a scholarly edition of Jonson's works in 1756. As with Shakespeare, there was debate about Spenser. Thomas Warton's *Observations on the Fairy Queen of Spenser* were in turn countered by William Huggins in *The Observer Observed* (1756). Publication, debate and the entrepreneurial activities of booksellers were crucial to the definition of a literary canon. This was not simply a matter of national pride and cultural celebration, but also the product of a need to assess historical and current literature in response to anxieties over quality and the relationship between standards and the pressures of the market.[17] Modern versions of Geoffrey Chaucer's *Canterbury Tales* appeared with some frequency, but tales judged indelicate, especially for female readers, such as those of the Miller, Reeve and Wife of Bath, might be omitted.[18] John Milton's masque presented at Ludlow in 1634, was revived from 1738 as a piece of public theatre, thanks to a successful adaptation by John Dalton who retitled it *Comus* after the sorcerer protagonist.

One aspect of the definition of the canon was the engagement with real and supposed forgeries. Thomas Chatterton (1752–1770) invented a fifteenth-century poet Thomas Rowley, allegedly a Bristol priest. The controversy over his works led to Chatterton's suicide and to contributions to the subject from major figures, Warton publishing *An Enquiry into the Authenticity of the Poems Attributed to Rowley* (1782). Interest in the canon also interacted with the opportunity to make money from compilations. As a result, collections frequently appeared, for example Samuel Derrick's *A Poetical Dictionary: or The Beauties of the English Poets* (1761). The sense of the value of the national theatrical tradition led to Charles Dibdin's five-volume *Complete History of the English Stage* (1800).

Similar views lay behind the interest in earlier English music, particularly Purcell and Handel. This led to cathedral festivals in music, as well as to the foundation first of the Academy of Vocal (later Ancient) Music in 1726, although the Academy also showed an interest in non-English composers. Later, in 1776, the concern with earlier music, especially that of Handel, contributed to the foundation of the fashionable Concert of Ancient Music, established by aristocrats led by John, 4th Earl of Sandwich. This was linked to a social and political conservatism, and, in the case of many subscribers, with an Evangelical piety.[19] Finally, this process led to the mighty Handel Commemoration celebrations of 1784, held over five days in Westminster Abbey with a choir and orchestra of over five hundred, an unprecedented number for England. The *Messiah* was performed at two of the concerts. These celebrations were so successful that they were repeated in 1785–87, 1790, and in 1791, the last with over one thousand performers, and in the presence of George III.[20] These were not the sole Handel concerts. Instead the celebrations encouraged other performances. At Drury Lane on 17 March 1786 'Redemption. A Selected Oratorio selected from the great and favourite Works of Mr Handel, that were performed at his commemoration' was staged.

There was also an interest in earlier music, such as the early seventeenth-century madrigals of John Wilbye which were much sung not only by the Madrigal Society, but also at the concerts of the Academy of Ancient Music and the Concert of Ancient Music. They were also reprinted in score in 1784, while major collections of madrigals appeared in 1765, 1768 and 1785. In 1779 John Smith, a chorister of the Chapel Royal and a glee-composer, published a collection of songs composed about 1500.

At the same time, this concern with earlier English music was matched by an interest in contemporary continental music. This was not only a case of the popularity of Haydn in London, a very different setting for the composer to his earlier life as court composer in the service of Prince Esterhazy in Hungary. The advertisement for 'Mr Clark's annual concert and ball' published in *Swinney's Birmingham and Stafford Chronicle* on 5 May 1791 noted that 'by particular desire, the grand overture that was performed at the Emperor's late coronation will open the performance'.

In literature, there was a movement away from Classical and towards native values and models. Entailing the searching and utilisation of a varied cultural inheritance in order to serve the needs of an apparently distinctive national culture, this led to the anglicanisation of Classical and Hebraic forms, techniques and preoccupations. John Dryden anglicised the epic and Abraham Cowley the ode, while the novel presented a new and accessible (to the literate) form.[21] With *Artexerxes* (1762), a translation of Metastaso's *Artaserse*, Thomas Arne produced an English equivalent to Italian opera, which enjoyed considerable success. The same year, in a less grand fashion, his *Love in a Village* was a successful vernacular pastiche.

The cult of the national past was seen with David Mallet and James

Thomson's masque *Alfred* (1740) with music by Thomas Arne, famous for the song 'Rule Britannia', and with William Mason's plays *Elfrida* (1772) and *Caractacus* (1776). Johann Christian Bach, the 'English Bach', had also paid tribute to this hero resisting the Romans, writing the opera *Carattaco* (1767) for the King's Theatre. In the 1730s and 1740s, merely to mention King Alfred was to make a political point about the need for national integrity and the defence of national honour in the face of Hanoverian influences, although Alfred could also serve as a symbol for England and Protestantism (and thus Hanover) against the Stuarts and Catholics.

Legal culture was similarly Anglicised. In 1731, English replaced 'Law French' as the language of authority in the common law courts; while English law was a subject of study. In 1713, Matthew Hale published his *History of the Common Law of England*, which linked the common law, Parliament and national identity. William Blackstone, appointed in 1758 the first Vinerian Professor of English Law at Oxford, published the *Commentaries on the Laws of England* (1765–69), in part to acclaim English common law against Roman law.

The domestic cultural tradition became stronger in the second half of the century, in part thanks to the institutionalisation of art, not least through the Royal Academy, established in 1768, and to greater national wealth. The Academy itself was the realisation of long-held ideas for an institution that would combine artistic education with national glory. In 1749, John Gwynn had published *An Essay on Design: Including Proposals for Erecting a Public Academy ... for Educating the British Youth in Drawing, and the Several Arts Depending Thereon*. Artists and craftsmen developed products of excellence in areas formerly dominated by foreign work: English silverware gained in importance, and ceramics produced in London and Staffordshire were admired for their beauty. For design, Wedgwood called on the artistic skills of Flaxman and Stubbs.[22] In painting, a modernised Classical style was popularised by Reynolds and taught at the Royal Academy. It served to provide grandiloquent dignity and a sense of destiny to those whose portraits he painted. Reynolds was particularly impressed by Raphael and what he saw as a Grand Style that could be introduced into English painting, but he displayed little interest in contemporary Italian artists.[23] On the stage, Garrick developed a naturalistic school of acting believed to be superior to continental acting methods.

Indeed, it has been argued that the elite cosmopolitanism of the early decades of the century was challenged by the rise of a national consciousness whose bourgeois champions sought to proclaim and define an English culture that would be recognisably superior to any other.[24] In particular, after the defeat of France in the Seven Years' War (1756–63), there was a self-confident vigour that greatly affected cultural life. Rococo influences were displaced in favour of a less obviously derivative art and dependent culture.[25] Although England, particularly London, remained very much a destination for foreign artists seeking work, the relationship with foreign artists was different to the situation in the first half of the century. Italian opera, however, remained a separate community, In the 1750s, Italian opera in London was in a state of very serious disarray, following a sequence of schisms, failures, bankruptcies and imprisoned or absconding managers. Managerial shortcomings were more than matched by the sense of artistic decline: indifferent performers and an over-reliance on the pasticcio had become perennial problems. New managers changed the system. The novelist Frances Brooke was a crucial figure in the revitalisation of the King's Theatre in the 1770s: she had drive and proved herself a very capable manager, both financially and in artistic planning. She was motivated by a conviction that she had been slighted by David Garrick when he rejected her play *Virginia*, and she set out to show that his artistic judgement was flawed. The links between London, and Rome and Naples were close. The English artistic community in Italy sent up-to-date information about singers, composers and scores back to London. Through her contacts with Ozias Humphry and others, Brooke was well informed about operas that were proving successful and gossip about opera stars, and popular scores were sent to London. The connection with Rome was particularly important in the supply of recent *opera buffe*, and works by Piccinni, Paisiello and Anfossi were sent to Brooke to be adapted for the King's Theatre. Charles Wiseman, the longstanding agent of the King's Theatre in Rome, sometimes referred to as Signor Carlo Wiseman, was a crucial musical broker, and Earl Cowper played a comparable role in Florence. The season as a whole could stand or fall by the reception of one singer, and Caterina Gabrielli's debut in 1776 in *Didone* was sensational, both for the publicity hype and for her reception, although this was followed by a debate over her true merits. Despite the sensation of her first appearance, Gabrielli failed to live up to audience expectations. Her reception provides an interesting example of London's attitude towards the vocal qualities of star singers, the debate focused on the issue of volume versus musicality. Gabrielli's lack of volume was equated with a lack of warmth or commitment, but others discerned a magical quality in her soft singing.[26]

Johann Christian Bach, the youngest son of Johann Sebastian Bach, who was hired in 1762 to compose Italian operas for the King's Theatre, London, producing a number, including *La Clemenza di Scipione* (1775), came out of this community into a wider public market as a result of the Hanover Square Concerts. In the second half of the century, in general the demands of the anonymous market were more important for artists than they had been, and those of private patronage correspondingly less significant. The latter, however, still played a role, as with the German-born and Italian-trained painter Johann or John Zoffany who moved to English in about 1758 and benefited from royal patronage. Angelica Kauffmann not only did decorative painting for Robert Adam, but, in 1781, married Antonio Zucchi, an Italian who worked on many Adam interiors.

The earlier sense of English cultural inferiority had also gone. In 1772, Reynolds depicted England as more dynamic than France:

> There is at least a dozen of their most able academicians come over to try their fortune among us and we hear of more coming. There is no employment for them in France, either from the poverty of the nation or from the declining of all arts amongst them except that of furnishing Europe with bauble.[27]

Philip James de Loutherbourg (1740–1812), a German-born Alsatian who left Paris for London in 1771, became chief designer of scenery for Garrick at Drury Lane Theatre, where he transformed scene painting. In part, this very much responded to current events. The *Morning Post, and Daily Advertiser* of 17 March 1786 advertised:

> Mr Loutherbourg's Eidophusikon, including the awful and pathetic scene of the storm and shipwreck, conveying a very striking idea of the late dreadful catastrophe of the *Halsewell* East Indiaman; and the Grand Scene from Milton; confessedly the Chef d'oeuvres of that eminent and incomparable artist ... The pauses necessary to change the scenery will be supplied with English readings and recitals.

Also a painter of landscapes in the Romantic style and of battle-scenes in the French Revolutionary War, such as *Admiral Duncan's Victory at Camperdown*, Loutherbourg depicted a dynamic country, most obviously in his scenes of industrialisation, especially *Coalbrookdale by Night*, although in other respects as well. His *A Midsummer Afternoon with a Methodist Preacher* captured the unregimented nature of individual faith.

While foreigners came to England, the English who went abroad did so not only to Europe but also to the British colonies. The latter had a growing and varied impact on domestic culture. Alongside prosaic information about developments in the colonies, there was the playing out of moral themes that the exoticism of colonial life permitted. Thus, the tale of 'Inkle and Yarico', published in the leading English periodical, The *Spectator*, on 13 March 1711, was one of humanity affronted, and morality breached, by slavery:

> Mr Thomas Inkle, an ambitious young English trader cast ashore in the Americas, is saved from violent death at the hands of savages by the endearments of Yarico, a beautiful Indian maiden. Their romantic intimacy in the forest moves Inkle to pledge that, were his life to be preserved, he would return with her to England, supposedly as his wife. The lovers' tender liaison progresses over several months until she succeeds in signalling a passing English ship. They are rescued by the crew, and with vows to each other intact, they embark for Barbados. Yet when they reach the island Inkle's former mercantile instincts are callously revived, for he sells her into slavery, at once raising the price he demands when he learns that Yarico is carrying his child.

This was but a stage in a tale that had surfaced in Richard Ligon's *History of the Island of Barbadoes* (1657), and whose iterations were to include George Colman the Younger's much-performed play *Inkle and Yarico* (1787),[28] which, in the fashion of the time, was provided with a happy ending. The popularity of the story reflected the way in which the transoceanic world could provide a setting for moral challenges. Slavery was the most important instance and provided critics with a variety of targets.[29] Thomas Day's first publication *The Dying Negro* (1773) criticised the American Patriots for supporting slavery (a theme he returned to in *Reflections on the Present State of England and the Independence of America*, 1782), but he went on to attack the war in his poems *The Devoted Legions* (1776) and *The Desolation of America* (1777).

Slavery was not the sole moral issue in European expansion that was considered, although it was one that was particularly at issue for Britain, the leading slave trader in the second half of the century. In 1792, Thomas Morton had considerable success with *Columbus*, a tale of doomed cross-cultural love set against the background of harsh

European expansion. England abroad was more clearly at issue when John Gay had the protagonist of *Polly* (1729), his ballad-opera sequel to *The Beggar's Opera*, travel to the West Indies in search of the transported Macheath.

Aside from morality, there was adventure. Exploration provided a staple for the world of print, as travel literature offered vivid accounts for a society interested in novelty, including fanciful tales of wonder.[30] Narratives such as William Dampier's *Voyage to New Holland in the Year 1699* (1703–9), William Funnell's *A Voyage Round the World* (1707) and Edward Cooke's *A Voyage to the South Sea and Round the World* (1712) helped create a sense of the Pacific and its surrounds that could be seized from the real and imagined grasp of Spain.[31] The difficulties of engaging with the problems posed by the now global character of maritime ambitions were also recounted: in *A Rake's Progress* (1735) Hogarth presented a madman trying to solve the problems of longitude on the madhouse wall. Individual works were given further prominence by being republished in collected works, such as Thomas Astley's *New General Collection of Voyages and Travels* (1745).

This also affected the world of fiction, particularly in Gulliver's voyage to Lilliput, which was located in the South Pacific, while Daniel Defoe's *Robinson Crusoe* was based on the marooning of the privateer Alexander Selkirk on Juan Férnandez in 1704–9. Fiction could be satirical in character, as in a pamphlet of 1739 that reflected an attitude seen as humorous that was at the same time disparaging, and also employed in this fashion against non-European people. Entitled *An Essay towards the Character of the Late Chimpanzee*, the subject was a female chimpanzee brought from West Africa in 1738, but presented as a lascivious 'lady': 'there was a gentleman always with her; whom some ladies (to prevent any reflections) called her uncle: But I can assure them he was no relation; but only her steward'.

As the colonies were overseas, their role also contributed to the maritime theme in national culture, which, was seen in works such as the ship and port paintings of Samuel Scott.[32] Compared to the West Indies and the oceans, other colonies had a smaller impact, but they still featured. The novelist Frances Brooke, in *The History of Emily Montague* (1769), offered descriptions of Canada's landscape and social life based on her period there as the wife of a garrison chaplain.[33] The impact of wealth gained overseas on English society became a stock scenario, whether the wealth derived from the East Indies, as with Samuel Foote's depiction of Sir Matthew Mite, the extortionist cum nabob, in his play *The Nabob* (1772), or the West Indies, as with Jane Austen's novel *Mansfield Park* (1814). Knowledge of the outer world was necessary to understand many allusions, not least a miscomparison by Mrs Malaprop in Sheridan's *The Rivals*: 'She's as headstrong as an allegory on the banks of the Nile'.

Britain's engagement with the wider, non-European world also led to the production of works that were only partly affected by continental prototypes. The painters who accompanied Cook on his voyages, such as William Hodges and John Webber, provided a powerful visual image of the South Seas, for example Hodges's *Monuments on Eastern Island*.[34] His *Tahiti Revisited* (1776) offered a vista of paradise, but was also influenced by Classical models as interpreted in the tradition of Claude Lorrain. Hodges (1744–97) was draughtsman on Cook's second voyage to the Pacific. He was subsequently employed by the Admiralty in finishing his drawings and in superintending their engraving for the published account of the voyages. He first exhibited at the Royal Academy with Pacific views. Painting in India between 1778 and 1784, Hodges produced works that were engraved for an English market fascinated by distant lands. Less successful as a painter of British landscapes and allegorical pictures, he retired from the profession, becoming a banker, although he failed in that career.[35]

The portrayal of the Pacific was taken further with the portraits in the Classical manner of denizens of the South Seas brought back to England, especially Omai, who was depicted as a very noble figure, for example in William Parry's portrait of him alongside Joseph Banks and Daniel Solander (1775–76). Hodges was not alone in painting in India.[36] The musicologist Charles Burney's son James sailed on Cook's second and third naval voyages, learning Polynesian and recording Polynesian music in his journal to help solve the problem whether harmony and counterpoint was understood in the South Seas.[37]

The impact of the non-European world was varied and widespread. Ceramics were greatly influenced not only by the United Provinces (Holland) but also by the Orient, the cultural pattern of which was fixed in William Chambers's *Designs of Chinese Buildings, Furniture, Dresses, Machines and Utensils* (1757). In the 1760s, drawing on Japanese *Kakiemon* designs and colours, the skilled painters of the Worcester factory produced more elaborate versions. Richly coloured and flamboyant, depicting dragons, phoenix and ho-ho birds, as well as exotic vegetation such as chrysanthemums and bamboo, this pottery reflected interest in the Orient. Gold was used for details and highlights. Teaware patterns such as *Rich Queen's* and *Jabberwocky* were very popular. Indeed, tea, chocolate, coffee and sugar created not only patterns of sociability but also a need and opportunity for a new sphere of design and decorative work, although Johnson also addressed the complaint that tea was degenerate.[38] In a different sphere, although also an aspect of conspicuous consumption, India and North America were sources of plants for English gardens. In the later decades of the century many parks had 'American Gardens' containing trees that were regarded as particularly fine in the autumn. During the century, over three hundred new American species were imported into England, with John Bartram of Philadelphia playing a crucial role from 1734. White cedar was one of his most popular introductions.

Britain's military success and commercial strength led to a triumphalist frame of mind in which credit was reflected on the national character and the political system. In the *Royal Magazine* of June 1760, Oliver Goldsmith proclaimed: 'Hail Britain, happiest of countries! happy in thy climate, fertility, situation, and commerce; but still happier in the peculiar nature of thy laws and government.' Victories encouraged for example the depiction of warships and other maritime themes on canvas.[39] Richard Paton exhibited paintings of recent successes, displaying Boscawen's victory off Lagos and the capture of the *Foudroyant* in pictures exhibited with the Society of Artists in 1762. The cartouche to a map of India published in 1782 by James Rennell, former Surveyor-General of the Bengal Presidency, showed Britannia receiving the sacred scriptures of India from a Brahman. Four years earlier, Spiridion Roma had been commissioned by the directors of the East India Company to paint the ceiling of their Leadenhall Street headquarters. His *The East Offering its Riches to Britannia* showed India and China, both as women, indeed presenting their riches. The expansion of British territorial power did not lessen the exoticism of the East, but instead increased interest in it, even though much remained fantasy, as in the successful *Tales of the Genii* (1764), a work, based on the *Arabian Nights*, by James Ridley, one of the many literary chaplains of the age. As with many literary works, the character of *The Tales* reflected the fact that they were originally published in parts.

Power in the Orient, however, produced a number of disturbing cultural and political resonances. It seemed to position Britain as the descendant not of republican Rome with its virtues and vital energies but of Imperial Rome with its self-indulgent decadence. The gain of an Indian-based Oriental empire encouraged comparison with imperial Rome because, unlike Britain's North American empire, but like that of imperial Rome, the new empire in India had no ethnic underpinning and was clearly imperial. Writers in the tradition of civic humanism, and, later, Romantic writers such as Byron, Shelley and de Quincey, searched for points of reference around which to discuss their anxieties about the effects of empire upon metropolitan culture; and imperial Rome was the obvious parallel.[40]

Triumphalism in part reflected the challenges Britain encountered, and these led to patriotic themes. The culture of patriotism was very varied in idioms, ranging from Charles Dibdin's musical farce *Plymouth in an Uproar* performed in 1779, the year in which France and Spain attempted invasion, to the quiet confidence of the heroic poses of generals in the portraits that matched those of assured landowners. Dibdin's farce followed Frederick Pilon's *The Invasion: or A Trip to Brighthelmstone* (Brighton), which was popular at Covent Garden in late 1778, while, appearing after the threat of invasion had receded, Sheridan's *The Critic* (1779) ridiculed the patriotic depiction of the danger in the shape of Puff's absurd *The Spanish Armada*. The audiences at Convent Garden also saw other works marking Britain's war effort, including *Illumination: or The Glazier's Conspiracy* (1779), a prelude based on the London illuminations after the popular acquittal of Admiral Keppel on a court martial for his conduct at the battle of Ushant in 1778, and *The Siege of Gibraltar,* a musical farce of 1780 celebrating the British success in resisting Spanish attack. The resolute defence of the fortress was also recorded on canvas, with Reynolds's portrait of its governor Lord Heathfield hung in Boydell's Shakespeare Gallery surrounded by four paintings of the siege by Richard Paton. Past and present greatness were therefore brought side by side. Family collections also recorded military service, as indeed did the family stories satirised by Laurence Sterne. At Ickworth the portraits include Admiral Augustus Hervey, later 3rd Earl of Bristol, showing him as a captain during the successful operations at Havana in 1762, and also John, Lord Hervey, eldest son of the 4th Earl, in the uniform of a captain, both by Gainsborough.

The 'pantomimical interludes' offered audiences at Birmingham's New Street theatre took note of the country's spreading power. For

17 August 1791, between Elizabeth Inchbald's *Next Door Neighbours* and the musical farce *Midas*, the audience was promised:

> a grand serious pantomime in one act called Soldiers' Festival, or The Night before the Battle ... with an exact representation of the siege of Quebec, an engagement between the English and French armies, and the death of General Wolfe.

Victory and heroic death[41] in 1759 still resonated, but for 22 August 1791 something more recent was promised:

> A pantomime exhibition called Botany Bay; or, A Trip to Port Jackson, with entire new scenery, painted for the occasion ... in which will be introduced a picturesque view of the coast of New South Wales ... arrival of the Grand Fleet, landing, reception, and employment of the convicts. To conclude with the ceremony of planting the British flag, on taking possession of a new discovered island, with a dance by the convicts, and the grand chorus of 'God Save the King'.

This followed 'A Touch of the Times: being a comic description of wonderful and strange events, particularly of those famous pugilists ...' and a new comedy, *Better Late Than Never*, and preceded 'The musical entertainment of Rosina'.

In 1777–83, James Barry had produced a set of paintings to decorate the Great Hall of the Society for the Encouragement of Arts, Commerce and Manufactures, a body, founded in 1754, that offered decorative medals and money to reward innovations in various fields, including the arts, which were seen as aesthetic capital that would benefit the nation.[42] The array of philosophers, scientists and others displayed by Barry in this set reached back to the ancient world, and culminated with modern British talent, for example poets from Homer to Goldsmith. Johnson and Arthur Young were both shown. To Barry and to his patrons, the British could be seen as the new Olympians, equal to the greatness of the past. Furthermore, the sculptor John Bacon (1740–99) produced a bronze statue of George III in the courtyard of Somerset House in a Roman costume holding the rudder of a ship attended by a majestic lion and above a colossal figure of Father Thames presented as a reborn Neptune. Spreading power was also seen in cultural terms, with English styles and stylists influential in the colonies, satisfying both public and private patronage.

The last decade of the century, however, posed new problems, as the French Revolution encouraged a domestic radicalism that challenged established suppositions. Many cultural figures were exhilarated or appalled by this challenge, sometimes both;[43] few were neutral. Romanticism thus had a clear political context and programme: in theme and content, many figures were engaged in a struggle for imaginative freedom. Wordsworth managed to make his fusion of political and personal awareness and commitment poetically intense, although his most overtly political poems were unpublished in the 1790s. In his poem *The French Revolution* (1790), William Blake represented the Bastille, the Parisian fortress stormed the previous year, in terms of a symbolic seven towers with the names Horror, Darkness, Religion, Order, Destiny, Bloody and God; Darkness including the cruelly-pinioned man in the iron mask. In *The Prelude*, Wordsworth, who arrived in France in 1790, wrote:

> ... 'twas a time when Europe was rejoiced,
> France standing on the top of golden hours,
> And human nature seeming born again.
> How bright a face is worn when joy of one
> Is joy of tens of millions.

Samuel Coleridge and Robert Southey also both initially supported the French Revolution, and it also provided them with a significant subject in their play *The Fall of Robespierre* (1794), although they were subsequently disillusioned with its violence and radicalism, creating a poetry that reflected the contradictions of their position, and of the Revolution.[44]

Romanticism was a term not used until the early nineteenth-century in relation to writers we now call Romantic. Partly as a consequence, Romanticism was a tendency, not a programme, but a central theme in this tendency was a reaction against earlier Classical cultural themes, especially the emphasis on restraint and order, and the role of a literary tradition focused on the Classical world. Romanticism, instead, embraced a diversity born of the individual experience of the artist and its capacity to engage with and inspire the imagination of the individual reader and spectator. In place of convention came an emphasis on the artist's individualism as a product of the integrity of innate vision, an emphasis that also encouraged a rethinking of past quality. This vision was of the spirit, rather than the mind, indeed of feeling unconfined by restraint, a tendency formerly ascribed in a pejorative fashion to women.[45] This holistic account led itself not to the compromises and restraints of order, but rather to a presentation of the vital soul of the individual, and thus of society. Breaking boundaries was largely a matter of changes within individual genres, but in some cases, such as that of Blake, spanned genres. Blake also exemplified the belief that the stress on the individual vision was truer than that on learned artistic behaviour.

In response to the radical drives of the period, a group of writers developed the novel as a means of social criticism pertinent to what they saw as the political issues of the time. The most striking result was William Godwin's *Things as They Are; or The Adventures of Caleb Williams* (1794), which in part was a literary vehicle for his *Enquiry Concerning Social Justice* (1793) and translated the problem of malignity from the depraved sin of Gothic novels to the pain stemming from inequity.[46] Thomas Holcroft's *Anna St Ives* (1792), Charlotte Smith's *Desmond* (1792), Mary Wollstonecraft's *The Wrongs of Woman: or Maria* (1798), and Godwin's *St Leon* (1799) were other radical political novels. The radical volatility of the period also encouraged anew the probing of imaginary foreign perspectives in order to throw light on the situation in England. In George Cumberland's *The Captive of the Castle of Senaar* (1798), the utopian society of the Sophians is introduced, a very different one to contemporary England, without oppression, property or marriage but, instead, with the rule of rational liberty. *Hermsprong: or Man As He Is Not* (1796) by Robert Bage (1728–1801), a novelist who ran a Staffordshire paper-mill, offered a radical critique of the social system, using the perspective of a Native American who personified the virtuous Noble Savage in a more modern setting; but with the radicalism tempered by an appreciation of the constraints of society. As a result, the hero in the end returns to his true role as part of the establishment, not a rejection of it.

Although these novels have enjoyed much attention, they were outweighed, at least in quantity, by the anti-Jacobin novels that appeared, especially after the French Revolutionary Terror of 1793–94, works such as Isaac D'Israeli's *Vaurien: or Sketches of the Times* (1797). These novels depicted English radicals as dangerous allies of French Jacobins, their secret intentions allegedly revealed by this connection, as well as personally immoral. In *Vaurien*, Mary Wollstonecraft was Miss Million, a backer of sex outside marriage, and Godwin Mr Subtile, 'the coldest blooded metaphysician of the age'. In contrast to these figures, the novels offered a defence of existing social arrangements, not least through a presentation of the nobility as the traditional leaders of society.[47] This literary offensive-defensive was matched in newspapers and periodicals, and was the cultural counterpart of the powerful Loyalist current of the period.[48] The general social context was an opposition to social mobility, industrialisation and urbanisation, in short a repositioning of the earlier rural tradition in more clearly political terms. This opposition also drew on well-established notions of the value of restraint, as with Anna Maria Porter's novel *Walsh Colville: or, A Young Man's First Entrance into Life* (1797), with the dangers of indulgence and sin now in part interpreted in political as well as moral terms.

When on 23 January 1793, the news of Louis XVI's execution in the Place de la Concorde two days earlier reached London, the play at the Haymarket came to an abrupt end when the audience shouted out 'No Farce, No Farce' and left. Loyalism had a variety of literary consequences. The unsuccessful playwright John Delap, for example, responded to the crisis of the 1790s with poems including *Sedition: an Ode Occasioned by His Majesty's Late Proclamation* (1792). This was a more pronounced instance of the anti-radical tendencies already seen in the 1770s and 1780s, especially in response to the radicalism linked to domestic support for the American Revolution. For example, the radicalism of the historian Catherine Macaulay led to serious criticism from the late 1770s.[49] In the crisis of the 1790s, there was also a stepping up of the regulation of opinion, not only with moves against sedition but also through the registration of printing presses, introduced in 1799. At the same time, Loyalism, at least in some variants, can be seen as a modernist argument because a major theme in Loyalist propaganda was to depict radical notions of equality as incompatible with a modern, commercial society.

There was also in the 1790s a more general process of cultural reinterpretation as part of the conservative patriotism that held such sway during the decade. In part, this focused on relations between Britain and the Continent, which were heavily politicised. In opposing the French Revolution, the elite identified themselves with nationalism, although they did so at the cost of discarding their old cosmopolitanism in favour of middle-class morality. The culture of the Victorian elite was thus determined by the reaction to the challenges of the late eighteenth century.[50] This is an over simplistic account of the process of cultural formation, but also one that captures the active reshaping seen in the period. This reshaping was not simply a response to domestic radicalism and French Revolution, but they were important in providing themes and motives. William Hodges' painted two large allegorical works, *The Effects of Peace* and *The Effects of War*, but when displayed in 1794 they offended Frederick, Duke of York, commander of the British forces in the Low Countries and son of George III. Without court favour, having earlier enjoyed official patronage, and failing to strike a successful public echo, Hodges gave up painting.

A more popular academician, James Northcote (1746–1831), a protégé of Reynolds, helped to form a particular image of the national past from 1784. His paintings included *The Murder of the Young Princes in the Tower, Sir William Walworth … Killing Wat Tyler*, and *The Revolution of 1688*. The Whig myth now as national celebration was also seen in Northcote's painting *The Landing of William of Orange at Torbay*, which was engraved by James Parker in 1801.

More generally, there was a powerful historical interest in English culture that is overly neglected. Plays on historical subjects, such as Richard Cumberland's *The Battle of Hastings* (1778), George Colman the Younger's *The Battle of Hexham* (1789) and *The Surrender of Calais* (1791), and Edward Jerningham's less successful *The Siege of Berwick: A Tragedy* (1793), were an important genre, *The Surrender of Calais* closing with

> Rear, rear our English banner high
> In token proud of victory!
> Where'er our god of battle strides,
> Laud sound the trump of fame!
> Where'er the English warrior rides,
> May laurelled conquest grace his name.

Epic poetry contributed to this patriotic fervour, for example Samuel Wilcocke's *Britannia: A Poem* (1797), which looked at ancient history. Epic poetry was also an aspect of the celebration of modern endeavour. Nelson's victory over the French at the battle of the Nile in 1798 led to W. Hildreth's *The Niliadian Epic Poem: Written in the Honour of the Glorious Victory of August 1798* (1799), as well as a host of shorter works, such as John Delap's *The Lord of Nile: An Elegy* (1799).

At the close of the century, the arts appeared to have a clear political dimension. Coleridge, Southey and Wordsworth all became disillusioned with the French Revolution and each, instead, became willing to support established notions of community and culture. It would be mistaken, however, to think of culture simply in political terms. There were also stylistic issues at work, for example in the theatre where, alongside populist themes, there was also a fashion for melodramatic Gothic sensation, and a more grandiose, if not histrionic, manner of acting associated in particular with Sarah Siddons and her brother John Philip Kemble and linked to the painterly values of the period.[51] This showiness was to be more generally true of the artistic life of the early years of the nineteenth century. Similarly, the extent to which Thomas Girtin's decision to use water colours as a worthy medium in their own right, rather than a preparation for work in oils, should be seen as political is unclear.

There was no cultural transformation at the close of the century, but rather a continuation of the complex and varied process of change that is overly simplified if it is discussed simply in terms of the French Revolution or, indeed, of Romanticism. What was clear was that the successful defiance of domestic radical change and of France ensured that the triumphant marketplace was not overthrown and did not have to accept direction. Although governmental roles were important,[52] entrepreneurs treating culture as a commodity whose value was set by the market remained the dominant figures, and this continued to be the case until the state came to play a greater role in cultural sponsorship in the late twentieth century.

Notes

Notes to Introduction

1. T. Whately, *Observations on Modern Gardening* (London, 1770), pp. 183–84.
2. *Political State of Great Britain*, October 1738, p. 300; *Gentleman's Magazine*, 7 (1738), pp. 532–3, 545.
3. Cambis to Amelot, French Foreign Minister, 23 October 1738, Paris, Quai d'Orsay, Archives du Ministere des Affaires Etrangères, Correspondance Politique, Angleterre (hereafter AE, CP, Ang.) 399 fols 224–6.
4. Amelot to Cambis, 30 October 1738, AE, CP, Ang. 399 fol. 227.
5. G. Mackaness, *Admiral Arthur Phillip, Founder of New South Wales 1738–1814* (Sydney, 1957), p. 204.
6. J. M. Black, *Eighteenth-Century Britain, 1688–1783* (Basingstoke, 2001).

Notes to Chapter 1: Arts and Amusements

1. N. McKendrick, J. Brewer and J. H. Plumb, *The Birth of Consumer Society: the Commercialisation of Eighteenth-Century England* (London, 1982); Brewer and R. Porter (eds), *Consumption and the World of Goods* (London, 1993); M. Berg and H. Clifford, *Consumers and Luxury: Consumer Culture in Europe, 1650–1850* (Manchester, 1999).
2. B. Allen, *Francis Hayman, 1708–1776* (London, 1989).
3. M. S. Wilson, 'Columbine's Picturesque Passage: The Demise of Dramatic Action in the Evolution of Sublime Spectacle on the London Stage', *Eighteenth Century*, 31 (1990), pp. 191–210.
4. M. Mack, *Alexcander Pope: A Life* (New Haven, Connecticut, 1985).
5. Buckinghamshire to Sir Charles Hotham, Hull, University Library, 12 July 1783, Hotham papers, 4/22.
6. Farmington, Connecticut, Lewis Walpole Library, Hanbury Williams papers, vol. 69, fols 80–81.
7. D. V. Erdman, 'Grub Street behind the skirts of Margaret Nicholson', *Factotum*, 12 (July 1981), pp. 25–27; A. H. Cash (ed.), '*An Essay on Woman*' *by John Wilkes and Thomas Potter: A Reconstruction of a Lost Book with a*

Historical Essay on the Writing, Printing, and Suppressing of this 'Blasphemous and Obscene' Work (New York, 2001); J. Peakman, *Mighty Lewd Books. The Development of Pornography in Eighteenth-Century England* (London, 2003).

8. J. Peakman, *Lascivious Bodies: A sexual history of the eighteenth century* (London, 2004), p. 15.

9. A. Vickery, *The Gentleman's Daughter: Women's Lives in Georgian England* (New Haven, Connecticut, 1998).

10. *Daily Gazetteer*, 14 April 1737.

11. Stone to James, 1st Earl Waldegrave, 30 May 1737, Chewton House, Waldegrave papers.

12. [Johnson], *A Compleat Vindication of the Licensers of the Stage* (London, 1739), p. 9.

13. J. C. D. Clark, *Samuel Johnson: Literature, Religion and English Cultural Politics from the Restoration to Romanticism* (Cambridge, 1994).

14. For an emphasis on modernity, J. Cannon, *Samuel Johnson and the Politics of Hanoverian England* (Oxford, 1994) and H. Hudson, *Samuel Johnson and the Making of Modern England* (Cambridge, 2003).

15. J. C. Beasley, 'Portraits of a Monster: Robert Walpole and Early English Prose Fiction', *Eighteenth-Century Studies*, 14 (1981), pp. 406–31.

16. B. A. Goldgar, *Walpole and Wits: The Relation of Politics to Literature, 1722–1742* (Lincoln, Nebraska, 1976); C. Gerrard, *The Patriot Opposition to Walpole: Politics, Poetry and National Myth, 1725–1742* (Oxford, 1995).

17. J. Andrews, *A Comparative View of the French and English Nations* (London, 1785), pp. 47–58.

18. R. Ballaster, *Seductive Forms: Women's Amatory Fiction, 1684–1740* (Oxford, 1992).

19. M. J. Cardwell, *Arts and Arms: Literature, Politics and Patriotism during the Seven Years War* (Manchester, 2004), p. 8.

20. For a possibly exaggerated view, W. Weber, *The Rise of Musical Classics in Eighteenth-Century England: A Study in Canon, Ritual and Ideology* (Oxford, 1992).

21. T. Furniss, *Edmund Burke's Aesthetic Ideology: Language, Gender, and Political Economy in Revolution* (Cambridge, 1993).

22. J. Loftis, *The Politics of Drama in Augustan England* (Oxford, 1963), p. 92.

23. J. Eglin, *Venice Transfigured: The Myth of Venice in British Culture, 1660–1797* (Basingstoke, 2001), pp. 47–49.

24. T. Mowl, *Gentlemen and Players: Gardeners of the English Landscape* (Stroud, 2000).

25. E. P. Thompson, *Customs in Common* (London, 1991).

26. T. Harris (ed.), *Popular Culture in England, c. 1500–1850* (Basingstoke, 1995).

27. D. Kutcha, *The Three-Piece Suit and Modern Masculinity: England, 1550–1850* (Berkeley, California, 2002), pp. 101, 163.

28. W. Gibson, ' "Pious Decorum": Clerical wigs in the Eighteenth Century', *Anglican and Episcopal History*, 65 (1996), pp. 145–62.

29. A. Buck, *Dress in Eighteenth-Century England* (London, 1980); N. Rothstein, *Silk Designs of the Eighteenth Century* (London, 1990); B. Lemire, *Fashion's Favourite: The Cotton Trade and the Consumer in Britain, 1660–1880* (Oxford, 1991); J. Ashelford, *The Art of Dress: Clothes and Society, 1500–1914* (London, 1996).

30. I. C. Bristow, *Architectural Colour in British Interiors, 1615–1840* (New Haven, Connecticut, 1996).

31. M. Warner and R. Blake, *Stubbs and the Horse* (New Haven, Connecticut, 2005).

32. S. Varey, *Space and the Eighteenth-Century English Novel* (Cambridge, 1990).

33. R. Voitle, *The Third Earl of Shaftesbury, 1671–1713* (Baton Rouge, Louisiana, 1984).

34. A. C. Kelly, *Swift and the English Language* (Philadelphia, Pennsylvania, 1988).

35. P. K. Monod, *Jacobitism and the English People, 1688–1788* (Cambridge, 1989).

36. P. Langford, *A Polite and Commercial People: England 1727–1783* (Oxford, 1989), p. 116.

37. C. Haydon, *Anti-Catholicism in Eighteenth-Century England, c. 1714–80: A Political and Social Study* (Manchester, 1993).

38. *Daily Post Boy*, 10 November, *St. James's Evening Post*, 11 November, *Fog's Weekly Journal*, 13 November 1731; *The Flying Post*, 3 February 1732; Edinburgh, National Archives of Scotland, GD. 267/7/20.

39. Huntingford to Addington, 17 September 1789, Exeter, Devon County Record Office, 152M/C1789/F99.

40. C. Haydon, 'The Gordon Riots in the English Provinces', *Historical Research*, 63 (1990), pp. 354–59.

41. C. Williams (ed.), *Sophie in London 1786* (London, 1933), pp. 94–95.

42. E. R. Delderfield, *Cavalcade by Candlelight: The Story of Exeter's Five Theatres* (Exmouth, 1950), p. 31; *The Morning Post, and Daily Advertiser*, 17 March 1786.

43. Samuel Johnson to Elizabeth Johnson, 24 June 1775, to his mother, 22 April 1776, Exeter, Devon Record Office, 5521M/F4/1.

44. H. Walpole, *Memoirs of King George II*, edited by J. Brooke (3 vols, New Haven, 1985), 3, 111; W. Cobbett (ed.), *Parliamentary History of England* (36 vols, London, 1806–20), 30, 189; L. W. Jennings (ed.), *The Correspondence and Diaries of John Wilson Croker* (3 vols, London, 1885), 1, 409.

45. Thomas to James Harris, 26 April 1746, Winchester, Hampshire County Record Office, 9M73 G309/31.

46. A. Fraser, 'The Dancing Dogs of Sadler's Wells and their Rivals', *Factotum*, 18 (March 1984), pp. 25–27.

47. Anon., 'The Bottle Cungerer', *Factotum*, 37 (September 1993), p. 27.

Notes to Chapter 2: The Crown

1. P. K. Monod, *Jacobitism and the English People, 1688–1788* (Cambridge, 1989).

2. R. Braverman, *Plots and Counterplots: Sexual Politics and the Body Politic in English Literature, 1660–1730* (Cambridge, 1993).

3. D. Burrows, *Handel and the English Chapel Royal* (Oxford, 2005).

4. L. R. N. Ashley, *Colley Cibber* (Boston, 1989).

5. R. McGuinness, *English Court Odes* (Oxford, 1971); D. Thame, 'Madness and Therapy in Maria Edgeworth's *Belinda*: Deceived by Appearances', *British Journal for Eighteenth-Century Studies*, 26 (2003), p. 271.

6. Christoph Friedrich Kreienberg, Hanoverian Resident in London, to Jean de Robethon, George's confidential secretary, 14 July 1713, Huntington Library, San Marino, California, HM 44710 fol. 57; D. Burrows, 'Handel and Hanover', in P. Williams (ed.), *Bach, Handel, Scarlotti: Tercentenary Essays* (Cambridge, 1980).

7. D. Burrows and R. D. Hume, 'George I, the Haymarket Opera Company and Handel's *Water Music*', *Early Music* (August 1991), pp. 323–33.

8. C. Gerrard, *The Patriot Opposition to Walpole: Politics, Poetry, and National Myth, 1725–1742* (Oxford, 1994).

9. *The Martial Face: The Military Portrait in Britain, 1760–1900*, volume to accompany exhibition by the Department of Art, Brown University (Providence, Rhode Island, 1991). I would like to thank Peter Harrington for discussing the subject with me.

10. J. Harris and M. Snodin (eds), *Sir William Chambers: Architect to George III* (London, 1996).

11. R. Alberts, *Benjamin West: A Biography* (Boston, Massachusetts, 1978).

12. J. Roberts (ed.), *George III and Queen Charlotte: Patronage, Collecting and Court Taste* (London, 2004), pp. 90–151; D. Watkin, *The Architect King: George III and the Culture of the Enlightenment* (London, 2004).

13. C. B. Johnson, 'A Documentary Survey of Theater in the Madrid Court during the First Half of the Eighteenth Century' (unpublished PhD. thesis, University of Los Angeles, 1974), pp. 277–78.

14. B. Cherry, 'The Devon Country House in the Late Seventeenth and Early Eighteenth Centuries', *Devon Archaeological Society*, 46 (1988), p. 100.

15. V. Carretta, *George III and the Satirists from Hogarth to Byron* (Athens, Georgia, 1990).

16. H. Hoock, *The King's Artists: The Royal Academy of Arts and the Politics of British Culture, 1760–1840* (Oxford, 2003).

Notes to Chapter 3: The Aristocracy

1. N. Scarfe (ed.), *A Frenchman's Year in Suffolk* (Woodbridge, 1988), p. 34.

2. J. Raven, *Judging New Wealth: Popular Publishing and Responses to Commerce in England, 1750–1800* (Oxford, 1992).

3. J. Cannon, *Aristocratic Century: The Peerage of Eighteenth-Century England* (Cambridge, 1984).

4. Lucas papers, Bedford, Bedfordshire Record Office, Lucas papers, 30/9/17/3.

5. M. Trinick, 'A New Acquisition: A Portrait of William Lemon', *Journal of the Royal Institution of* Cornwall, new series, 2 (1992), p. 126; P. McKay, 'A Patron of Promise: Charles, 7th Earl of Northampton', *Northamptonshire Past and Present*, 8 (1992–93), pp. 271–72; R. Wilson and A. Mackley, *Creating Paradise: The Building of the English Country House, 1660–1880* (London, 2000), pp. 25–26.

6. C. S. Smith, 'Supply and Demand in English Country House Building, 1660–1740', *Oxford Art Journal*, 11 (1988), pp. 3–9. See also, J. Summerson, 'The Classical Country House in Eighteenth-Century England', *Journal of the Royal Society of Arts*, 107 (1959), pp. 539–87.

7. C. Christie, *The British Country House in the Eighteenth Century* (Manchester, 2000).

8. A. Smith, 'Sherborne Castle: From Tudor Lodge to Country House', *Local Historian*, 25 (1995), pp. 231–41.

9. C. Ridgway, *Sir John Vanbrugh: A Biography* (London, 1987).

10. T. Barnard and J. Clark (eds), *Lord Burlington: Architecture, Art and Life* (London, 1995).

11. As argued by G. Worsley, *Classical Architecture in Britain: The Heroic Age* (New Haven, Connecticut, 1995).

12. R. Wittkower, *Palladio and English Palladianism* (London, 1974); S. Parissien, *Palladian Style* (London, 1994).

13. Proctor to Agneta Yorke, 13 September 1772, Cambridge, Cambridgeshire Record Office, Yorke papers, 408/F2.

14. E. Harris and N. Savage, *British Architectural Books and Writers, 1556–1785* (Cambridge, 1990).

15. M. McCarthy, *The Origins of the Gothic Revival* (London, 1987); M. Aldrich, *Gothic Revival* (London, 1994).

16. J. M. Crook, *The Greek Revival: Neo-Classical Attitudes in British Architecture, 1760–1870* (London, 1995).

17. D. Stillman, *English Neoclassical Architecture* (London, 1989).

18. T. Gray (ed.), *Devon Country Houses and Gardens* (Exeter, 2001), p. 149.

19. BL, Add. MS, 74062.

20. S. Houfe, 'A Northamptonshire Lady in France: The Travel Diaries of Lady Pomfret', *Northamptonshire Past and Present*, 51 (1998), p. 33.

21. C. Gilbert, *The Life and Work of Thomas Chippendale* (London, 1978); J. Sellars (ed.), *The Art of Thomas Chippendale: Master Furniture Maker* (Harewood, 2000).

22. P. Kirkham, *The London Furniture Trade, 1700–1870* (London, 1988); C. Edwards, *Eighteenth-Century Furniture* (Manchester, 1996).

23. For illustrations, J. R. Millburn, 'J. Kirk, Engraver', *Bookplate Journal*, new series, 1 (2003), pp. 31, 33.

24. S. Deuchar, *Sporting Art in Eighteenth-Century England: A Social and Political History* (New Haven, Connecticut,1988).

25. J. Harris, *The Artist and the Country House: A History of Country House and Garden View Painting, 1540–1870* (London, 1979).

26. M. E. Burkett and D. Sloss, *Read's Point of View: Paintings of the Cumbrian Countryside* (Bowness, 1995).

27. R. Guilding, *Marble Mania: Sculpture Galleries in England, 1640–1840* (London, 2001); M. Baker, *Figured in Marble: The Making and Viewing of Eighteenth-Century Sculpture* (London, 2001).

28. J. Cornforth, *Early Georgian Interiors* (New Haven, Connecticut, 2004).

29. J. Martin, *Wives and Daughters: Women and Children in the Georgian Country House* (London, 2004), pp. 36–37.

30. W. Gibson, *Enlightenment Prelate: Benjamin Hoadly, 1676–1761* (Cambridge, 2004), pp. 294–95.

31. S. Parissien, *Adam Style* (London, 1992).

32. C. Christie, *The British Country House in the Eighteenth Century* (Manchester, 2000).

33. D. Harris, *The Nature of Authority: Villa Culture, Landscape and Representation in Eighteenth-Century Lombardy* (University Park, Pennsylvania, 2003), p. 185.

34. B. Wragg, *The Life and Works of John Carr of York* (York, 2000).

35. P. Willis, *Charles Bridgeman and the English Landscape Garden* (Newcastle, 2002). The gardens at Hampton Court laid out under William III by George London have recently been returned to their original form.

36. J. Harris, *The Palladian Revival: Lord Burlington, His Villa and Garden at Chiswick* (New Haven, Connecticut, 1994).

37. M. I. Wilson, *William Kent: Architect, Designer, Painter, Gardener, 1685–1748* (London, 1984); J. D. Hunt, *William Kent: Landscape Garden Designer* (London, 1987).

38. Scarfe (ed.), *A Frenchman's Year in Suffolk*, pp. 35–36.

39. P. Wade-Martins (ed.), *An Historical Atlas of Norfolk* (Norwich, 1993), pp. 110–11; D. Dymond and E. Martin (eds), *An Historical Atlas of Suffolk* (Ipswich, 1988), pp. 86–87; G. Foard, 'Ecton: Its Lost Village and Landscape Park', *Northamptonshire Past and Present*, 8 (1993–94), pp. 341–51.

40. Proctor to Yorke, 15 July 1764, 13 Sept. 1772, Cambridge, Cambridgeshire Record Office, Yorke papers, 408/F2.

41. Hamilton's masterly use of the landscape at Painshill to create entrancing vistas is becoming more apparent due to the 'garden archaeology' of recent years.

42. D. Watkin, *Athenian Stuart: Pioneer of the Greek Revival* (London, 1992).

43. T. Gray (ed.), *Travels in Georgian Devon: The Illustrated Journals of the Reverend John Swete, 1789–1800* (Exeter, 1997), p. xv.

44. Report of debate sent with Chavigny to Chauvelin, 6 February 1736, AE, CP, Ang. 393.

45. G. Worsley, *The British Stable: An Architectural and Social History* (New Haven, Connecticut, 2004).

46. T. Whately, *Observations on Modern Gardening* (London, 1770), pp. 190–91.

47. M. Wills, *Gibside and the Bowes Family* (Chichester, 1995), pp. 43–47; G. Clarke, 'Grecian Taste and Gothick Virtue: Lord Cobham's Gardening Programme and Its Iconography', *Apollo*, 97 (1973), pp. 56–67; R. Hewlings, 'Chiswick, House and Gardens: Appearance and Meaning', in Barnard and Clark (eds), *Lord Burlington*, pp. 81–89, 106–21.

48. Lyttelton to Elizabeth Montagu, 21 July 1762, BL, RP 2377i.

49. T. Williamson, *Polite Landscapes: Gardens and Society in Eighteenth-Century England* (Stroud, 1995).

50. Johnson, *The History of Rasselas, Prince of Abyssinia* (London, 1759), chapter 20.

51. E. Dumbauld, *Thomas Jefferson: American Tourist* (Norman, Oklahoma, 1946), pp. 79–80; J. D. Hunt and P. Willis (eds), *The Genius of the Place* (3rd edn, Cambridge, Massachusetts, 1988).

52. A. Tinniswood, *The Polite Tourist: A History of Country House Visiting* (London, 1998).

53. L. Harris (ed.), *Robert Adam and Kedleston: The Making of a Neo-Classical Masterpiece* (London, 1987).

54. T. Williamson, 'Estate Management and Landscape Design', in C. Ridgway and R. Williams (eds), *Sir John Vanbrugh and Landscape Architecture in Baroque England, 1690–1730* (Stroud, 2000), p. 28.

55. G. Tyack, 'Country Houses *c.* 1500-*c.* 1750', in J. Dils (ed.), *An Historical Atlas of Berkshire* (Reading, 1998), p. 60

56. Scarfe (ed.), *A Frenchman's Year in Suffolk*, p. 36.

57. J. Rosenheim, *The Emergence of a Ruling Order: English Landed Society, 1650–1750* (London, 1998).

58. P. Ayres, *Classical Culture and the Idea of Rome in Eighteenth-Century England* (Cambridge, 1997).

59. L. Davidoff, *Best Circles: Society, Etiquette and the Season* (London, 1973).

60. D. Pearce, *London's Mansions: The Palatial Houses of the Nobility* (London, 1986); C. S. Sykes, *Private Palaces: Life in the Great London Houses* (London, 1985).

61. M. Wild, 'Revisiting Christopher Smart's *Midwife*: Alexander the Great and the Terrible Old Lady', *British Journal for Eighteenth-Century Studies*, 27 (2004), pp. 279–92.

Notes to Chapter 4: Religion

1. L. Jardine, *On a Grander Scale: The Outstanding Career of Sir Christopher Wren* (London, 2002), pp. 414–24.

2. W. Gibson, *Church, State and Society, 1760–1850* (London, 1994) and *The Church of England, 1688–1832* (London, 2000).

3. D. Nalbach, *The King's Theatre 1704–1867: London's First Italian Opera House* (London, 1972), p. 35.

4. Reynolds to Lord Grantham, 20 July 1773, Bedford, County Record Office, Lucas papers, 30/14/326/2.

5. A. Asfour and P. Williamson, *Gainsborough's Vision* (Liverpool, 1999).

6. B. Hornby, 'A Place in History through Memoirs', *Northamptonshire Past and Present*, 51 (1998), pp. 31–32.

7. T. Friedman, *James Gibbs* (London, 1984).

8. Eg. G. Clarke, 'Winterborne Tomson: Church Repairs in 1774–75', *Notes and Queries for Somerset and Dorset*, 32 (1990), pp. 804–7.

9. M. McDermott, 'West Gallery at All Saints' Church, Trull', *Notes and Queries for Somerset and Dorset*, 34 (1997), p. 89.

10. M. Trinick, 'A New Acquisition: A Portrait of William Lemon', *Journal of the Royal Institution of Cornwall*, new series 2, 1 (1992), p. 124; B. Robins (ed.), *The John Marsh Journals: The Life and Times of a Gentleman Composer, 1752–1828* (Stuyvesant, New York, 1998).

11. F. Warren and I. Cockman, *Music in Portsmouth, 1789–1842* (Portsmouth, 1998), pp. 1–4.

12. D. Bindman (ed.), *John Flaxman* (London, 1979).

13. N. Temperley, *The Music of the English Parish Church* (2 vols, Cambridge, 1979).

14. R. Smith, *Handel's Oratorios and Eighteenth-Century Thought* (Cambridge, 1995).

15. *Swinney's Birmingham and Stafford Chronicle*, 4 April 1776.

16. Ex inf. Reg Ward.

17. M. F. Marshall and J. Todd, *English Congregational Hymns in the Eighteenth Century* (Lexington, Kentucky, 1982); D. Davie, *The Eighteenth-Century Hymn in England* (Cambridge, 1993); H. Guest, *A Form of Sound Words: The Religious Poetry of Christopher Smart* (Oxford, 1989).

18. W. Shaw, *The Three Choirs Festival: The Official History of the Meetings of the Three Choirs of Gloucester, Hereford and Worcester, c. 1713–1953* (Worcester, 1954).

19. J. Mitchell, 'Bible Publishing in Eighteenth-Century Britain', *Factotum*, 20 (May 1985), p. 18.

20. P. R. Backscheider, *Daniel Defoe: Ambition and Innovation* (Lexington, Kentucky, 1986), pp. 173–77.

21. J. L. Altholz, *The Religious Press in Britain, 1760–1900* (New York, 1989).

22. H. Forster, 'The Centenaries of Edward Young', *British Journal for Eighteenth-Century Studies*, 6 (1983), p. 152.

23. M. F. Marshall (ed.), *The Poetry of Elizabeth Singer Rowe, 1674–1737* (Lewiston, New York, 1988).

24. A. Reddick, *The Making of Johnson's Dictionary, 1746–1773* (Cambridge, 1990).

25. P. Rawlings, *Drunks, Whores and Idle Apprentices: Criminal Biographies of the Eighteenth Century* (London, 1992).

Notes to Chapter 5: The Middling Orders

1. T. C. W. Blanning, *The Culture of Power and the Power of Culture: Old Regime Europe, 1660–1789* (Oxford, 2001).

2. R. Leppert, *Music and Image: Domesticity, Ideology and Socio-Cultural Formation in Eighteenth-Century England* (London, 1988).

3. J. Sekora, *Luxury: The Concept in Western Thought, Eden to Smollett* (Baltimore, 1977); E. J. Clery, C. Franklin and P. Garside (eds), *Authorship, Commerce and the Public: Scenes of Writing, 1750–1850* (Basingstoke, 2002), p. 20.

4. D. Donald, *The Age of Caricature: Satirical Prints in the Age of George III* (London, 1996).

5. L. Lippincott, *Selling Art in Georgian London: The Rise of Arthur Pond* (New Haven, Connecticut, 1983); S. H. A. Bruntgen, *John Boydell, 1719–1804: A Study of Art Patronage and Publishing in Georgian London* (New York, 1985); I. Pears, *The Discovery of Painting: The Growth of Interest in the Arts in England, 1680–1768* (New Haven, Connecticut, 1988);

D. H. Solkin, *Painting for Money: The Visual Arts and the Public Sphere in Eighteenth-Century England* (London, 1993).

6. C. B. Bailey, 'Aspects of the Patronage and Collecting of French Painting in France at the End of the Ancien Régime' (unpublished D.Phil thesis, University of Oxford, 1985), pp. 31–35.

7. H. Playford, *The Second Book of the Pleasant Musical Companion* preface (4th edn, London, 1701), cited in R. McGuinness, '"The Medium is the Message": Some Aspects of Music and the London Press *c.* 1670–*c.* 1700', *Factotum*, 25 (February, 1988), p. 15.

8. S. Sadie, 'Concert Life in Eighteenth Century England', *Proceedings of the Royal Musical Association*, 85 (1958–9), pp. 17–30; E. Hobhouse (ed.), *The Diary of a West Country Physician, 1684–1726* (London, 1934); T. Fawcett, *Music in Eighteenth Century Norwich and Norfolk* (Norwich, 1979); C. Hogwood and R. Luckett (eds), *Music in Eighteenth-Century England: Essays in Memory of Charles Cudworth* (Cambridge, 1983); J. Burchell, *Polite or Commercial Concerts? Concert Management and Orchestral Repertoire in Edinburgh, Bath, Oxford, Manchester, and Newcastle, 1730–1799* (New York, 1996); B. Robins (ed.), *John Marsh Journals* (Stuyvesant, New York, 1998); D. W. Jones (ed.), *Music in Eighteenth-Century Britain* (Aldershot, 2000); S. Wollenberg and S. McVeigh (eds), *Concert Life in Eighteenth-Century Britain* (Aldershot, 2004).

9. F. Warren and I. Cockman, *Music in Portsmouth, 1789–1842* (Portsmouth, 1988), p. 3.

10. H. C. Robbins Landon, *Haydn in London, 1791–95* (London, 1976); S. McVeigh, *Concert Life in London from Mozart to Haydn* (Cambridge, 1993).

11. F. Lynch, *The Independent Patriot* (London, 1737), dedication, pp. 2, 23, 25, 42, 50.

12. John Ley to his mother, 19 October 1793, Exeter, Devon Record Office 63/2/11/6.

13. G. Sheldrick (ed.), *The Accounts of Thomas Green, 1741–1790* (Hertford, 1990); N. Scarfe, *Innocent Espionage: The La Rochefoucauld Brothers' Tour of England in 1785* (Woodbridge, 1995), p. 208.

14. J. Brewer and R. Porter (eds), *Consumption and the World of Goods* (London, 1993); L. Weatherill, *Consumer Behaviour and Material Culture in Britain, 1660–1760* (2nd edn, London, 1996).

15. P. Lewis, *Fielding's Burlesque Drama* (Edinburgh, 1987); R. D. Hume, *Henry Fielding and the London Theatre, 1728–1737* (Oxford, 1988).

16. H. Crane, *Playbill: A History of the Theatre in the West Country* (Plymouth, 1980), p. 39.

17. I. Mackintosh and G. Ashton (eds), *The Georgian Playhouse: Actors, Artists, Audiences and Architecture, 1730–1830* (London, 1975). For a vivid account

of a performance in Falmouth, E. Jaggard, 'James Boswell's Journey through Cornwall, August–September 1792', *Journal of the Royal Institution of Cornwall* (2004), p. 29.

18. J. Lafler, *The Celebrated Mrs Oldfield: The Life and Art of an Augustan Actress* (Carbondale, Illinois, 1989).

19. D. Burrows and R. D. Hume, 'George I, the Haymarket Opera Company and Handel's Water Music', *Early Music* (August 1991), p. 330.

20. L. W. Conolly, *The Censorship of English Drama, 1737–1824* (San Marino, California, 1976); V. J. Leisenfeld, *The Licensing Act of 1737* (Madison, Wisconsin, 1984).

21. J. Campbell, *Natural Masques: Gender and Identity in Fielding's Plays and Novels* (Stanford, California, 1995).

22. J. Brewer, *The Pleasures of the Imagination: English Culture in the Eighteenth Century* (London, 1997).

23. R. Porter, *Enlightenment: Britain and the Creation of the Modern World* (London, 2000).

24. A. Braham, *The Architecture of the French Enlightenment* (London, 1989).

25. N. Salway, 'Women Pianists in Late Eighteenth-Century London', in S. Wollenberg and S. McVeigh (eds), *Concert Life in Eighteenth-Century Britain* (Aldershot, 2004), pp. 273–90.

26. R. Lonsdale (ed.), *Eighteenth-Century Women Poets: An Oxford Anthology* (Oxford, 1989).

27. C. Ingrassia, *Authorship, Commerce and Gender in Early Eighteenth-Century England: A Culture of Paper Credit* (Cambridge, 1998).

28. J. Pearson, *The Prostituted Muse: Images of Women and Women Dramatists, 1642–1737* (New York, 1988); K. Kendall (eds), *Love and Thunder: Plays by Women in the Age of Queen Anne* (London, 1988); J. Raven, *British Fiction, 1750–1770: A Chronological Check-List* (London, 1987).

29. M. Wood, *'Studious to Please': A Profile of Jane West, an Eighteenth-Century Author* (Donington, 2003).

30. C. Tuite, *Romantic Austen: Sexual Politics and the Literary Canon* (Cambridge, 2002).

31. J. Todd, *The Sign of Angelica: Women, Writing and Fiction, 1660–1800* (London, 1989); R. W. Uphaus and G. M. Foster (eds), *The 'Other' Eighteenth Century: English Women of Letters, 1660–1800* (East Lansing, Michigan, 1991); C. Turner, *Living by the Pen: Women Writers in the Eighteenth Century* (London, 1992).

32. A. Stott, *Hannah More: The First Victorian* (Oxford, 2002).

33. Advertisement in *Jackson's Oxford Journal*, 3 July 1790.

34. J. Todd (ed.), *The Collected Letters of Mary Wollstonecraft* (London, 2003), pp. 1–3.

35. Diary of Countess of Pomfret, 8 June 1748, Leicester, Leicestershire Record

Office DG 7/4/12a; *The Letters and Journals of Lady Mary Coke* (4 vols, Edinburgh, 1889–96) I, p. 86; E. J. Climenson (ed.), *Elizabeth Montagu* (2 vols,London, 1906), I, p. 293; Montagu to Elizabeth Carter, 24 November 1759, San Marino, California, Huntington Library, Montagu papers, 3031.

36. W. Gibson, 'Recent Work in Local History and Archives, 2002–2004', *Archives*, 29 (2004), p. 65.

37. J. Martin, *Wives and Daughters: Women and Children in the Georgian Country House* (New Haven, Connecticut, 2004), p. 238.

38. B. M. Benedict, 'The "Curious Attitude" in Eighteenth-Century Britain: Observing and Owning', *Eighteenth Century Life*, 14 (1990), pp. 86–92.

39. Sheridan, *The Rivals* I, ii.

40. K. S. Green, *The Courtship Novel, 1740–1820: A Feminised Genre* (Lexington, Kentucky, 1991).

41. J. Epstein, *The Iron Pen: Frances Burney and the Politics of Women's Writing* (Bristol, 1989).

42. J. Cradock, *Literary and Miscellaneous Memoirs* (London, 1826), p. 67.

43. J. Pearson, *Women's Reading in Britain, 1750–1835: A Dangerous Recreation* (Cambridge, 1999).

44. See pp. 78, 143.

45. B. Dolan, *Josiah Wedgwood. Entrepreneur to the Enlightenment* (London, 2004), p. 328.

46. R. Porter, *The Making of Geology* (Cambridge, 1977).

47. J. Smail, *The Origins of Middle-Class Culture: Halifax, Yorkshire, 1660–1780* (Ithaca, New York, 1994); C. B. Estabrook, *Urban and Rustic England: Cultural Ties and Social Spheres in the Provinces, 1660–1780* (Manchester, 1998); P. Clark, *British Clubs and Societies, 1580–1800* (New York, 2000).

48. W. A. Speck, *Literature and Society in Eighteenth-Century England: Ideology, Politics and Culture, 1680–1820* (London, 1998), pp. 107–11.

49. Thomas Pelham to Lord Pelham, 19 December 1777, BL, Add. MS 33127, fol. 374.

Notes to Chapter 6: Pleasures of the Many

1. BL, Add. MS 36972, fol. 88.

2. R. Scribner, 'Is a History of Popular Culture Possible?', *History of European Ideas*, 10 (1989), pp. 175–91; T. Harris (ed.), *Popular Culture in England, c. 1500–1850* (London, 1994), pp. 1–27.

3. C. Bergstrom, 'Purney, Pastoral and the Polymorphous Perverse', *British Journal for Eighteenth-Century Studies*, 17 (1994), pp. 149–63.

4. C. Vialls and K. Collins (eds), *A Georgian Country Parson: The Rev. John Mastin of Naseby* (Northampton, 2004), p. 12.

5. *Maggs Brothers Catalogue 1293* (2003), p. 178.

6. K. Thomas, *Religion and the Decline of Magic* (London, 1971); R. M. Isherwood, 'Popular Musical Entertainment in Eighteenth-Century Paris', *International Review of the Aesthetics and Sociology of Music*, 9 (1978), pp. 295, 308; J. A. Sharpe, *Early Modern England* (London, 1987), p. 285; S. Pedersen, 'Hannah More meets Simple Simon: Tracts, Chapbooks, and Popular Culture in late eighteenth-century England', *Journal of British Studies*, 25 (1986), p. 87;

7. I have benefited from listening to a paper on Beaumont by Jonathan Barry.

8. See also S. S. Genuth, *Comets, Popular Culture and the Birth of Modern Cosmology* (Princeton, New Jersey, 1997).

9. Anon., *Some Considerations on the Establishment of the French Strollers* (London, 1749); Anon., *An Impartial State of the Case of the French Comedians* (London, 1750); Anon., *A Serious Address to the Thinking Part of the Inhabitants of Westminster* (London, 1750); BL, Add. MS 35378, fol. 22; *Westminster Gazette*, 11 January 1777

10. Arbuthnot to Sir Robert Murray Keith, 25 June 1784, BL, Add. MS 35532, fol. 77.

11. J. Thorp, 'Sign of a Harlequin', *Factotum*, 38 (February 1994), pp. 7–10.

12. M. S. Wilson, 'Columbine's Picturesque Passage: The Demise of Dramatic Action in the Evolution of Sublime Spectacle on the London Stage', *Eighteenth Century*, 31 (1990), p. 198.

13. Henry Ley to John Ley, 4 March 1793, Exeter, Devon Record Office, 63/2/11/6.

14. L. Hughes, 'Ablesimov's *Mel'nik*: A Study in Success', *Study Group on Eighteenth-Century Russia Newsletter*, 9 (1981), p. 31.

15. E. Waterhouse, *Gainsborough* (London, 1966), pp. 23–25, 29–34.

16. B. Chesley, 'Probable Sources for Garrick's Pantomime', *Notes and Queries*, new series, 36 (March 1989), p. 61.

17. P. J. de Gategno, *James MacPherson* (Boston, Massachusetts, 1989).

18. A. Johnston, *Enchanted Ground: The Study of Medieval Romance in the Eighteenth Century* (London, 1964); B. H. Davis, *Thomas Percy: A Scholar-Cleric in the Age of Johnson* (Philadelphia, Pennsylvania, 1989).

19. A. L. Owen, *The Famous Druids* (Oxford, 1962).

20. J. Goodridge, *Rural Life in Eighteenth-Century Poetry* (Cambridge, 1995).

21. R. Greene, *Mary Leapor: A Study in Eighteenth-Century Women's Poetry* (Oxford, 1993).

22. M. Waldron, *Lactilla, Milkwoman of Clifton: The Life and Writings of Ann Yearsley, 1753–1806* (Athens, Georgia, 1996); D. Landry, *The Muses of Resistance: Laboring-Class Women's Poetry in Britain, 1739–1796* (Cambridge, 1990); H. G. Klaus, 'Mary Collier (1688?–1762), *Notes and Queries*, new series, 47 (2000), pp. 201–4.

23. D. Dugaw, *Warrior Women and Popular Balladry, 1650–1850* (Cambridge, 1989).

24. M. J. Lomas, 'Militia and Volunteer Wind Bands in Southern England in the Late Eighteenth and Early Nineteenth Centuries', *Journal of the Society for Army Historical Research*, 67 (1989), pp. 154–66, and 'The Wiltshire Militia Band, 1769-c. 1831', *Wiltshire Archaeological and Natural History Magazine*, 85 (1992), pp. 93–100.

25. Vialls and Collins, *Georgian Country Parson*, p. 7.

26. G. R. Seaman, 'Eighteenth-Century English Periodicals and Music', *British Journal for Eighteenth-Century Studies*, 7 (1984), p. 72.

27. M. T. Davis (ed.), *London Corresponding Society, 1792–1799* (6 vols, London, 2002) III, p. 133.

Notes to Chapter 7: Books and Newspapers

1. C. Pickford, 'Bedford Stationers and Booksellers', *Factotum*, 15 (October 1982), p. 23.

2. J. Feather, *The Provincial Book Trade in Eighteenth-Century England* (Cambridge, 1985).

3. K. T. Winkler, *Handwerk und Markt: Druckerhandwerk, Vertriebswesen, und Tagesschrifttum im London 1695–1750* (Stuttgart, 1993); R. Taylor, *Goldsmith as Journalist* (London, 1992).

4. J. M. Black, 'Political Allusions in Fielding's "Coffee-House Politician"', *Theoria*, 62 (1984), pp. 45–56.

5. *Swinney's Birmingham and Stafford Chronicle*, 1 June 1775.

6. R. M. Wiles, *Serial Publication in England before 1750* (Cambridge, 1957); R. D. Mayo, *The English Novel in the Magazines, 1740 to 1815* (Evanston, Illinois, 1962); J. L. Defoe, 'Defoe Serialized', *Factotum*, 19 (1984), pp. 21–23.

7. H. Berry, 'Promoting Taste in the Provincial Press: National and Local Culture in Eighteenth-Century Newcastle upon Tyne', *British Journal for Eighteenth-Century Studies*, 25 (2002), p. 14.

8. *Mist's Weekly Journal*, 11 February 1727.

9. The *Morning Post, and Daily Advertiser*, 7 March 1786.

10. J. Carré, 'Burlington's Literary Patronage', *British Journal for Eighteenth-Century Studies*, 5 (1982), pp. 26–27.

11. M. K. Flavell, 'The Enlightened Reader and the New Industrial Towns: A Study of the Liverpool Library, 1758–1790', *British Journal for Eighteenth-Century Studies*, 8 (1985), pp. 17–35.

12. P. Kaufman, *Libraries and Their Users* (London, 1969), pp. 36–64.

13. R. J. Goulden, 'Edmund Baker and Jasper Sprange', *Factotum*, 38 (February 1994), p. 19.

14. P. Phillips, *Diary*, 2 vols (1780), II, p. 31.

15. Anon., *Reflections on Ancient and Modern History* (Oxford, 1746), p. 25.

16. Anon., *Reflections*, p. 26.

17. Montagu to Elizabeth Carter, 16 July 1762, San Marino, Huntington Library, Montagu papers, 3079.

18. J. Richetti, *The English Novel in History, 1700–1780* (London, 1998).

19. J. E. Tierney (ed.), *The Correspondence of Robert Dodsley, 1733–1764* (Cambridge, 1988).

20. P. Garside, 'Thomas Lockett's Catalogue of Novels', *Factotum, Occasional Paper, 3* (London, no date), p. 11.

21. L. Lipking, *Samuel Johnson: The Life of an Author* (Cambridge, Massachusetts, 1998).

22. R. Myers and M. Harris (eds), *Fakes and Frauds: Varieties of Deception in Print and Manuscript* (Winchester, 1989); J. Feather, *Publishing, Piracy and Politics: An Historical Study of Copyright in Great Britain* (London, 1994).

23. R. Sweet, *The Writing of Urban Histories in Eighteenth-Century England* (Oxford, 1997).

24. R. Rolt, *An Impartial Representation of the Conduct of the Several Powers of Europe*, 4 vols (London, 1747–50), I, x.

25. R. Rolt, *Lives of the Principal Reformers*, p. ix.

26. R. Rolt, *Lives*, p. 195.

27. R. Rolt, *Impartial Representation*, I, p. x.

28. P. Limborch, *History of the Inquisition* (London, 1731), p. xv.

29. *Mist's Weekly Journal*, 21 December 1723, 11, 18 January 1724; *London Journal*, 10 October 1730; *Daily Courant*, 26 August, 30 September 1734.

30. N. McKendrick, 'The Commercialisation of Leisure: Botany, Gardening and the Birth of a Consumer Society', in S. Cavaciocchi (ed.), *Il tempo libero: economia e società, seccoli. XIII-XVIII* (Prato, 1995), p. 598.

31. L. Lipking, *The Ordering of the Arts in Eighteenth-Century England* (Princeton, New Jersey, 1970).

32. A. Reddick, *The Making of Johnson's Dictionary, 1746–1773* (Cambridge, 1990).

33. C. Siskin, *The Work of Writing: Literature and Social Change in Britain, 1700–1830* (London, 1998); K. O'Brien, 'The History Market in Eighteenth-Century England', in I. Rivers (ed.), *Books and Their Readers in Eighteenth-Century England: New Essays* (London, 2001), p. 116.

Notes to Chapter 8: Styles

1. 4th edn (London, 1735), pp. 119–20.

2. T. Fawcett, *Music in Eighteenth-Century Norwich and Norfolk* (Norwich, 1979).

3. J. Sparrow, 'An Oxford Altar-Piece', *Burlington Magazine*, 102 (1960), pp. 4–9.

4. W. C. Shrader, 'Some Thoughts on Rococo and Enlightenment in Eighteenth Century Germany', *Enlightenment Essays*, 6 (1975), pp. 61–62.

5. A. Blunt (ed.), *Baroque and Rococo* (London, 1978).

6. R. Wendorf, *The Elements of Life: Biography and Portrait Painting in Stuart and Georgian England* (Oxford, 1990).

7. F. H. Ellis, *Sentimental Comedy: Theory and Practice* (Cambridge, 1991).

8. J. Todd, *Sensibility* (London, 1986); J. Mullan, *Sentiment and Sociability: The Language of Feeling in the Eighteenth Century* (Oxford, 1988).

9. E. R. Delderfield, *Cavalcade by Candlelight: The Story of Exeter's Five Theatres* (Exmouth, 1950), p. 25.

10. Samuel Johnson to his sister Elizabeth, 9 March 1774, 6 February 1775, to his father, 23 February 1775, Exeter, Devon Record Office, 5521 M/F4/1.

11. H. Honour, *Neo-Classicism* (London, 1968).

12. A. M. Wilson, *Diderot* (New York, 1972), p. 463.

13. Reynolds to Lord Grantham, 2 May 1774, Bedford, Bedfordshire Record Office, Lucas papers, 30/14/32b/3.

14. F. Salmon, *Building on Ruins: The Rediscovery of Rome and English Architecture* (London, 2001).

15. J. M. Levine, *The Battle of the Books: History and Literature in the Augustan Age* (Ithaca, New York, 1991); D. Spadafora, *The Idea of Progress in Eighteenth-Century Britain* (New Haven, Connecticut, 1990).

16. *Morning Post and Daily Advertiser*, 17 March 1786.

17. D. Jacobson, *Chinoiserie* (London, 1993).

18. M. Butler, *Romantics, Rebels and Reactionaries: English Literature and its Background, 1760–1830* (Oxford, 1981).

19. A. Janowitz, *England's Ruins: Poetic Purpose and the National Landscape* (Oxford, 1990).

20. T. Whately, *Observations on Modern Gardening* (London, 1770), p. 155.

21. F. P. Lock, *Edmund Burke I, 1730–1784* (Oxford, 1998), pp. 91–124.

22. E. J. Clery, *The Rise of Supernatural Fiction, 1762–1800* (Cambridge, 1995).

23. *Henry Fuseli*, Tate Gallery exhibition catalogue (London, 1975).

24. B. Sutcliffe (ed.), *Plays by George Colman the Younger and Thomas Morton* (Cambridge, 1983), p. 10.

25. N. Penny, 'An Ambitious Man: The Career and Achievement of Sir Joshua Reynolds', from N. Penny (ed.), *Reynolds* (London, 1986), p. 39.

26. Frances Crewe, journal, BL, Add. MS 37926, fol. 107.

27. Pitt to James Oswald, 19 September 1751, Hockworthy, autograph volume no. 6, printed in *Memorials of the Public Life and Character of the Right Hon. James Oswald of Dunnikier* (Edinburgh, 1825), pp. 112–14.

Notes to Chapter 9: London and the Provinces

1. J. G. Links, *Canaletto* (2nd edn, London, 1994); D. Buttery, *Canaletto and Warwick Castle* (Chichester, 1992).

2. G. Rozman, *Urban Networks in Russia, 1750–1800, and Premodern Periodization* (London, 1976), p. 243.

3. For London's cultural role over the following decades, C. Fox, *London World City, 1800–1840* (New Haven, 1992).

4. G. Kahan (ed.), *George Alexander Stevens and 'The Lecture on Heads'* (Athens, Georgia, 1984).

5. W. Albert, *The Turnpike Road System in England, 1663–1840* (London, 1972).

6. BL., Add. 58213, fol. 216.

7. J. N. Summerson, *Georgian London* (London, 1988).

8. For an excellent recent study of a fashionable West End milieu, R. Garnier, 'Grafton Street, Mayfair', *The Georgian Group Journal*, 13 (2003), pp. 210–72.

9. E. McKellar, *The Birth of Modern London: The Development and Design of the City, 1660–1720* (Manchester, 1999).

10. L. D. Schwarz, *London in the Age of Industrialisation: Entrepreneurs, Labour Force and Living Conditions, 1700–1850* (Cambridge, 1992).

11. R. G. W. Anderson, M. L. Caygill, A. G. MacGregory and L. Syson (eds), *Enlightening the British: Knowledge, Discovery and the Museum in the Eighteenth Century* (London, 2004).

12. J. N. Cox, *Seven Gothic Dramas, 1789–1825* (Athens, Ohio, 1992).

13. M. Sands, *The Eighteenth-Century Pleasure Gardens of Marylebone, 1737–1777* (London, 1987).

14. W. A. Speck, *Literature and Society in Eighteenth-Century England: Ideology, Politics and Culture, 1680–1820* (London, 1998), pp. 107–08.

15. Bowlby to Sir Charles Hotham, 29 December 1749, Hull, University Library, Hotham papers 4/3.

16. R. Porter, 'Science, Provincial Culture and Public Opinion in Enlightenment England', *British Journal for Eighteenth-Century Studies*, 3 (1980), pp. 20–46.

17. P. J. Corfield, *The Impact of English Towns, 1700–1800* (Oxford, 1982); P. Borsay, *The English Urban Renaissance: Culture and Society in the Provincial Town, 1660–1770* (Oxford, 1989); P. Clark (ed.), *The Cambridge Urban History of Britain, II. 1540–1845* (Cambridge, 2000); P. Borsay and L. Proudfoot (eds), *Provincial towns in early modern England and Ireland: Change, convergence and divergence* (Oxford, 2002).

18. P. Hembry, *The English Spa, 1560–1815: A Social History* (London, 1990).

19. D. Mannings, 'Notes on Some Eighteenth-Century Portrait Prices in Britain', *British Journal for Eighteenth-Century Studies*, 6 (1983), pp. 190–91.

20. W. Ison, *Georgian Buildings of Bath, from 1700 to 1830* (London, 1948); P. Borsay, *The Image of Georgian Bath, 1700–c. 2000: Towns, Heritage and History* (Oxford, 2000); M. Reed, 'The transformation of urban space, 1700–1840', in P. Clark (ed.), *The Cambridge Urban History of Britain, II: 1540–1840* (Cambridge, 2000), p. 634; D. E. Shuttleton, 'Mary Chandler's *Description of Bath* (1733): A Tradeswoman Poet of the Georgian Urban Renaissance', in R. Sweet and P. Lane (eds), *Women and Urban Life in Eighteenth-Century England* (Aldershot, 2003), pp. 173–94.

21. Ones currently open include Fenton House in Hampstead, Maister House in Hull, Lawrence House in Launceston, and Wordsworth House in Cockermouth

22. Samuel Johnson to his sister Elizabeth, 17 March 1775, Exeter, Devon Record Office, 5521 M/F4/1. See also A. Dain, 'Assemblies and Polite Leisure in East Anglia', *Suffolk Review*, new series, 28 (1997), pp. 2–22.

23. S. Varey, *Space and the Eighteenth-Century English Novel* (Cambridge, 1990).

24. N. Briggs, *John Johnson, 1732–1814: Georgian Architect and County Surveyor of Essex* (Chelmsford, 1991); A. White, *The Buildings of Georgian Lancaster* (Lancaster, 1992).

25. M. Farr (ed.), *The Great Fire of Warwick, 1694* (Warwick, 1992).

26. H. Berry, 'Creating Polite Space: The Organisation and Social Function of the Newcastle Assembly Rooms', in Berry and J. Gregory (eds), *Creating and Consuming Culture in North-East England, 1660–1830* (Aldershot, 2004), p. 138.

27. S. Rosenfeld, *The Georgian Theatre of Richmond and its Circuits: Beverley, Harrogate, Kendal, Northallerton, Ulverston and Whitby* (York, 1984).

28. Advertisement in *Swinney's Birmingham and Stafford Chronicle*, 4 August 1791.

29. T. Fawcett, 'Eighteenth-Century Art in Norwich', *Walpole Society*, 46 (1976–78), pp. 71–90; N. Surry, *Art in a Dockyard Town: Portsmouth, 1770–1845* (Portsmouth, 1992); M. E. Burkett, *Christopher Steele 1733–1767 of Acre Walls, Egremont* (Kendal, 2003).

30. E. Saunders, *Joseph Pickford and Derby: A Georgian Architect* (Stroud, 1993).

31. D. L. Bates, 'All Manner of Natural Knowledge: the Northampton Philosophical Society', *Northamptonshire Past and Present*, 8 (1993–94), pp. 372–73.

32. T. Fawcett, 'Measuring the Provincial Enlightenment: The Case of Norwich', *Eighteenth Century Life*, 8 (1982), pp. 20–23.

33. C. Nicholson, *Writing and the Rise of Finance: Capital Satires of the Early Eighteenth Century* (Cambridge, 1994).

34. R. J. Mayhew, *Enlightenment Geography. The Political Languages of British Geography, 1650–1850* (Basingstoke, 2000), pp. 141–67, esp. pp. 142–43.

35. E. Moir, *The Discovery of Britain: The English Tourists, 1540–1840* (London, 1964); I. Ousby, *The Englishman's England: Taste, Travel and the Rise of Tourism* (Cambridge, 1990).

36. M. Andrews, *The Search for the Picturesque: Landscape, Aesthetics and Tourism in Britain, 1760–1800* (Aldershot, 1989).

37. Exeter, Devon Record Office, Z19/2/10a.

38. T. Gray (ed.), *Travels in Georgian Devon: The Illustrated Journals of the Reverend John Swete, 1789–1800* (Exeter, 1997), pp. xiv, 161.

39. M. Mack, *The Garden and the City: Retirement and Politics in the Later Poetry of Pope, 1731–1743* (Toronto, 1969).

Notes to Chapter 10: Home and Abroad

1. B. Redford, *Venice and the Grand Tour* (New Haven, Connecticut, 1996); A. Wilton and I. Bignamini (eds), *Grand Tour: The Lure of Italy in the Eighteenth Century* (London, 1996).

2. J. Harris, *The Palladian Revival: Lord Burlington, His Villa and Garden at Chiswick* (New Haven, Connecticut, 1994); T. Barnard and J. Clark (eds), *Lord Burlington: Architecture, Art, and Life* (London, 1995).

3. W. Dean and J. M. Knapp, *Handel's Operas, 1704–1726* (Oxford, 1987).

4. L. Werkmeister, *A Newspaper History of England, 1792–1793* (Lincoln, Nebraska, 1969), p. 164; P. Wagner, *Eros Revived: Erotica of the Enlightenment in England and America* (London, 1990), pp. 3–4, 206.

5. PRO. SP. 100/3, 6 June 1722.

6. R. Pound, '"Fury after licentious pleasures": *A Rake's Progress* and concerns about luxury in eighteenth-century England', in R. Simon and C. Woodward (eds), *A Rake's Progress: From Hogarth to Hockney* (London, 1997), p. 20.

7. V. Lange, *The Classical Age of German Literature, 1740–1815* (London, 1982), eg. pp. 52, 59, 66; J. B. Knudsen, *Justus Möser and the German Enlightenment* (Cambridge, 1986), pp. 58–60, 148; B. Fabian, *The English Book in Eighteenth-Century Germany* (London, 1992); J. S. Toomre, 'Sumarokov's Adaptation of Hamlet …', *Study Group on Eighteenth-Century Russia*, 9 (1981), pp. 6–20; E. J. Simmons, *English Literature and Culture in Russia, 1533–1840* (Cambridge, Massachusetts, 1935).

8. P. Ayres, *Classical Culture and the Idea of Rome in Eighteenth-Century England* (London, 1997).

9. L. J. Colley, *Britons: Forging the Nation, 1707–1837* (New Haven, Connecticut, 1992).

10. C. Gerrard, *The Patriot Opposition to Walpole: Politics, Poetry, and National Myth, 1725–1742* (Oxford, 1994).

11. *Weekly Miscellany*, 8 March 1735.

12. Lynch, *Independent Patriot* (London, 1737), pp. 27–28.

13. M. Duffy, *The Englishman and the Foreigner* (Cambridge, 1986).

14. L. Fox, *A Splendid Occasion: the Stratford Jubilee of 1769* (Oxford, 1973).

15. E. Tomarken, *Samuel Johnson on Shakespeare: The Discipline of Criticism* (Athens, Georgia, 1991); M. Walsh, *Shakespeare, Milton, and Eighteenth-Century Literary Editing: The Beginnings of Interpretative Scholarship* (Cambridge, 1997); J. Gondris (ed.), *Reading Readings: Essays on Shakespeare Editing in the Eighteenth Century* (London, 1998).

16. J. Bate, *Shakespearean Constitutions: Politics, Theatre, Criticism, 1730–1830* (Oxford, 1989).

17. J. B. Kramnick, *Making the English Canon: Print Capitalism and the Cultural Past, 1700–1770* (Cambridge, 1999).

18. B. Bowden, *Eighteenth-century Modernizations from the Canterbury Tales* (Woodbridge, 1991).

19. W. Weber, *The Rise of Musical Classics in Eighteenth-Century England: A Study in Canon, Ritual and Ideology* (Oxford, 1992); N. A. M. Rodger, *The Insatiable Earl: A Life of John Montagu, 4th Earl of Sandwich* (London, 1993), p. 119–20.

20. C. Burney, *An Account of the Musical Performances ... in Commemoration of Handel* (London, 1785); H. Johnstone, 'A Ringside Seat at the Handel Commemoration', *Musical Times*, 125 (1984), pp. 632–36; W. Weber, 'The 1784 Handel Commemoration as Political Ritual', *Journal of British Studies*, 28 (1989), pp. 43–69.

21. H. D. Weinbrot, *Britannia's Issue. The Rise of British Literature from Dryden to Ossian* (Cambridge, 1993).

22. R. Reilly, *Wedgwood* (London, 1989).

23. A. Wilton, *The Swagger Portrait: Grand Manner portraiture in Britain from Van Dyck to Augustus John, 1630–1930* (London, 1992).

24. G. Newman, *The Rise of English Nationalism: A Cultural History* (New York, 1987).

25. L. Colley, 'The English Rococo', in M. Snodin (ed.), *Rococo: Art and Design in Hogarth's England* (London, 1984), p. 17.

26. I. Woodfield, *Opera and Drama in Eighteenth-Century London: The King's Theatre, Garrick and the Business of Performance* (Cambridge, 2001).

27. Reynolds to Lord Grantham, 3 April 1772, Bedford, Bedfordshire Record Office, Lucas papers 30/14/326/1.

28. F. Felsenstein (ed.), *English Trader, Indian Maid: Representing Gender, Race, and Slavery in the New World. An Inkle and Yarico Reader* (Baltimore, Maryland, 1999).

29. D. Turley, *The Culture of English Anti-Slavery, 1780–1860* (London, 1991).

30. M. Lincoln, 'Tales of Wonder, 1650–1750', *British Journal for Eighteenth-Century Studies*, 27 (2004), pp. 219–32.

31. G. Williams, *The Great South Sea: English Voyages and Encounters, 1570–1750* (New Haven, Connecicut, 1997).

32. G. Quilley, '"All Ocean is her Own": The Image of the Sea and the Identity of the Maritime Nation in Eighteenth-Century British Art', in G. Cubitt (ed.), *Imagining Nations* (Manchester, 1998), pp. 132–52.

33. L. McMullen, *An Odd Attempt in a Woman: The Literary Life of Frances Brooke* (Vancouver, 1983).

34. B. Smith, *Imagining the Pacific: In the Wake of the Cook Voyages* (New Haven, Connecticut, 1992).

35. I. C. Stuebe, *The Life and Works of William Hodges* (London, 1979).

36. M. Archer, *Early Views of India: The Picturesque Journey of Thomas and William Daniell, 1786–1794* (London, 1980).

37. Rodger, *Insatiable Earl*, p. 121.

38. R. Emmerson, *British Teapots and Tea Drinking, 1700–1850* (London, 1992); P. B. Brown, *In Praise of Hot Liquors: The Study of Chocolate, Coffee and Tea Drinking, 1600–1850* (York, 1995).

39. Quilley, 'All Ocean is Her Own', pp. 132–52.

40. N. Leask, *British Romantic Writers and the East: Anxieties of Empire* (Cambridge, 1993).

41. A. E. Wolfe-Aylward, *The Pictorial Life of Wolfe* (Plymouth, 1933); A. McNairn, *Behold the Hero: General Wolfe and the Arts in the Eighteenth Century* (Montreal, 1999); N. Rogers, 'Brave Wolfe: the making of a hero', in K. Wilson (ed.), *A New Imperial History: Culture, Identity and Modernity in Britain and the Empire, 1660–1840* (Cambridge, 2004), pp. 239–59.

42. D. G. C. Allan and J. Abbott (eds), *The Virtuoso Tribe of Arts and Sciences: Studies in the Eighteenth-Century Work and Membership of the London Society of Arts* (London, 1992).

43. J. Todd, *Mary Wollstonecraft: A Revolutionary Life* (London, 2000).

44. N. Wordsworth, *Wordsworth and Coleridge: The Radical Years* (Oxford, 1988).

45. M. B. Ross, *The Contours of Masculine Desire: Romanticism and the Rise of Women's Poetry* (Oxford, 1990).

46. K. W. Graham, *The Politics of Narrative: Ideology and Social Change in William Godwin's Caleb Williams* (New York, 1990).

47. M. O. Grenby, *The Anti-Jacobin Novel: British Conservatism and the French Revolution* (Cambridge, 2001).

48. *Poetry of the Anti-Jacobin* (London, 1799).

49. B. Hill, *The Republican Virago: The Life and Times of Catherine Macaulay Graham, Historian* (Oxford, 1992).

50. G. Newman, *The Rise of English Nationalism: A Cultural History, 1740–1830* (2nd edn, London, 1998).

51. S. West, *The Image of the Actor: Verbal and Visual Representation in the Age of Garrick and Kemble* (London, 1991).

52. H. Hoock, *The King's Artists: The Royal Academy of Arts and the Politics of British Culture, 1760–1840* (Oxford, 2003).

Selected Further Reading

Ackerman, J., *The Villa: Form and Ideology of Country Houses* (London, 1990).

Agnew, J.-C., *Worlds Apart: The Market and the Theater in Anglo-American Thought, 1550–1750* (Cambridge, 1986).

Aldrich, M., *Gothic Revival* (London, 1994).

Altick, R. D., *The Shows of London: A Panoramic History of Exhibitions, 1600–1862* (Cambridge, Mass., 1978).

Altick, R. D., *Paintings from Books: Art and Literature in Britain, 1760–1900* (Columbus, Ohio, 1985).

Altick, R. D., *The English Common Reader: A Short History of the Mass Reading Public, 1800–1900* (Chicago, 1957).

Andrews, M., *The Search for the Picturesque: Landscape, Aesthetics and Tourism in Britain, 1760–1800* (Aldershot, 1989).

Backschneider, R. R., *Daniel Defoe: His Life* (Baltimore, 1992).

Ballaster, R., *Seductive Forms: Women's Amatory Fiction from 1684 to 1740* (Oxford, 1992).

Barker-Benfield, G. J., *The Culture of Sensibility: Sex and Society in Eighteenth-Century Britain* (Chicago, 1992).

Barnard, T., and Clark, J. (eds), *Lord Burlington: Architecture, Art, and Life* (London, 1995).

Barrell, J., *The Political Theory of Painting from Reynolds to Hazlitt* (New Haven, 1986).

Barrell, J. (ed.), *Painting and the Politics of Culture: New Essays on British Art, 1700–1850* (Oxford, 1992).

Barry, J. and Brooks, C. (eds), *The Middling Sort of People: Culture, Society and Politics in England, 1550–1800* (Basingstoke, 1994).

Battestin, M. C. and R. R., *Henry Fielding: A Life* (London, 1989).

Beard, G. W., *Upholsterers and Interior Furnishing in England, 1530–1840* (New Haven, 1997).

Bell, I. A., *Literature and Crime in Augustan England* (London, 1991).

Bermingham, A., and Brewer, J. (eds), *The Consumption of Culture, 1600–1800: Image, Object, Text* (London, 1995).

Bevis, R. W., *English Drama: Restoration and Eighteenth Century, 1660–1789* (London, 1988).

Bindman, D., *Hogarth and his Times* (London, 1997).

Bindman, D., *William Blake: His Art and Times* (London, 1982).

Black, J., *Eighteenth-Century Britain, 1688–1783* (Basingstoke, 2001).

Black, J., *Italy and the Grand Tour* (London, 2003).

Borsay, P., *The English Urban Renaissance: Culture and Society in the Provincial Town, 1660–1770* (Oxford, 1989).

Brewer, J., and Porter, R. (eds), *Consumption and the World of Goods* (London, 1993).

Brewer, J., *The Pleasures of the Imagination: English Culture in the Eighteenth Century* (London, 1997).

Brownell, M. R., *Alexander Pope and the Arts of Georgian England* (Oxford, 1978).

Burrows, D., *Handel* (Oxford, 1994).

Burrows, D. (ed.), *The Cambridge Companion to Handel* (Cambridge, 1997).

Burrows, D. and Dunhill, D., *Music and Theatre in Handel's World: the Family Papers of James Harris 1732–80* (Oxford, 2002).

Butler, M., *Romantics, Rebels and Reactionaries: English Literature and its Background, 1760–1830* (Oxford, 1981).

Castle, T., *Masquerade and Civilization: The Carnivalesque in Eighteenth-Century English Culture and Fiction* (Stanford, California, 1986).

Christie, C., *The British Country House in the Eighteenth Century* (Manchester, 2000).

Clark, P., *British Clubs and Societies, 1580–1800* (New York, 2000).

Clark, P. (ed.), *The Cambridge Urban History of Britain, II: 1500–1840* (Cambridge, 2000).

Clifford, H., *Silver in London: The Parker and Wakelin Partnership, 1760–1776* (New Haven, 2004).

Cohen, M., *Fashioning Masculinity: National Identity and Language in the Eighteenth Century* (London, 1996).

Colley, L., *Britons: Forging the Nation* (New Haven, 1992).

Copley, S., and Garside, P. (eds), *The Politics of the Picturesque: Literature, Landscape and Aesthetics since 1770* (Cambridge, 1994).

Daunton, M., *Progress and Poverty: An Economic and Social History of Britain, 1700–1850* (Oxford, 1995).

Denvir, B., *The Eighteenth Century: Art, Design and Society, 1689–1789* (London, 1984).

Dobson, M., *The Making of the National Poet: Shakespeare, Adaptation, and Authorship, 1660–1769* (London, 1992).

Doody, M. A., *The Daring Muse: Augustan Poetry Reconsidered* (Cambridge, 1985).

Downie, J. A., *To Settle the Succession of the State: Literature and Politics 1678–1750* (Basingstoke, 1994).

Eagleton, T., *The Rape of Clarissa: Writing, Sexuality and Class Struggle in Samuel Richardson* (Oxford, 1982).

Edwards, C., *Eighteenth-Century Furniture* (Manchester, 1996).

Eglin, J. *Venice Transfigured: The Myth of Venice in British Culture, 1660–1797* (Basingstoke, 2001).

Estabrook, C. B., *Urban and Rustic England: Cultural Ties and Social Spheres in the Provinces, 1660–1780* (Manchester, 1998).

Everett, N., *The Tory View of Landscape* (New Haven, 1994).

Feather, J., *The Provincial Book Trade in Eighteenth Century England* (London, 1985).

Ford, B., *The Cambridge Cultural History of Britain: Eighteenth-Century Britain* (Cambridge, 1992).

Fowler, J. and Cornforth, J. *English Decoration in the Eighteenth Century* (London, 1978).

Golby, J. M. and Purdue, A. W., *The Civilisation of the Crowd: Popular Culture in England, 1750–1900* (London, 1984).

Goldgar, B., *Walpole and the Wits: The Relation of Politics to Literature, 1722–1742* (London, 1976).

Greene, D. (ed.), *Samuel Johnson* (Oxford, 1984).

Grundy, I., *Lady Mary Wortley Montagu: Comet of the Enlightenment* (Oxford, 1999).

Harris, E. *British Architectural Books and Writers, 1556–1785* (Cambridge, 1990).

Harris, T. (ed.), *Popular Culture in England, c. 1500–1850* (Basingstoke, 1995).

Hogwood, C., and Luckett, R. (eds), *Music in Eighteenth-Century England: Essays in Memory of Charles Cudworth* (Cambridge, 1983).

Hoock, H., *The King's Artists: The Royal Academy of Arts and the Politics of British Culture, 1760–1840* (Oxford, 2003).

Hume, R. D., *Henry Fielding and the London Theatre, 1728–1737* (Oxford, 1988).

Hunter, J. P., *Before Novels: The Cultural Contexts of Eighteenth-Century English Fiction* (London, 1990).

Johnstone, H. D., and Fiske, R. (eds), *The Blackwell History of Music in Britain, IV: The Eighteenth Century* (Oxford, 1990).

Jones, R. W., *Gender and the Formation of Taste in Eighteenth-Century Britain: The Analysis of Beauty* (Cambridge, 1998).

Jones, S., *The Cambridge Introduction to Art: The Eighteenth Century* (Cambridge, 1985).

Kelly, G., *The English Jacobin Novel, 1780–1805* (Oxford, 1976).

Kidson, A. (intro.), *George Romney, 1734–1802*, catalogue of National Portrait Gallery Collection (London, 2002).

Klein, L., *Shaftesbury and the Culture of Politeness: Moral Discourse and Cultural Politics in Early Eighteenth-Century England* (Cambridge, 1994).

Langford, P., *A Polite and Commercial People: England, 1727–1783* (Oxford, 1989).

Langford, P., *Englishness Identified: Manners and Character, 1650–1850* (Oxford, 2000).

Lemire, B., *Dress, Culture and Commerce: The English Clothing Trade Before the Factory* (London, 1997).

Leppert, R., *Music and Image: Domesticity, Ideology and Socio-Cultural Formation in Eighteenth-Century England* (London, 1993).

Lewis, P. and Wood, N. (eds), *John Gay and the Scriblerians* (London, 1988).

Lonsdale, R. (ed.), *Eighteenth-Century Women Poets: An Anthology* (Oxford, 1989).

Lonsdale, R. (ed.), *The New Oxford Book of Eighteenth Century Verse* (Oxford, 1984).

Lucas, J., *England and Englishness: Ideas of Nationhood in English Poetry, 1688–1900* (London, 1990).

Mack, M., *Alexander Pope: A Life* (New Haven, 1985).

McVeagh, J. (ed.), *All Before Them: English Literature and the Wider World, 1660–1780* (London, 1990).

Mullan, J., *Sentiment and Sociability: The Language of Feeling in the Eighteenth Century* (Oxford, 1988).

Newman, G., *The Rise of English Nationalism: A Cultural History, 1740–1830* (London, 1987).

Nicholson, C. (ed.), *Alexander Pope: Essays for the Tercentenary* (Aberdeen, 1988).

Nokes, D., *John Gay: A Profession of Friendship* (Oxford, 1995).

Nokes, D., *Raillery and Rage: A Study of Eighteenth-Century Satire* (Brighton, 1987).

Nussbaum, F. (ed.), *The New Eighteenth Century* (London, 1987).

Paulson, R., *Hogarth* (London, 1991–93).

Pears, I., *The Discovery of Painting: The Growth of Interest in the Arts in England, 1680–1768* (New Haven, 1988).

Pearson, J., *Women Reading in Britain, 1750–1835* (Cambridge, 1999).

Peters, J. S., *Congreve, the Drama, and the Printed Word* (Stanford, California, 1990).

Pittock, M., *Poetry and Jacobite Politics in Eighteenth-Century Britain and Ireland* (Cambridge, 1994).

Pittock, M., *Inventing and Resisting Britain: Cultural Identities in Britain and Ireland, 1685–1789* (Basingstoke, 1997).

Pointon, M., *Hanging the Head: Portraiture and Social Formation in Eighteenth-Century England* (New Haven, 1993).

Porter, R., *English Society in the Eighteenth Century* (London, 1982).

Porter, R., *Enlightenment: Britain and the Creation of the Modern World* (London, 2000).

Probyn, C. T., *English Fiction of the Eighteenth Century, 1700–1789* (London, 1987).

Pugh, S. (ed.), *Reading Landscape: Country-City-Capital* (Manchester, 1990).

Raven, J., Small, H. and Tadmor, N. (eds), *The Practice and Representation of Reading in England* (Cambridge, 1997).

Reilly, R., *Wedgwood* (London, 1989).

Richetti, J. (ed.), *Cambridge Companion to the Eighteenth-Century Novel* (Cambridge, 1996).

Rivers, I. (ed.), *Books and their Readers in Eighteenth-Century England* (Leicester, 1982).

Rogers, P., *Essays on Pope* (Cambridge, 1993).

Rogers, P., *Samuel Johnson* (Oxford, 1993).

Rogers, P., *The Augustan Vision* (London, 1974).

Rompkey, R., *Soame Jenyns* (Boston, 1984).

Ross, A., and Woolley, D. (eds), *Jonathan Swift* (Oxford, 1984).

Rowe, A., *Garden Making and the Freman Family: A Memoir of Hamels, 1713–33* (Hertford, 2002).

Sekora, J., *Luxury: The Concept in Western Thought, Eden to Smollett* (Baltimore, 1977).

Shoemaker, R. B., *Gender in English Society, 1650–1850: The Emergence of Separate Spheres?* (London, 1998).

Smail, J., *The Origins of Middle-Class Culture: Halifax, Yorkshire, 1660–1780* (Ithaca, 1994).

Smith, R., *Handel's Oratorios and Eighteenth-Century Thought* (Cambridge, 1995).

Snodin, M. (ed.), *Rococo: Art and Design in Hogarth's England* (London, 1984).

Snodin, M. and Styles, J. (eds), *Design and the Decorative Arts: Georgian Britain, 1714–1837* (London, 2004).

Speck, W. A., *Literature and Society in Eighteenth-Century England: Ideology, Politics and Culture, 1680–1820* (London, 1998).

Speck, W. A., *Society and Literature in England, 1700–60* (Dublin, 1983).

Spencer, J., *The Rise of the Woman Novelist: From Aphra Behn to Jane Austen* (Oxford, 1986).

Summerson, J. N., *Architecture in Britain, 1530–1830* (London, 1991).

Swarbrick, A. (ed.), *The Art of Oliver Goldsmith* (London, 1984).

Tinniswood, A., *The Polite Tourist: Four Centuries of Country House Visiting* (London, 1998).

Todd, J., *Sensibility: An Introduction* (London, 1986).

Turley, D., *The Culture of English Anti-Slavery, 1780–1860* (London, 1991).

Varey, S., *Space and the Eighteenth-Century Novel* (Cambridge, 1990).

Vickery, A., *The Gentleman's Daughter: Women's Lives in Georgian England* (New Haven, 1998).

Ward-Jackson, P., *English Furniture Design of the Eighteenth Century* (London, 1984).

Weatherill, L., *Consumer Behaviour and Material Culture in Britain, 1660–1760* (London, 1988).

Weber, W., *The Rise of Musical Classics in Eighteenth-Century England: A Study in Canon, Ritual, and Ideology* (Oxford, 1992).

Williamson, T., *Polite Landscapes: Gardens and Society in Eighteenth-Century England* (Stroud, 1995).

Woollenberg, S. and McVeigh, S. (eds), *Concert Life in Eighteenth-Century Britain* (Aldershot, 2004).

Worsley, G., *Classical Architecture in Britain: The Heroic Age* (New Haven, 1995).

Index